Rethinking
Human Adaptation

Also of Interest

Human Adaptability: An Introduction to Ecological Anthropology, Emilio F. Moran

Sociobiology: Beyond Nature/Nurture? Reports, Definitions and Debate, edited by George W. Barlow and James Silverberg

Biology and the Social Sciences: An Emerging Revolution, edited by Thomas C. Wiegele ·

A Systems View of Man, Ludwig von Bertalanffy, edited by Paul A. LaViolette

The Women of Rural Asia, Robert Orr White and Pauline Whyte

India: Cultural Patterns and Processes, edited by Allen G. Noble and Ashok K. Dutt

Resource Managers: North American and Australian Hunter-Gatherers, edited by Nancy M. Williams and Eugene S. Hunn

Involuntary Migration and Resettlement: The Problems and Responses of Dislocated People, edited by Art Hansen and Anthony Oliver-Smith

*Available in hardcover and paperback.

A Westview Special Study

Rethinking Human Adaptation:
Biological and Cultural Models
edited by Rada Dyson-Hudson and Michael A. Little

Most anthropologists agree that a comprehension of adaptation and adaptive processes is central to an understanding of human biological and behavioral systems. However, there is little agreement among archeologists, cultural anthropologists, and human biologists as to what adaptation means and how it should be analyzed. Because of this lack of a common underlying theory, method, and perspective, the subdisciplines have tended to move apart, and anthropology is no longer the integrated science envisaged at its inception in the nineteenth century.

In this book, the authors--both biological and cultural anthropologists--use a common theoretical framework based on recent evolutionary, ecological, and anthropological theory in their analyses of biological and social adaptive systems. Although a synthesis of the subdisciplines of anthropology lies somewhere in the future, the original essays in this volume are a first attempt at a unified perspective.

Dr. Rada Dyson-Hudson is associate professor in the Department of Anthropology, Cornell University. In the past, she was associate professor and research associate in the Department of Pathobiology at the School of Hygiene, Johns Hopkins University. Her attempt to reconcile the implications of natural selection theory with a commitment to social equality led to a rethinking of human adaptation and, among other things, the organization of the symposium at the American Anthropological Association of which this book is a result. *Dr. Michael A. Little* is professor of anthropology at the State University of New York at Binghamton. He has been scientific coordinator of the Human Adaptability Section of the International Biological Program and is coauthor of *Ecology, Energetics, and Human Variability* (1976).

Rethinking
Human Adaptation:
Biological and
Cultural Models

edited by Rada Dyson-Hudson
and Michael A. Little

Westview Press / Boulder, Colorado

A Westview Special Study

Copyright © 1983 by Westview Press, Inc.

Published in 1983 in the United States of America by
   Westview Press, Inc.
   5500 Central Avenue
   Boulder, Colorado 80301
   Frederick A. Praeger, President and Publisher

Library of Congress Catalog Card Number 82-83813
ISBN 0-86531-511-6

Composition for this book was provided by the editors
Printed and bound in the United States of America

Contents

Tables

Figures

Acknowledgments

The editors acknowledge the following people for help, in a variety of ways, in the preparation of this book: Barbara Donnell, Davydd J. Greenwood, Glenn Hausfater, Robert Netting, Lynne Rienner, and Coraleen Rooney. We thank, particularly, Kenneth A. R. Kennedy, who commented on the entire manuscript. We thank, also, the contributors to this book for their patience.

R. D-H.
M.A.L.

Introduction

The concept of adaptation is central to an understanding of human biology and behavior. Although biologists' studies of adaptation are firmly rooted in Darwin's theory of evolution through natural selection,
anthropologists generally deal with morphological, physiological, and behavioral (cultural) adaptations as if
they represent quite different phenomena. In this book,
we suggest that Darwinian theory can provide a body of
theory appropriate for the analysis of both biological
and cultural adaptation. Only by focusing on interactive
patterns in biological and behavioral systems can we understand human biological and cultural adaptive responses.
    In their analysis of human biology and behavior, the
authors in this volume approach adaptation from an interactive rather than a deterministic mode. Dyson-Hudson
presents a model for the development of all human phenotypes which emphasizes that these must be based not only
on evolved genetic programs but also on the environmental
information encountered during the entire lifetime of the
individual. Kellum and Haas demonstrate that deterministic models cannot deal adequately with biological phenomena such as the variations in human sex ratios at
birth and variations in human reproductive success in
high Andean populations. Interactive models are also
clearly required for an understanding of human behavioral
adaptations traditionally studied by cultural ecologists
and ecological anthropologists. Moran, Dow, and Boone
demonstrate the importance of considering environmental
variables in assessing the adaptiveness of spatial mobility, "primitive" warfare, and warfare in complex and
hierarchical societies. Smith shows that, by using interactive models based on a synthesis of neo-Darwinian
theory with evolutionary ecology, human behavioral adaptations can be analyzed within the theoretical framework
of recent advances in biology.
    Anthropology has, since its inception, been identi-
fied as an integrated biological and social science.
However, in recent years the sub-fields have tended to
move apart in method, theory, and content. The contributions to this book, by sociocultural and biological anthropologists, treat adaptation within the framework of recent
evolutionary theory. This is a positive trend and we firmly believe that only by these integrated approaches can
adaptation in human populations be fully understood.

1
An Interactive Model of Human Biological and Behavioral Adaptation

Rada Dyson-Hudson

Editors' Summary: In the first chapter, Rada Dyson-Hudson emphasizes an evolutionary perspective, based on Darwinian theory, on human biological and behavioral adaptation. Her approach differs from more deterministic scientists in its attempt to deal with the environmental lability of most human genetic systems and the tight interaction among behavioral, biological, and environmental features of human populations. Dyson-Hudson believes that if there is to be a unified theory of biological and cultural adaptation, it must be based on an explicit recognition that natural selection is the only force which can generate and maintain adaptation.

EVOLUTION AND ADAPTATION

The concepts of evolution and adaptation are widely used in both the biological and social sciences. However, there is often a great difference in the way the terms are used in these respective disciplines. This means that while biologists and social scientists may appear to be discussing the same thing, they are often, in fact, attempting to analyze and explain quite different phenomena.

In the first part of this paper, I review the different ways in which the concept of adaptation is used in the biological and social sciences, and then develop an interactive model that can help us to understand both biological and behavioral adaptation within a single theoretical framework. Then, I discuss what evolutionary theory leads us to predict about the relative importance of genes vs. environments in the genesis of specific phenotypes in particular species. Finally, I suggest that focusing on gene-environment interactions can help us to understand both adaptive and maladaptive human behaviors.

Biological Definitions

Charles Darwin's original definition of evolution was 'descent with modification.' He attributed changes

1

in phyletic lineages (changes in populations through
time) to the process of natural selection--the accumulation in populations of favorable hereditary variations
through differential survival and reproduction of individuals within those populations (Darwin 1859). Mendel
recognized the particulate nature of hereditary variation
and his 'laws' formed the basis for population genetics.
The melding of Mendel's theory of particulate inheritance
with Darwin's theory of evolution through natural selection (termed neo-Darwinian theory) underlies much of current evolutionary theory, and a definition of organic
evolution now widely accepted by biologists is "a change
in gene frequencies from generation to generation" (Wilson 1975:584). This definition differs from Darwin's
original formulation, since the forces leading to changes
in the gene pool (micro-evolution) include the random
processes of mutation and genetic drift, as well as the
non-random processes of gene flow (due to migration of
individuals), selective mating, and natural selection.
And random processes may also be implicated in macro-
evolutionary trends within phyletic lineages, and patterns of divergence and extinction of species (Raup
1977). Although not all evolutionary biologists agree
that natural selection plays the major role in organic
evolution, there is general agreement that natural selection is the mechanism by which organisms adapt to their
environment: that "Natural selection is the only acceptable explanation for the genesis and maintenance of
adaptation" (Williams 1966: vii, italics mine).
    Biological adaptation can be broadly defined as the
fit between an organism and the external world in which
it lives (Lewontin 1978:213). More specifically, adaptation is generally taken to refer to any feature of an organism which contributes to its survival and reproduction. Although adaptation is sometimes viewed as the
process of evolutionary change by which the organism
provides better and better 'solutions' to the 'problems
set by the environment, it is important to recognize
that, since environments are constantly changing, there
is, in fact, no end to adaptation. Organisms do not become better and better adapted, but rather the adaptation
process consists of a series of fine adjustments in the
organism according to the environmental conditions at a
given time, and the variability in the population. Hence
there is no pinnacle of organic evolution. Some species
in the face of constantly changing environments either
have 'preadaptations' to the changed environments--that
is characteristics evolved as adaptations to one environment which, fortuitously, enable an individual to survive
in a different environment; and/or have sufficient
heritable--genetically based--variation of the right kind
to change adaptively, to track the environment. Other
species become extinct.

Selective pressures depend on the nature of the environment, and the ways in which selective pressures in the environment can operate are constrained by the heritable variation present in the population. Thus organic evolution does not have a predictable direction. A species may, for example, adapt by evolving into larger or smaller forms; into more complex or simpler organisms; into social or solitary individuals.

Much of evolutionary biology has consisted of working out an adaptationist program, in which the evolutionary biologist assumes that each aspect of an organism's morphology, physiology, and behavior has been molded by natural selection as a solution to a problem posed by the environment. The biologist then constructs a plausible argument about how each part functions as an adaptive device. Developing adaptive explanations is fraught with difficulties (see Lewontin 1978: 216-228 for a discussion of some of these). For example, the assertion of universal adaptation is difficult to test, "because simplifying assumptions and ingenious explanations can almost always result in an ad hoc adaptive explanation" (Lewontin 1978: 230). However, as Lewontin stresses, an all-out adaptationist program must be adopted because if a weaker form of evolutionary explanation is accepted, and only some proportion of cases are explained by adaptation, it "would leave the biologist free to pursue the adaptationist program in the easy cases and leave the difficult ones to the scrap heap of chance" (1978: 230).

Some adaptive explanations can be tested. One method is testing how well predictions based on genetic and ecological theory fit the characteristics, behaviors, organizations found in real-life situations. (See Alexander and Tinkle 1981. Krebs and Davies 1981 and Wilson 1975 are reviews of the biological literature. Chagnon and Irons 1979, 1981; Dyson-Hudson and Smith 1978; McCay 1981; and Winterhalder and Smith 1981, apply these theories to humans. See also Smith Chapter 2.)

Furthermore neo-Darwinism theory has reached the stage where authors of adaptive explanations do not have a free rein: they must conform to certain rules in framing their 'just-so-stories'. The requirements for an evolutionary argument about a particular attribute of a specific organism, include the following:[1] (see Dyson-Hudson 1979 for a more detailed discussion of these points).

1. A characteristic must be a meaningful trait, that is, it must have been a unit under natural selection.

2. A characteristic must be heritable, that is, some of the variation of that characteristic within the population must (in the evolutionary past) have been due to genetic differences among individuals.

3. A characteristic must have contributed to reproductive success. More accurately, a characteristic must
have contributed to 'inclusive fitness', that is, the individual's contribution to the gene pool of future generations, as measured by personal reproductive success,
plus the reproductive success of relatives, with relative's contribution devalued in proportion to their genetic distance.
4. Selection must have been strong enough to modify
the character within the time span available.
5. Alternative explanations must be explored.
6. It must be recognized that a characteristic can
change its function during the evolutionary history of a
species.
7. If an adaptive argument is used, the reason why
other organisms in similar niches (with similar roles in
the environment) have not evolved the same characteristics must be considered.
8. Adaptiveness must be defined in an explicit environmental context.
9. Since natural selection generally operates
through differential survival and reproduction of individuals rather than of groups, evolved traits should be
adaptive primarily to individuals, and only secondarily
to higher levels of organization. Thus, adaptation
should be attributed to no higher level of organization
than is demanded by the evidence.
    Although no adaptive explanation can possibly meet
these stringent criteria because we do not have sufficient knowledge and understanding of past environments
and of the functioning of organisms within these, nonetheless they are extremely useful because they make it
possible to identify inadequate adaptive explanations--
those which clearly violate some or all of these requirements.
    In summary, there is a general consensus among neo-
Darwinian theorists that evolution does not occur according to a pre-ordained plan, that adaptation is the product of natural selection, and that natural selection
generally operates at lower rather than higher levels of
organization. It operates at the level of the individual
(or possibly even gene complexes), rather than at the
level of the group, the population, the species, the society or the 'culture'. Evolutionary theory has developed to a stage which makes it possible to make rules
for formulating adaptive explanations and, at least in
some cases, adaptive explanations can be tested.

Definitions Used by Anthropologists

    Among anthropologists dealing with human adaptation,
there is no consensus as to the meaning of the terms
'evolution' and 'adaptation'; nor is there any set of
rules for writing evolutionary and adaptive explanations

which would be acceptable to the large body of scholars
interested in human adaptation. It is not possible in
this chapter to review the diversity of views, but some
examples will be cited. Some biological anthropologists
focus on adaptation as morphological and physiological
adjustments which occur during growth and development
(cf. Haas, chapter 3). Others study biological phenomena
such as human genetics, mating systems, and fertility.
In contrast, for many cultural ecologists evolution refers to the process of social change through which egalitarian societies develop into complex and hierarchical
societies--through which 'primitive' societies inevitably
'progress' to become more and more like modern 'civi-
lized' societies. According to these theorists, extant
societies represent stages in a progression from egalitarian through tribal to ranked societies and states (cf.
Fried 1967).
     Inspired by the work of Leslie White (1943) and F.
W. Cottrell (1951), some cultural ecologists have focused
on energy use as the indicator of the level of adaptation. For example, according to Y. A. Cohen (1974:46)
"Adaptation in man is the process by which he makes effective use for productive ends of the energy potential
of his habitat. . . . He accomplishes this by harnes-
sing increasingly effective sources of energy and by
shaping his institutions to meet the demands of each
energy system so he can make maximum use of it." Although Cohen does not define the terms 'efficient', or
'effective', he appears to use them to mean a greater
dependence on non-food energy (e.g. hydroelectric power,
fossil fuels, etc.). This leads him to equate the stages
of adaptation with the trajectory of cultural change
based on greater and greater energy consumption which led
to present-day Western society. For example, he concludes that although "some hunter-gatherers . . . enjoy
a greater abundance of food than their horticultural
neighbors; we nevertheless speak of the latter as repre-
senting a higher level of development because horticulture is a strategy based on more efficient energy systems" (Cohen 1974:47).
     Rappaport (1971b) defines adaptation as:

     . . . the process by which organisms or groups of
     organisms, through responsive changes in their
     states, structures, or compositions, maintain
     homeostatis in and among themselves in the face of
     both short-term environmental fluctuations and
     long-term changes in the composition or structure
     of their environments. (p. 60)

While for Sahlins (1964):

     . . . adaptation implies maximizing the social life
     chances. But maximization is almost always a com-

promise, a vector in the internal structure of culture and the external pressure of environment. (p.
136)

Bennett (1976) recognizes the importance of the concept
of behavioral adaptation, which he defines as:

. . . the coping mechanisms that humans display in
obtaining their wants or adjusting their lives to
the surrounding milieu, or the milieu of their lives
and purposes. (p. 246)

He views the concept of adaptation as providing a framework which focuses "on the active mode of human engage-
ment with natural phenomena" and allows for "the inclu-
sion of society as a part of the environment with which
men cope." (See Alland 1975, Alland and McCay 1974, and
Hardesty 1977 for other views on human adaptation.)

    Marvin Harris, another major figure in cultural-eco-
logical theory, also views adaptation as central to an
understanding of human behavior. He strongly rejects the
notion that 'progress' is adaptive; and seeks to explain
such 'riddles of culture' as India's sacred cow, Jewish
and Muslim prohibitions on eating pork, and Aztec canni-
balism, as adaptive cultural phenomena (Harris 1974,
1977).

    However, it is not possible to discern any rules under-
lying his ingenious adaptive explanations of human culture, except for the assumption that many, but not all,
cultural phenomena can best be understood as adaptive responses to the material world, with adaptation meaning
survival of the group, not the individual.

    Cultural ecologists usually view the population, the
species, the group, or the culture, as the unit of adaptation and adjustment. For example Cohen states that "at
each successive stage of cultural evolution man is better
adapted for the survival of his group--that is, the survival of his adaptive unit--and in turn, of the species
as a whole" (1974:47). Harris also regularly uses group
benefit as the criterion of adaptive behavior. For example, he suggests that: "Reciprocity is a form of economic exchange that is primarily adapted to the conditions in which the stimulation of intensive extra productive efforts would have an adverse effect upon group
survival" (1974:126). Organic evolution through natural
selection operating at the level of the individual is
virtually never invoked by cultural ecologists as the
underlying reason for human adaptive behavior.

    Anthropologists are becoming increasingly aware of
the ethnocentric bias of the idea that cultural evolution represents progress toward becoming more and more
like us (see Greenwood and Stini 1977:409-426). Also,
there is a growing recognition that the group level of
analysis which characterizes cultural evolutionary theory

in the social sciences has not yielded the kind of theoretical strides that biologists have made by focusing on
individual selection through natural selection (Van den
Berghe 1978:36). Some anthropologists are turning to
neo-Darwinian theory in their attempts to understand
human behavior (see articles and references in Chagnon
and Irons 1979, 1981, Winterhalder and Smith 1981). However, despite these recent advances in the application
of evolutionary theory to human behavior, biological and
behavioral adaptation are still very generally dealt with
as if they represent totally different processes. It is
very widely assumed that nature--as represented by the
genes--is the prime force in human morphological and physiological adaptation. In contrast, although some biologists and anthropologists have suggested that certain
human behaviors are strongly genetically programmed,
nurture--the environment in the broadest sense--is
generally assumed to be the prime force in human behavioral (cultural) adaptation.

GENE-ENVIRONMENT INTERACTIONS

An emphasis on the dichotomies genes/environment,
nature/nurture has hindered our understanding of adaptive
processes. As Lewontin (1974) observed, one of the difficulties in the full understanding of genetic/environ-
mental effects in the past arose from a confusion between
the concepts of analysis of alternative causes (genes or
environments) and the analysis of interacting causes
(genes and environments). However, the interactions between genes and environments is now being documented in
anthropological research. On the one hand, recent work
in biological anthropology (e.g. Haas 1980b) documents
that some human responses to high altitude which have
often been attributed to biological adaptations cannot
be understood without taking into consideration environmental variables (see Haas, Chapter 3). On the other
hand, the extent to which sociobiological and ecological
theory is successful in predicting and/or explaining certain human behaviors (Chagnon and Irons 1979, 1981;
Winterhalder and Smith 1981) suggests that, despite the
strong influence of environment on how humans behave,
there is an evolved genetic program underlying some aspects of human behavior.
The growing understanding of gene action also makes
it clear that both genetic and environmental information
must be involved in the genesis of any phenotype, be it
morphological, physiological, or behavioral. The unique
information encoded in the DNA of the fertilized egg is
always necessary for the development of each and every
individual and all phenotypic attributes--how each individual looks, functions, and behaves--must be based to
some degree on genetic information. Also there is a continuous exposure of each and every individual to the en-

8

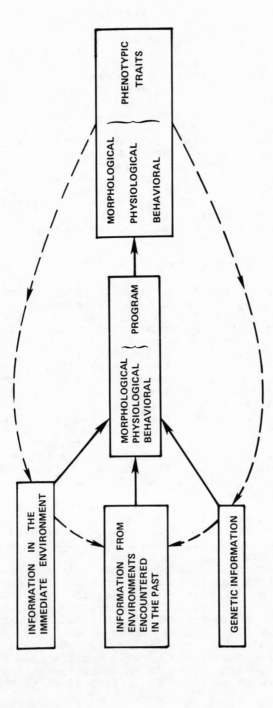

Figure 1.1. A model specifying the gene-environment interactions in the development of morphological, physiological and behavioral phenotypes.

9

vironment as the information encoded in the DNA is translated into an individual's phenotype. Therefore all
phenotypic traits must also be influenced to some degree
by environments. An individual's phenotype is the product of genetic information interacting with diverse environments through time.

I shall now present a model which makes explicit the
interactions between genes and environments, and show
that this model can help us to understand both biological
and behavioral adaptation within a single theoretical
framework.

An Interactive Model

The model (Figure 1.1) focuses on the complex interactions between genetic and environmental information in
the development of specific phenotypic traits. It postulates that the information from the immediate environment
and information from environments encountered during an
individual's entire lifespan interact with information
encoded in the DNA to generate a program which in turn
generates each morphological, physiological, and behavioral trait. This model takes into account that genetic
information encoded in the DNA molecules influences the
development of a particular phenotype. It distinguishes
between information from environments encountered in the
past (encoded through ontogenesis in morphology, physiology, and behavior) which conditions an individual to respond in particular ways, and information in the immediate environment (a stimulus) which generates a specific
response. The morphological, physiological, or behavioral program which generates a specific phenotypic trait
is a 'black box' and represents all the physiological and
neurological structures and functions within an individual which go to generate that particular morphological, physiological, or behavioral trait.

Closed vs. Open Genetic Programs

To understand adaptive processes it is important to
recognize that the degree to which genetic information
specifies a particular phenotypic trait varies. Some
traits are based on closed genetic programs that, in environments which allow the individual to survive, provide
all the information necessary to specify the development
of that particular phenotypic trait. However, many
traits are based on open genetic programs, which allow
and/or require the input of environmental information
during the translation into phenotype (Mayr 1974). Open
genetic programs result in genetic plasticity.

For example, the genes must carry all the information necessary for the development of the whole complex
of behaviors characteristic of the European cuckoo, since
these are parasitic birds and their young are invariably

reared by foster parents who possess behavior patterns
very different from those of either nestling or adult
cuckoos (Welty 1975:166-167, 324-326). In contrast young
male white-crowned sparrows isolated from adults before
they were two weeks old, even if they can hear their own
voices, develop songs with only some of the species-specific characteristics and without dialect elaborations
of the song of adult white-crowned sparrows. In this
species, the fully developed song pattern is learned during the first 100 days of life from hearing adult males
sing, and the local dialects of song which have developed
in this species are culturally transmitted elaborations
of the species-specific genetic program (Marler and
Tamura 1964).
    Open genetic programs vary greatly in the specifi-
city of information which can or must be incorporated.
For example, attachment behavior in mallard ducks which
leads to following behavior and later to species recognition, is irreversibly learned (imprinted) within the
first day after hatching. However, only caretakers which
are less than about three feet gall, and constantly emit
quacking noises similar to an adult mallard, elicit this
behavior (Lorenz 1952:42-43). In this case, both the
time and the nature of the relevant environmental information is highly specified. In contrast, human verbal
communication systems are constantly being modified by
environmental information. New words can always be incorporated into a person's vocabulary, and as long as
he/she has learned a primary language before puberty,
he/she can continue to learn new languages throughout
his/her life. Nevertheless, human linguistic capability
is a species-specific trait with a detailed neurological
basis and must therefore also have detailed genetic
specifications (Lenneberg 1967).

SELECTION FOR CLOSED VS. OPEN GENETIC PROGRAMS

    There is a widespread belief that morphological
traits, being material and relatively unchanging, must
be more specified by genetic information than are physiological functions, while behaviors, which are necessarily
ephemeral, are least influenced by the genes. However,
"hygienic" behavior in honey-bees (uncapping the cell if
a larva dies, and removing the corpse) is inherited in a
simple Mendelian fashion, with one dominant gene U (for
uncapping), and one dominant gene R (for removing the
larva) (Rothenbuhler 1964a and 1964b). In contrast, two
forms of locust which are morphologically so distinct
that they had been described as separate species were
found to be the solitary and gregarious forms of a
single species, and which form develops is determined by
environmental factors--the degree of crowding during development (Chapman 1976:40-49; Uvarov 1966). Clearly,
it is not possible to use the distinction between morpho-

logical, physiological, and behavioral traits to decide
a priori the nature of the genetic vs. environmental
contribution to the development of a particular trait.
To do so we must turn to evolutionary theory.

Life History Characteristics and Evolutionary Theory

Evolutionary theory does enable us on the basis of
the life history characteristics and the evolutionary
history of a particular species to make predictions
about the degree to which a specific phenotypic trait in
that species will be influenced by genetic vs. environmental information (Mayr 1974). In small-brained,
shortlived species, particularly those with
non-overlapping generations which are dependent on a
narrow range of food sources, closed genetic programs
are effective ways of transmitting information about
adaptive phenotypic traits from one generation to the
next. Indeed, closed programs are widespread among
so-called lower animals. Closed genetic programs are
also efficient ways of generating adaptive traits in a
very predictable environment. But when traits are
generated by closed programs, phenotypic changes often
cannot track environmental change, particularly if
environments change rapidly in unpredictable ways:
extinction of the species is likely to occur before
phenotypic adjustments can be made. Therefore for
species evolving in unpredictably changing environments
open genetic programs are of considerable selective advantage, because they enable individuals to retain
extensive flexibility toward components of the
environment. A species living in a wide variety of
habitats also is more likely to have open genetic
programs governing morphological, physiological, and
behavioral traits than is a species living in a narrow
range of habitats.
Humans are members of a wide-ranging, long-lived,
large-brained, omnivorous species. Infants are very im-
mature at birth, and a long period of prenatal care is
required. Hominids evolved in Africa during the Miocene
and Pliocene, when that continent was experiencing
extensive geological perturbations leading to widespread
and unpredictable habitat changes (Andrews and Van
Couvering 1975). When Homo spread from Africa to all
the temperate and tropical regions of the Eurasian
continent, the whole world was experiencing the drastic
and unpredictable climatic oscillations of the
Pleistocene. This led to the expansion and contraction
of continental and mountain glaciers and to widespread
and unpredictable habitat changes (Butzer 1971). Thus
the species characteristics and evolutionary history of
Homo makes it very likely that natural selection has
favored the evolution in humans of very open genetic

programs governing morphological, physiological, and
behavioral traits.

Categories of Behavioral Phenotypes

It is also possible to specify what kinds of behavioral phenotypes are most likely to be governed by open
vs. closed genetic programs (Mayr 1974). Genetic programs specifying intra-specific and inter-specific communicative behaviors--those in which there is a signal
and a responding partner, and therefore a narrow range
of 'correct' responses--are more likely to be based on
relatively closed genetic programs than are programs
specifying the development of non-communicative behaviors. Inter-specific communication consists of
specialized signals between two species, and according
to Mayr (1974) can include searching behaviors of predators, and predator-thwarting behaviors of prey. Intra-
specific communication includes behaviors such as
species recognition, intra-specific agonistic displays,
and parent-offspring interactions in species with
parental care. Non-communicative behaviors include, for
example, food selection, foraging strategies, and
habitat preference (Mayr 1974). Although they may
involve some display, social behaviors such as
territoriality, dominance, altruism, and aggression (as
opposed to agonistic displays) are also largely non-communicative behaviors.
Studies of human biology and behavior confirm these
predictions that human phenotypic traits will be largely
based on open genetic programs, and that non-communicative behaviors will have extremely open genetic
programs. Biological anthropologists studying human
adaptations to cold, to heat, and to high altitude, have
documented the importance of environmental as well as
genetic information in the development of adaptive
phenotypes (see articles in Damon 1975). Those human
behaviors which are most narrowly specified by genetic
programs--which are most stereotyped, most predictable,
most universal--are facial expressions, gestures, and
other forms of non-verbal communication which transmit
information about the affective state of the individual
to other members of the species (Eibl-Eibesfeldt 1971;
Morris et al. 1979). In contrast, non-communicative
behaviors such as dominance, territoriality, and
aggression, clearly vary markedly with learning, and
according to the environment in which the specific
behavioral response occurs (see e.g., Dyson-Hudson and
Smith 1978). Attempts to analyze these complex human
social behaviors which ignore or underestimate the
importance of environmental information (e.g. Ardrey
1966; Lorenz 1966; Wilson 1978) have been widely criticized by anthropologists (e.g. Alland 1972; Dyson-Hudson
1979; Montagu 1968) as ignoring the complexity and

diversity of these behaviors both within and between
human groups.

APPLYING AN INTERACTIVE MODEL TO HUMAN BEHAVIOR

Many natural and social scientists are very reluc-
tant to acknowledge a genetic basis for human behavior
because they believe that to do so means that they must
accept genetic determinism, and deny the importance of
culture and learning (e.g. see articles in Montagu
1968). For example, in his rebuttal of Lorenz's claim
that aggression is innate, Montagu states that "the
notable thing about human behavior is that it is learned
. . . everything a human being does as such he has had
to learn from other human beings" (1968:xii). Another
important reason for rejecting the idea that natural
selection has influenced human behavior is that theories
of genetic determination of human behavior have been
used to justify racism, and sexism, in Western society
(see AASftP 1977).
However, it is not legitimate to reject a
scientific theory simply because we dislike its
philosophical, political, or social implications. The
working out of adaptationist programs to try to explain
human behavioral traits is a legitimate enterprise for
anthropologists concerned with human evolution.
However, it must be recognized that these adaptive
explanations are hypotheses, not scientific truths. If
we are to develop a unified theory of human adaptation,
these adaptive explanations must specifically relate to
natural selection theory, must be formulated as testable
hypotheses, and must be tested. They must not be
presented as scientific facts, to be used as the basis
for policy decisions.
In the following sections, I shall discuss some
human communicative behaviors, and some
non-communicative behaviors frequently cited as
influenced by organic evolution.

Intra-Specific Communicative Behaviors

Human non-verbal communicative behaviors appear to
have a relatively large genetic component, to be
governed by relatively closed genetic programs.
Eibl-Eibesfeldt (1971:11-13) documents that children
born both deaf and blind nonetheless smile and laugh
when they are happy, and weep, stamp their feet, clench
their fists, and frown, when they are angry. He also
documents cross-cultural similarities in flirting
behavior of girls (p. 48-49); in non-verbal expressions
of shame (p. 50-52), and in threat behavior of men (p.
55-56). (See also Morris et al., 1979). Clearly,
genetic information is very important in the genesis of
these behaviors. However, even though smiling, laughing,

frowning, and crying can develop apparently without learning, they cannot usefully be described simply as 'genetically determined'. Laughter and tears do not occur in vacuo but rather are responses to particular kinds of environmental stimuli some of which may be universal, and some of which are culture-specific. The response to a baby's smile is almost always a smile, and a person tripping, falling, and dropping the bundles he/she is carrying elicits laughter in many different cultures. However, much humor is culture-specific. For example, cartoons in the New Yorker magazine elicit laughter only among people of a particular social stratum acquainted with the culture of New York City. Although the genetic programs which govern the patterns of motor responses in much of human non-verbal communication appear to be relatively closed, information from environments encountered in the past can strongly condition what stimulus elicits a particular non-verbal response.

The many elements in the environment which influence the genesis of mother-infant interactions, a complex of behaviors involving a great deal of intra-specific communicative behavior, has been studied in Western and non-Western societies (e.g. Brazelton 1969, Konner 1977). Although it might seem that a simple genetic program (care for your infant) would be highly adaptive and would have evolved as a closed genetic program this is not, in fact, the case. A great deal of learning is involved in human maternal care of infants, and appropriate responses by the infant are very important in generating appropriate responses in parents (Brazelton 1969).

The openness of this genetic program makes sense when the life history of the human species is considered. Although the human gestation period is shorter than some other large mammals (e.g. camels, elephants), humans invest a great deal more time and energy in raising of their offspring than do other species. Gestation costs the human mother about 80,000 kilocalories, while nursing for only one year requires 306,000 kcal (WHO 1973:79). During most of human evolutionary history mothers probably nursed their infants for up to three years; and carrying the children as they gathered wild foods added enormously to the energetic cost of raising children (Blurton Jones and Sibley 1978; Lee 1972). These high energy demands precluded further pregnancies until the infant was weaned so it was adaptive for a mother to make this enormous energetic investment in a neonate only if the infant was likely to survive to adulthood and to reproduce successfully. If not, it would improve the mother's reproductive success to abandon the neonate and become pregnant again (Daly and Wilson 1981:406). Humans appear to have evolved an open program for mother-infant bonding, with attachment most likely to occur if the infant responds to the mother in ways which indicate that it is healthy and normal (Brazelton 1969).

The Anomaly of Language

Language is a human behavioral trait which is an intra-specific communicative behavior but is based on a very open genetic program. This strongly suggests that the selective pressures favoring the development of verbal communication are quite different from the selective pressures leading to the evolution of non-verbal communication in humans and other species. That language did not evolve to its present complexity simply as part of a signaling system to elicit specific behavioral responses is supported by the fact that in many cases speech is far less reliable for transmitting information about human motivational states than are gestures and other forms of non-verbal communication. In contrast, human language is far more effective than is non-verbal communication for communicating information about environmental conditions and their variations in space and time.

The selective pressures leading to the evolution of language may have been analogous to those leading to the evolution billions of years ago of complex molecules as carriers of hereditary information. The evolution of DNA allowed the process of adaptation to occur at enormously more rapid rates than had previously been possible because through natural selection information about successful adaptations to past environments was encoded in the DNA and transmitted to future generations. Language can perform essentially this same function since through speech, people can transmit information about successful adaptations to past environments. However, natural selection takes many generations to encode information about individual adaptive behaviors into the DNA of the gene pool of the species, while language can encode information about adaptive behaviors into the cultural pool of the population in a single generation or less. Furthermore, only relatively simple messages can be transmitted through the genes while language can transmit highly complex messages with conditional clauses and complex subjects and objects. Also the use of language enables an individual to transmit information selectively--for example to transmit accurate information to kin and friends, and inaccurate information to strangers.

The emergence of this new mode for encoding and transmitting information about adaptation to environments must certainly have contributed to the dramatic increase in the abundance and range of the hominid lineage. In, perhaps, less than a million years, members of this lineage evolved from creatures restricted to tropical savanna habitats and colonized virtually all of the tropical and temperate regions of the Eurasian land mass.

16

Non-Communicative Behaviors

Some writers have implied that complex human behaviors such as territoriality, aggression, dominance,
and cultural evolution, are determined by the genes.
Ardrey (1966:4-5) claims that "Man . . . is as much a
territorial animal as is a mockingbird singing in the
clear California night. If we defend the title to our
land or the sovereignty of our country, we do it for
reasons no different, no less innate, no less ineradi-
cable, than do lower animals." Lorenz (1966) suggests
that aggression in humans is an instinct which cannot be
eradicated but can best be dealt with by discharging the
aggressive drive in relatively benign forms of behavior,
such as sports. Tiger (1970) believes that an evolved
propensity for males to form bonds, and to be dominant,
makes it inevitable that women will be poorly represented
in high political office. Wilson (1978:88-96) considers
that the emergence of complex, hierarchical, nationalis-
tic, male-dominated societies results from the hyper-
trophy (extreme growth) of human behavioral traits that
evolved while hominids were hunter-gatherers. Apparently
he believes that these evolved traits are genetically
strongly programmed concluding that "we will not . . .
eliminate the hard biological sub-structure until such
time, many years from now, when our descendents learn how
to change the genes themselves" (96-97).
In fact, territoriality, dominance, aggression, and
cultural evolution are not intra-specific communicative
behaviors, so it is very unlikely indeed that they would
be based on closed genetic programs. More important,
they are not behavioral traits--they were not units under
selection during the human evolutionary past. A discussion of dominance and human hierarchies will illustrate
this point.

Dominance

If dominance were an evolutionary trait--the unit
under selection--then it follows that, since the dominants in an hierarchically organized society leave more
offspring, the frequency of dominants in any population
will increase until ultimately the whole population becomes dominant. Clearly this is an impossibility. One
individual cannot be dominant unless others are submis-
sive. The individuals who succeed in being dominant
leave more offspring (are 'winners' in the 'game' of
reproduction). Those who do not succeed may either waste
energy in unsuccessful attempts to be dominant, or adopt
alternative strategies whereby they salvage some reproductive success. The behavior which would lead to the
greatest reproductive success is being able to evaluate
environmental variables (such as size and strength of
competing males as compared to one's own strength and

size) and correctly choose the 'winner' or 'facultative
alternative' strategy. This 'capacity to choose correctly', rather than 'dominance' is the trait on which
selection must be operating. (See footnote 2 for a brief
discussion, with references, of the application of game
theory to analyses of behavioral strategies.)

Human Hierarchies

Some cultural ecologists have attempted to explain
the extremely rapid and independent origin at the end of
the Pleistocene of very hierarchical societies--'pristine
states'--in terms of group benefit. For example Carneiro
(1970a) suggests that early states formed in response to
competition among groups over circumscribed resources.
Others suggest that complex and hierarchical societies
arose through the interaction of a variety of social and
environmental factors (see Wright 1977).
I shall propose a model to account for the variation
in human hierarchical organization based on the aggregate
consequences of individual behavioral strategies which
vary predictably according to variations in the environment (see also Dyson-Hudson 1979, 1980). This postulates
that hierarchies will develop only where resources are
economically controllable, that is, where the cost of
controlling resources is less than the benefits gained.
In these situations the 'winner' strategy is to control
resources, since whoever gains control of resources is
likely to have greater reproductive success. (The association between economic and reproductive success is discussed in footnote 3.)
Individuals who are not members of the controller
group have three options. They can make do with marginal
resources, or they can try to gain access to desirable
resources either by affiliation with the controllers, or
by overthrowing them. The degree to which 'losers' can
be denied access to controllable resources, and therefore
the degree to which a society becomes hierarchical, depends on the nature of the resources themselves (the more
concentrated they are, the more they can be controlled)
and also on the environmental, social, cultural, and
technological means available to defend those resources
(e.g. the larger the controlling group, and the better
their weapons and military organization, the more likely
they are to be able to exclude others). The 'losers'
will choose the affiliative or the overthrow strategy depending on their perceptions of the expected costs and
benefits of these alternative strategies. Therefore
those in control will attempt to maximize the apparent
as well as actual benefits of affiliation, and the apparent as well as actual costs of attempted overthrow.
Areas where the earliest states developed all had
similar environments and subsistence strategies: grain
was cultivated in arid regions along seasonally flooded

rivers, and land, harvested food, and sometimes water
could be relatively easily controlled by a few individuals. I suggest that these hierarchical societies arose
as individuals or coalitions of individuals gained control of the dense but limited resources and took measures
to consolidate that control. Many features which characterize early states, such as armies, roads, and buildings
for food storage, have been interpreted as functioning
to defend the group against outsiders. However these
could also have served to protect the 'controllers'
against overthrow. And organized religions with monu-
mental buildings and a powerful priesthood which characterize early state societies could have served to validate the position of the 'controllers', and helped to
convince the 'affiliators' that the overthrow strategy
would bring down divine as well as secular retribution.
There are many steps between individual behavior
strategies (control: migrate, affiliate, or overthrow)
and complex and hierarchical societies. And since it is
impossible to reconstruct the behavior of individuals in
the prehistoric past, there is no way to prove (or dis-
prove) that adaptive individual behavioral tendencies
contributed to the origin of early hierarchical societies. However, it is evident in modern societies that
changes in resource controllability can lead to changes
in social stratification. (See Dyson-Hudson 1979, 1980
for some examples. Also see Boone Chapter 6 for a model
based on individual behavioral alternatives applied to
analyzing hierarchies and warfare in Medieval and Renais-
sance Europe.)

EVOLUTION AND MALADAPTATION

A widely held misconception is that a behavioral
phenotype which has evolved through natural selection is
'natural', and therefore is adaptive. Since adaptiveness
relates to a specific environmental context, if environments differ markedly from those experienced during the
evolutionary history of a species it is, in fact, unlikely that an evolved behavior will be adaptive.
A clear example for this is provided by Tinbergen's
(1951:44-46) classic studies of sign stimuli, and super-
normal sign stimuli (termed super-normal releases by
American ethologists). He found that animals often respond to signals--that only a portion of the total stimulus configuration acts as an effective cue in releasing
a specific behavior pattern. The approach of the red
spot on the side of an adult herring gull's bill is a
signal for the baby gull to gape; and the courting behavior of a male three-spined stickleback before a pregnant female is dependent on at least two sign-stimuli,
the swollen abdomen and the special posturing movement
of the female. Presenting an animal with an abnormal
stimulus which exaggerates the special cues can lead to

maladaptive responses, as exemplified by the Oystercatcher trying to incubate a giant model of an egg in
preference to her own (see Figure 1.2). People who
choose to eat highly sweetened and/or salted, very
crunchy 'junk foods', instead of a more nutritionally
balanced diet, may well be responding to supernormal sign
stimuli.

Figure 1.2. Oystercatcher reacting to a giant egg in
    preference to a normal egg (foreground) and a herring
    gull's egg (left). (With permission from Tinbergen,
    1951.)

    Evolved behaviors can also lead to maladaptive be-
haviors in changed environments, if a signal for an
evolved behavioral response becomes uncoupled from reproductive success. For example, natural selection may have
led to the evolution of behavior directed toward proximate signals (e.g. striving for economic success, and for
sexual pleasure) which, in past environments have led to
greater reproductive success.[3] The fact that many people
choose to buy a car, or a larger home, rather than having
more children, may have its roots in a historical association between economic success and reproductive success
which no longer exists in Western society.

CONCLUSIONS

    Adaptation and adaptability are often dealt with as
if they were distinct phenomena, with adaptation based

on organic evolution, and adaptability based on environmental variables (e.g., Moran 1979:1-20). In fact, both
adaptation and adaptability are the result of selective
processes. The capacity to adapt through developmental,
acclimatizational, and regulatory adjustments has evolved
through natural selection, and is constrained by genetic
information as well as being influenced by the environment.

Similarly, biological and cultural adaptation are
often dealt with as if they result from different processes. For example, Durham suggests that cultural
change occurs through a selective process which is parallel to, but independent of, natural selection, and that
cultural selection may complement natural selection by
retaining over time those cultural variants whose net effect best enhances the inclusive fitness of individuals
(Durham 1979:56-57). While ecological anthropologists
have often attributed cultural practices as varied as
warfare (Vayda 1961), ritual regulation of hunting of
wild game (Rappaport 1967) and the prohibition of sexual
intercourse during lactation (Stott 1962) to "population
self-regulation," these must ultimately result from group
selection, not individual selection.

However, Durham's theory is inadequate, because selective processes leading to cultural adaptation over
time cannot exactly parallel selective processes leading
to changes in the gene pool. Unlike genetic change, cultural change is not the passive result of these selective
processes. Rather it is directed by human motivations
and human learning capacities, which in turn are influenced by neurological structures and functions which
evolved through natural selection.[4] While the group
level analyses of ecological anthropologists are based
on the ecological theory of Wynne-Edwards (1962), this
is now rejected by animal ecologists (see Clutton Brock
and Harvey 1978:1-33 for a summary of the arguments).

I believe that, in order to match the strides made
in recent years in animal ecology, ecological anthropologists must develop a unified theory of human biological
and cultural (biocultural) adaptation: that this must
ultimately be based on Darwinian theory--on a recognition
that natural selection acting at the level of the individual, not the group, is the only force which can generate and maintain adaptation. I suggest that an interactive model which specifically takes into account that all
phenotypes are responses to environmental as well as genetic information, can help us to develop general theories of human adaptation, and to avoid deterministic
theories which are justly criticized as being scientifi-
cally untenable, and serving to validate the sexist,
racist, elitist status quo (AASftP 1977, Dyson-Hudson
1979).

If we are to make advances in anthropological
theory, adaptive explanations of human behavior should

be framed as testable hypotheses, based on predictions
derived from Darwinian theory (see Smith Chapter 2 in
this book). At a minimum, they should not violate the
rules for framing adaptive explanations which follow from
natural selection theory (Boone Chapter 6). Although it
is certain that all of human biology and behavior cannot
be explained in terms of natural selection theory, I believe that we should nonetheless attempt to relate human
biological and behavioral phenotypes to adaptations to
past and present environments. We will never know how
much of human biology and behavior can be understood
through a careful application of evolutionary theory unless we work toward this goal. Social scientists who believe a priori that natural selection theory will prove
inadequate for analyses of human interactions with their
environment--that human societies have emergent properties which require other paradigms for analysis--should
seek to develop a separate body of theory, rather than
borrowing concepts from evolutionary biology, and applying them in inappropriate ways.

ACKNOWLEDGMENTS

It is impossible to acknowledge all the people who
have contributed to this chapter, since it is the out-
growth of almost four decades of exposure to evolutionary
theory--as a research assistant to Th. Dobzhansky; as a
high school and college student attending talks of Ernst
Mayr, G. G. Simpson, G. L. Stebbins, Konrad Lorenz and
others; as a graduate student at Oxford working under A.
J. Cain and P. M. Sheppard and joining in seminars and
field work directed by Nikko Tinbergen; and as an independent researcher attending lectures and discussions led
by R. Levin, S. J. Gould, David Hull, and others at a
summer program on "The Biological and Social Perspective
on Human Nature" sponsored by the Society for the Human-
ities. Bruce Wallace, Davydd Greenwood, and William Pro-
vine have responded critically and helpfully, as I have
tried to develop my ideas on human biocultural adaptation. Colleagues and students in the Anthropology Department at Cornell University have challenged what to
me seemed self-evident truths, and forced me to re-formu-
late and clarify my presentation. Eric Smith and Donna
Zahorik read the semi-final drafts of the manuscript.
Jackie Livingstone drew Figure 1.2. The secretaries in
the Anthropology Department helped with the typing. However, although many people have contributed to this chapter, I alone am responsible for the views expressed here.

NOTES

1. These requirements for an evolutionary argument
are based on the following sources: 1 through 7, Levins

1977; 8, Slobodkin and Rapoport 1974; and 9, Williams, 1966.

2. Maynard Smith and others have formalized the application of game theory to the evolution of behavior, and developed models of evolutionarily stable strategies which predict what proportion of actors behaving in specified alternative ways will be stable in a given population given a defined set of alternatives. (See Maynard Smith 1976; Maynard Smith and Parker 1976; Maynard Smith and Price 1973.)

3. The relationship between economic success and/or social status, and reproductive success, has been explored by Barkow (1977), Chagnon et al. (1979); and Irons (1979c, 1980). Other studies which document this relationship include Easterlin (1968), Frisch (1978), Herlihy (1973) and Kahn and Strageldin (1979). Irons (1977) suggests that this relationship of fertility with economic and/or social status may no longer exist in modern industrial societies, because the novelty of modern social environments is such that the proximate behavioral mechanisms which were adaptive in pre-industrial societies are no longer adaptive.

4. Recent studies of learning clearly document Hamburg's (1963, 1968) theory that through natural selection, animals have evolved so that they readily learn those behaviors which were adaptive in environments regularly encountered during their evolutionary history, and are 'contra-prepared' to learn non-adaptive behaviors (see e.g. Shettleworth 1972, Seligman and Hager 1972, Hinde and Stevenson-Hinde 1973).

2
Evolutionary Ecology and the Analysis of Human Social Behavior

Eric Alden Smith

Editors' Summary: Eric Smith in this chapter expands on some of the ideas presented in the previous chapter to outline the field of evolutionary ecology, a rapidly developing area in ecology. Much of the theory is drawn from the animal ecology literature, but the work takes on an added dimension with its application to human populations. Smith points out that both evolutionary ecology and sociobiology are based on natural selection theory, and he recognizes individual benefit as a major criterion for adaptation. However sociobiology is based on genetic theory, while evolutionary ecology focuses on regularities in flexible phenotypic responses to problems and opportunities presented by the environment. Smith argues on logical and empirical grounds that ecological models and environmental variables are more useful in predicting patterns of human adaptation than are the narrowly genetic models of sociobiology. This fits well with Dyson-Hudson's conclusion on theoretical grounds that many human behaviors are based on very open rather than closed genetic programs.

INTRODUCTION

The Problem

The primary scientific mandate of anthropology is "to account for the evolution of the global inventory of sociocultural differences and similarities" (Harris 1975: 454). General systems of explanation for this domain have been advanced repeatedly over the years, and continue to compete for disciplinary pre-eminence. Prominent contributions include cultural ecology (Steward 1955), cultural evolutionism (White 1959), cultural materialism (Harris 1968, 1979), economic maximization theory (Schneider 1974), and--most recently--sociobiology (Chagnon and Irons 1979).

My aim here is to discuss yet another analytical approach--that body of theory known as evolutionary ecology. This approach, a branch of biology formalized in the last two decades, offers a unique set of analytical tools not duplicated by any existing specialty. I believe this theory has great potential for anthropological applications. While I hold that evolutionary ecology has certain inherent advantages over the anthropological "paradigms" mentioned above, I feel it is an approach generally compatible with all of them. Thus, we need not discard our current favorite theoretical approach in order to take advantage of theory from evolutionary ecology.

In essence, evolutionary ecology combines the basic elements of Darwinian (natural selection) theory with an emphasis on phenotypic and behavioral flexibility as adaptive responses to various kinds of ecological problems and opportunities. Because it offers ways of analyzing adaptive strategies without relying on genetic models, evolutionary ecology is of direct relevance to current discussion and analysis of human biological and cultural (biocultural) adaptation as represented by the set of papers contained in this volume. Evolutionary ecology has much to contribute to attempts at understanding the role of Darwinian processes in human adaptation and cultural transmission, and I believe that this theory can help us find a "middle way" between the rock of genetic determinism and the hard place of cultural autonomy.

An Outline

In this essay, I wish to sketch out the structure of evolutionary ecology, compare and contrast it with other approaches to explaining human behavioral diversity, and provide a brief summary of the nascent research program that is beginning to apply this body of theory to anthropological problems and data.

Accordingly, I first outline the scope, history, and mode of inquiry characterizing general evolutionary ecology. This body of theory is then compared and contrasted with those of its closest anthropological analogues: cultural ecology, human sociobiology, cultural materialism, and economic anthropology. Substantive applications of theory from evolutionary ecology to anthropological questions are summarized. Four topical areas are covered in this review: foraging strategies, spatial organization, life history strategies, and niche theory. These areas were chosen because I view them as the segments of evolutionary ecology most readily applicable to anthropological research.

THE LOGIC OF EVOLUTIONARY ECOLOGY

Scope and History

About twenty years ago, Robert MacArthur (e.g., 1958, 1960, 1961), building on the accomplishments of the previously isolated disciplines of population ecology and

evolutionary theory, crystallized a certain type of analytical approach now known as evolutionary ecology. This
approach represents an attempt to introduce theoretical
rigor to ecology, and to integrate several areas of population biology. As outlined in detail below, evolutionary ecology approaches problems by developing mathematical models derived from the basic postulates of natural
selection theory (as well as microeconomics), and deduces
testable hypotheses concerning behavioral or population
processes from these models.

While empirical tests have lagged somewhat behind
theory formulation (Stearns 1981; Wiens 1976: 110), field
research in behavioral ecology has been strongly affected
by these theoretical developments. Not only ecological
theorizing but, in fact, a great deal of empirical research on animal behavior, has been guided by theories
and models developed in evolutionary ecology. Excellent
overviews of this rapidly expanding field of inquiry are
now available (Cody and Diamond 1975; Emlen 1973; Krebs
and Davies 1978; May 1976; Pianka 1978; Roughgarden
1979).

Logic and Mode of Inquiry

Evolutionary ecology embraces a wide range of
topics, from analysis of strategies at the level of individual organisms to complex models of community structure
and coevolution. Anthropologists, being single-species
specialists, will probably find theory dealing with individual strategies to be of greatest use. The application of evolutionary ecological analysis to the behavior
of individuals of a single species involves a definite
sequence of steps. First, a research problem amenable
to ecological analysis is chosen (such as the subsistence system of a particular population in a particular
habitat). Next, an adaptive problem facing members of
the study population must be defined in a manner con-
gruent with natural selection theory (e.g., choosing the
optimal diet from an array of potential prey types). In
order to operationalize costs and benefits of alternative
strategies, a proximate goal or currency must be chosen
that is believed to be highly correlated with fitness
(e.g., the net rate of energy capture).

One must then choose an existing model, or generate
a new model, suitable for investigating the problem
(e.g., the MacArthur-Pianka optimal diet model discussed
below). The model is employed to deduce a cost-benefit
equation of some sort that specifies what form an optimal
solution should take (e.g., prey items should be added
to the diet in rank order of decreasing pursuit efficiency until the decrease in search time is offset by the
increase in pursuit time, such that the net energy capture rate is maximized). At that point, one must also
specify the constraints facing an optimal solution (e.g.,

is prey distribution random or patchy?). Given all these
steps, the researcher can deduce a set of hypotheses applicable to the specific case being investigated. Finally, these hypotheses can be tested by examining evidence on the fit between predicated (hypothetically optimal) and observed behavioral patterns. The results of
such tests can suggest modifications of the model, the
constraints, the cost-benefit currency, or the research
methods.

ANTHROPOLOGICAL APPLICATIONS

Currently, at least four main areas of research in
evolutionary ecology with clear anthropological implications can be discerned: (1) the study of foraging
strategies; (2) research on mating systems and life-history strategies; (3) the study of spatial organization
and group formation; and (4) the interrelated topics of
niche theory, population dynamics, and community structure. Each of these areas has produced work relevant to
the analysis of human social behavior, and each has motivated anthropological applications. The following sections review studies applying theory from these areas to
anthropological problems, stressing the new light thus
shed on aspects of human behavioral ecology. Rather than
detail the methods and results of these studies, I focus
on the heuristic value of evolutionary ecology models,
and their analytical advances over more orthodox approaches in ecological anthropology.

Foraging Strategies

In evolutionary ecology, the study of subsistence
strategies has led to the development of a group of
models labelled "optimal foraging theory" (reviews in
Kamil and Sargent 1981; Krebs 1978; Pyke et al. 1977;
Schoener 1971). This body of theory is concerned with
several topics, including prey choice and diet breadth,
foraging group size, optimal patch choice, and optimal
patterns of movement and time allocation during foraging.
Given the strong anthropological interest in subsistence strategies, any systematic body of theory dealing
with food procurement has obvious relevance. Hence, it
is not surprising that the bulk of anthropological applications of evolutionary ecology have been concerned with
foraging strategies--particularly those of hunter-
gatherers, where the connection with extant ecological
models is the most direct (Winterhalder 1981a). Of the
various topical areas included within optimal foraging
theory, that of optimal group size has perhaps the most
direct implications for human social behavior (Smith
1981). However, even a topic like optimal diet breadth
has strong implications for understanding human settlement patterns--a factor of obvious social importance.

The optimal diet model of MacArthur and Pianka (1966), alluded to earlier, can be used to illustrate the manner in which foraging theorists employ models to generate explanatory hypotheses. This particular model, illustrated in Figure 2.1, assumes what is termed a fine-grained relationship between forager and prey, such that foragers search for all prey types simultaneously and encounter the different types "randomly"--in direct proportion to their environmental abundance. (This is in contrast with other models, which apply to coarse-grained situations, where prey types are distributed in a "patchy" manner, and search is more selective.) Since, in this model, search is not charged to particular prey types, the available types can be rank-ordered by a ratio of average values (e.g., in calories) per unit of pursuit time, where "pursuit" includes capture, processing, and consumption time as well. The forager's goal is to choose the array of prey types that will maximize the total expected benefit per unit of foraging time, including both pursuit times (for all prey types chosen) and search time. As illustrated in the graph, the division into search time and pursuit time generates two opposing cost curves. As a forager widens its diet by adding prey types of lower and lower rank, pursuit costs averaged over the entire array of types increases; however, with a widened diet breadth, less time is "wasted" in search because a smaller proportion of all types encountered are rejected. How generalized or specialized should one be? The solution generated by the model is that prey types should be "added," in descending rank order, until the decreasing search costs are exactly offset by the increasing pursuit costs. This maximizes the total returns pre unit foraging time.

This model yields many predictions, only two of which will be noted here (see Pyke 1977, and Winterhalder 1981a, for further discussion). First, since changes in abundance affect only the search curve, the decision to add or drop an item from the diet should be based only on the abundance of higher-ranked prey types already included in the optimal diet, and not on the abundance of that prey type itself. No matter how common, inefficiently-pursued prey types should not be taken if they lie to the right of the intersection of the two curves (i.e., if adding this type will depress the overall rate of return from foraging). Second, when high-ranked resources are abundant, diets should be highly specialized, while scarcity of such resources selects for generalized diets--irrespective of the overall diversity of different habitats. These and other predictions have obvious implications for research on hunter-gatherer subsistence (Winterhalder and Smith 1981). Such models are responsive to rapid changes in subsistence choices, not only as a function of environmental change but also with regard to changes in pursuit methods (due to alterations

28

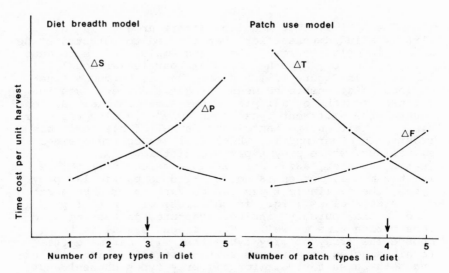

Figure 2.1.   The MacArthur-Pianka foraging strategy
    models.   (After MacArthur and Pianka 1966, and Winter-
    halder 1977.)
    <u>Optimal diet breadth model</u>.   The ΔS curve plots de-
    creasing search costs, and the ΔP curve increasing pur-
    suit costs, as prey types are added to the diet (in
    descending rank order of net return per unit pursuit
    time).   The optimal diet occurs at the intersection of
    the two curves, when decreasing search costs exactly
    offset increasing pursuit time and total foraging time
    per unit return is minimized (see arrow).   <u>Optimal</u>
    <u>patch choice model</u>.   The ΔT curve measures decreasing
    between-patch travel time, and the ΔF curve increasing
    within-patch foraging time, per unit return, as patch
    types are added to the foraging itinerary (in descend-
    ing rank order of net return per unit foraging time
    within patches).   Increasing the number of patch types
    decreases time spent traveling between (and/or search-
    ing for) foraging areas, but increases the average
    time cost per unit return within patches, as lower
    quality patch types are added to the itinerary.   The
    optimal number of patch types maximizes the overall
    return rate, given by the intersection of the two
    curves (see arrow).

in technology, social organization, or even information
networks).

Among anthropologists, archaeologists have thus far
been the most active in applying optimal foraging models.
Optimal prey selection has been modeled by Jochim (1976),
Perlman (1976), Bayham (1979), Yesner (1981), and Keene
(1979a, 1979b), each using a somewhat different approach
or set of simplifying assumptions. While direct tests
of diet breadth models using archaeological materials are
rarely feasible, the models do serve two other important
purposes. First, they provide a solid conceptual basis
for challenging prevailing commonsense views of hunter-
gatherer behavior and the nature of the archaeological
record. For example, the widely-held view that foragers
(human or otherwise) harvest prey in proportion to the
environmental availability is contrary to predictions of
certain optimal diet models, as discussed above. Second,
optimal diet models can facilitate archaeological recon-
structions of prehistoric subsistence systems, given
knowledge of past environments and foraging technology
(Jochim 1976; Keene 1981).

While archaeologists have led the way in applying
foraging theory to anthropological cases, ethnographic
applications are beginning to appear. Winterhalder
(1977, 1981b) produced the first field study on human
foraging strategies explicitly guided by optimal foraging theory. Working with the Boreal Forest Cree, Winterhalder examined predictions from the optimal diet breadth
and optimal patch choice models (see his Figure 1) developed by MacArthur and Pianka (1966). He documented a
qualitative agreement between predictions from these
models and contemporary Cree patterns of prey selection
and habitat usage, as well as preliminary congruence with
predictions from Horn's (1968) model of spatial organization and Charnov's (1976) "marginal value theorem" on
patterns of time allocation. Winterhalder was also able
to show that the historical patterns of Cree dietary
change, when considered from the point of view of changing search and pursuit costs due to technological innova-
tion, were at least consistent with optimal diet theory.

O'Connell and Hawkes (1981) have carried out some
preliminary tests of optimal diet breadth and patch
choice models with ethnographic data on Alyawara (Australian Aborigine) plant gathering. Though their results
are mixed, detailed quantitative data on Alyawara foraging is often consistent with predictions from the models
concerning energy efficiency maximization. O'Connell and
Hawkes also show that optimal foraging theory can shed
much light on the prehistory of hunter-gatherer foraging
strategies on the Australian continent. My own field research on Hudson Bay Inuit (Canadian Eskimo) foraging
strategies provides quantitative tests of foraging efficiency hypotheses in four areas--diet breadth and prey
choice, hunt type choice, time allocation, and optimal

foraging group size (Smith 1980, 1981). Results of these tests indicate that much of the variation in Inuit foraging behavior is predicted quite closely by foraging strategy models--even when the effects of participation in a cash economy and use of motorized vehicles are incorporated into the analysis.

Thus far, tests of hypotheses drawn from optimal foraging theory have been quite successful in accounting for diversity in various aspects of the subsistence systems of prehistoric and contemporary hunter-gatherers (Winterhalder and Smith 1981). Equally important, an awareness of this relatively sophisticated set of models has prompted a growing number of anthropologists to re-examine some currently popular but rather simplistic approaches to human subsistence behavior. For hunter-gatherer studies in particular, optimal foraging theory offers a partial resolution of the dilemma of how to account for the diversity of human foraging adaptions without abandoning the search for general theory (a point developed in detail in Smith and Winterhalder 1981).

Spatial Organization

Ecological study of spatial organization is a somewhat more diffuse area of inquiry than that concerned with foraging strategies. The focus is on such topics as territoriality, resource competition, and predator defense, as these relate to group formation or dispersion (reviews in Brown and Orians 1970; Bertram 1978; Davies 1978). Of special relevance to anthropology is the ecology of territorial behavior, which has been a controversial matter among social scientists (Dyson-Hudson and Smith 1978).

Wilmsen (1973) was perhaps the first anthropologist to apply an evolutionary ecological model to human social behavior; in particular, he argued that Horn's (1968) model of group formation in relation to resource dispersion and predictability helped account for the range of sizes observed in hunter-gatherer local bands. While Wilmsen did not apply Horn's model to particular societies, Heffley (1981) has begun this task with analyses of spatial organization and settlement patterns among three Northern Athapaskan societies. She showed that Athapaskan groups aggregate and disperse in response to the spatiotemporal concentration and predictability of key resources, such as caribou, in the manner predicted by Horn's model. It is interesting that in this case, some uniquely human attributes, such as information exchange, can be easily incorporated into the ecological model, while others, such as resource storage, are more difficult to incorporate.

Dyson-Hudson and Smith (1978) adapted evolutionary ecological theory, especially the "economic defendability" model of territoriality (Brown 1964), to analyze

cross-cultural variation in spatial organization. We
argued that territoriality is expected to develop only
when the benefits of exclusive use outweigh the costs of
territory defense, and that this is only likely to occur
when key resources are relatively predictable in space
and time, and of moderate density. Unpredictable and/or
scarce resources do not repay a territorial strategy,
while superabundant resources can be shared at no cost
(see Figure 2.2).

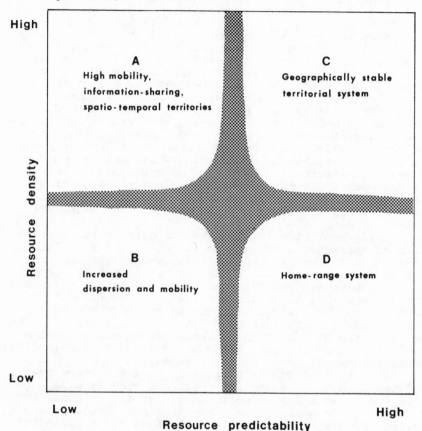

Figure 2.2. The economic defendability model of spatial
    organization. Low predictability of key resources
    favors mobility, and militates against territorial
    systems, while high resource density favors either ex-
    clusive use or co-operative exploitation, depending on
    defense costs and resource predictability. Combina-
    tions of these two factors (in conjunction with re-
    source utilization capabilities) produce the various
    optimal patterns of spatial organization illustrated.
    (From Dyson-Hudson and Smith 1978.)

The topically-related area concerning the evolutionary ecology of mating systems differs from life-history theory in a greater concern with social behavior and a lesser emphasis on demographic processes. Theory in this area is less developed than that concerning life history strategies (reviews in Clutton-Brock and Harvey 1978; Emlen and Oring 1977; Halliday 1978; Orians 1969; and Wittenberger 1979). Nevertheless, since explanation of variation in mating systems addresses matters of longstanding interest to anthropologists, the ecological theory is deserving of closer examination.

Much interest has focused on explaining the distribution of polygynous vs. monogamous mating systems. For example, the "polygyny threshold" model (Verner and Willson 1966; Orians 1969) predicts that females will choose a polygamous union whenever already-mated males control sufficient resources to offset the cost of sharing these with other females (see Figure 2.3). In other words, polygyny is more likely to develop when resources are unevenly distributed among males and their families, and polygynous males are expected to be "wealthier" in resources convertible into offspring while polygynous females are expected to roughly equal monogamous females in reproductive output. These predictions, and others that can be derived from the model (Gowaty 1981, Wittenberger 1981), are certainly amenable to test with anthropological data.

Emlen and Oring (1977) have discussed further varieties of mating systems, and their ecological correlates. They identify several types of polygynous systems: resource-defense polygyny (as in the Orians model), female-defense polygyny, and male-dominance polygyny. Emlen and Oring argue that the spatiotemporal distribution of resources, particularly their density and degree of clumping, often will determine the optimal distribution of females, which will in turn determine which mating system is likely to evolve (cf. Wrangham 1979 for an application of this idea to pongid social systems).

As yet, ecological theories of mating systems are relatively unrefined and untested, and clearly more complex models will be needed to deal with the cultural refinements of human systems. Nevertheless, evolutionary ecology provides some intellectual tools for explaining variation in human mating systems, and it would seem worthwhile to put these tools to use.

Theory of the Niche and Community Structure

The most dynamic and complex area of inquiry in evolutionary ecology is the study of niche evolution, competition, and community structure (reviews in Armstrong and McGelee 1980; Cody and Diamond 1975; Diamond 1978; May 1974; and Wiens 1977). This literature is far too large and complex even to survey here. I suggest that

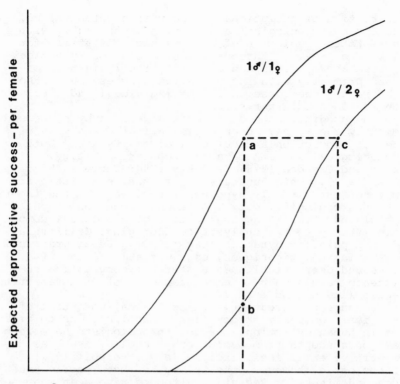

Figure 2.3. The resource-threshold model for the occurrence of polygyny. Expected reproductive success of
females is plotted as a function of the quantity of
resources controlled by her mate. The exact shape of
the curves is hypothetical, but it is assumed that any
such curve will be monotonically increasing to an
asymptote, as shown here. The model assumes that males
allocate resources to mates and their offspring, and
that females choose among males so as to maximize expected reproductive success. For any given quantity
of resources, females mated monogamously have greater
expected reproductive success than females mated polygynously (e.g., the difference between points a and b).
If there is sufficient variance in male-controlled resources, however, females may do better by mating
polygynously with a wealthy male than by mating monogamously with a poorer male. The difference in wealth
necessary to equalize the reproductive success of
monogamous and polygynous females is the "polygyny
threshold" (e.g., the difference between points a and
c). (After Orians 1969.)

this portion of evolutionary theory is a potential gold-
mine for anthropological applications, especially with
regard to the evolution of complex social systems--for
unlike the previous three areas of evolutionary ecology
surveyed above, niche and community theory is not concerned primarily with <u>individual</u> strategies, but rather
with tracing the consequences of individual and population trends for larger systems.

The predictions and insights generated by niche and
community theory have been employed in the analysis of
modes of production and cultural diversity among both
archaeological and ethnographic populations (e.g.,
Chasko and Cashdan 1978; Hardesty 1980; Terrell 1977;
Yellen 1977). Unfortunately, there has been little attempt to test directly hypotheses derived from the theory
with anthropological data. A recent exception is the
careful and stimulating application of ecological competition theory to the analysis of aboriginal California
Indian population dynamics (Gage 1979). Using graphical
and statistical techniques, Gage was able to show that
humans and deer established a state of competitive co-
existence regulated by the abundance of other interacting
species (acorns and fish).

Perhaps the greatest anthropological potential of
ecological community theory lies in applications to problems in human evolution. Paleoanthropologists have long
drawn on concepts from evolutionary ecology, such as the
competitive exclusion principle (e.g., Wolpoff 1971).
All too often, however, the theory has been poorly understood and misused. Recently, attempts have been made to
use the theory in a more appropriate fashion (Shaklee and
Shaklee 1975; Winterhalder 1980, 1981c). As demonstrated
by Winterhalder in particular, theory from evolutionary
ecology is a rich source for developing testable hypotheses for explaining the human evolutionary record.
Paleoanthropological research would undoubtedly benefit
from intensive application of this theory.

DISCUSSION

Having briefly surveyed evolutionary ecology and its
initial anthropological applications, something remains
to be said about the relation of this approach to other
types of inquiry. In particular, what, if anything, does
evolutionary ecology offer that is not already available
from cultural ecology, economic anthropology, cultural
materialism, or sociobiology?

Relations to Sociobiology

The relation to sociobiology is complex. Contemporary neo-Darwinian research on behavioral adaptation is
guided by two major bodies of theory: evolutionary genetics and evolutionary ecology. General sociobiology rep-

resents a synthesis of these two areas, and the boundary
between sociobiology and evolutionary ecology cannot be
mapped, if it exists at all. However, human sociobiology
is a special case, for at least two reasons. First, research in human sociobiology has thus far exhibited an
excessive emphasis on evolutionary genetics, to the virtual exclusion of ecological theory (Dyson-Hudson 1979;
Smith 1979). Second, sociobiological analysis of a
single species, human or otherwise, must move beyond the
high level of generality inherent in genetically-focused
models if it is to contribute much to understanding behavior that is unique to the species. This is totally
aside from the question of how to analyze the tremendous
variability exhibited by humans in their social behavior,
which makes the models of evolutionary genetics even more
limited in their explanatory power.

Evolutionary ecology seems naturally suited for
dealing with the behavioral variability so characteristic
of our species. The main differences between the evolutionary ecological approach and the genetically-focused
models that dominate human sociobiology are as follows.
First, while both approaches are ultimately founded on
the logical postulates of natural selection theory, evolutionary ecology emphasizes operationally-defined cost-
benefit measures that, unlike fitness, can be empirically
measured for particular traits or options. In practice,
the fitness value of specific choices, traits, or even
alleles is extremely difficult to measure, since many of
each are summed in any individual's life history. This
problem is only compounded when dealing with a long-
lived, multiple-breeding, behaviorally complex species
such as Homo sapiens. In many cases, however, there is
no good operational alternative to fitness as a currency
for testing sociobiological hypotheses. This may con-
strain sociobiological inquiry to cases amenable to analysis with long-term, retrospective data bases. This
difference, while more methodological than theoretical,
means that it will often be easier to test (falsify)
ecological hypotheses than sociobiological ones.

Second, evolutionary ecological models make minimal
assumptions about the genetic causes of behavioral variability: only a genetically modifiable capacity for
adaptive decision-making need be assumed in applying
these models (Durham 1976a, 1978; Smith 1980). On this
score, sociobiological models exhibit variable degrees
of reliance on genetic determinism. It seems likely that
human sociobiology will move increasingly away from assumptions, heuristic or otherwise, of simple genetic determinism and towards a more interactive view (Alexander
1979, Irons 1979b). If so, this difference between
ecological and sociobiological approaches to explaining
human behavior will diminish or even disappear.

The third major difference between the ecological
and the sociobiological approaches, as they have been ap-

plied so far, concerns the level of explanation addressed
and the types of evidence employed by each. Evolutionary
ecology focuses on the interaction of phenotypic potentials with environmental parameters. Accordingly, behavioral plasticity and environmental variability are
given central roles in the theory (Emlen 1976, 1980).
In contrast, most models employed in human sociobiology
focus on genetic asymmetries and other features associated with Mendelian inheritance (Thomas et al. 1979).
This difference in the focus of inquiry leads to differences in the level of inquiry, even for research on the
same topic.

An example of this is provided by the topic of mating systems. As noted above, evolutionary ecologists
have devoted much effort to understanding how ecological
costs and benefits select for particular mating systems.
On the other hand, sociobiologists interested in human
mating systems have focused almost exclusively on coeffi-
cients of genetic relatedness and kin selection arguments. For example, Kurland (1979) has presented a careful sociobiological argument about the role of paternity
uncertainty in determining the occurrence of matriliny
and the avunculate. However, because he stops at the genetic level, his efforts tell us very little about the
ultimate determinants of mating systems--why does paternity certainty vary cross-culturally? Kurland himself
admits this limitation of the genetic level of explanation (pp. 175-76), but because of his sociobiological
emphasis on genetic relatedness he has little to say
about the ecological determinants of the phenomenon he
is investigating.

Let me stress that the issue I am raising here is
not whether the sociobiological model is correct or not,
but whether it is being applied fully and correctly.
Even the simplest model of kin selection, which holds
that genetic "altruism" is adaptive whenever k > 1/r
(Hamilton 1963), must necessarily include ecological factors (Smith 1979). My criticism of human sociobiologists
is that too often they rest their argument on an assessment of genetic relatedness (r) alone, leaving out the
complex and crucial factors that determine the costs and
benefits (k) of alternative forms of reproductive investment. The primary theory dealing with such costs and
benefits has been developed in the field of evolutionary
ecology, not evolutionary genetics.

In summary, whether we are analyzing insect, avian,
or human social systems, selective forces are always
going to be ecological, and purely genetic models of
adaptation are inherently incomplete (Slatkin and Maynard Smith 1979: 233ff; Smith 1979). This does not mean
that genetically-focused models are somehow mistaken or
useless; rather, it suggests that since ecological and
genetic theory are complementary, researchers interested
in the application of evolutionary theory to human be-

havior should cultivate an interactive, integrated approach.

Relation to Anthropological Theory

In anthropological theory, the areas of cultural ecology, economic theory, and cultural materialism are most directly related to the analytical framework of evolutionary ecology. I believe that evolutionary ecology offers advances over these other approaches in both logic and methods, but that it by no means makes them obsolete. Intellectual relations in these cases should be primarily symbiotic rather than competitive.

Steward's (1955) cultural ecology has defined the dominant approach in ecological anthropology up to the present time. Although cultural ecology has been modified, by borrowing concepts and methods from general ecology (e.g., Vayda and Rappaport 1968) or systems theory (e.g., Flannery 1972), the basic inductive method has scarcely been altered (Smith and Winterhalder 1981). Priority is given to subsistence in explaining cultural variation, but the reason for this causal priority is never deductively justified. The tendency of cultural ecologists to state postulates and results in functionalist terms is also subject to criticism (Friedman 1979; Orans 1975; Orlove 1980; Smith and Winterhalder 1981; cf. Rappaport 1977), as is the theoretically and empirically unjustified reliance on systemic teleology and group selection (Bates and Lees 1979; Richerson 1977). Of course, evolutionary ecology is also a functionalist theory. However, the functional relationships are logically deduced from Darwinian postulates, do not assume purposeful behavior at the level of social or ecological systems, and are empirically testable.

The framework of cultural materialism (Harris 1968, 1979) is closely related to cultural ecology, although in this case the primary determinants of cultural diversity are broadened to embrace "the material conditions of life"--a diffuse set of factors never rigorously defined, and thus subject to much disputation (cf. Richardson and Boyd 1980). While Harris (1968: 520) has compared the "materialist" research strategy of cultural materialism to the "adaptive" research strategy of evolutionary theory, this compassion seems inappropriate. The principles of natural selection are of value as a deductive basis for generating hypotheses because they can be framed in rigorous logical and mathematical terms, and because they can in turn be derived from such well-established forces as heredity, variability, competition, and differential reproduction. In addition, natural selection and its attendant processes can be defined operationally in terms of gene frequency changes or differential propagation of offspring. The principles of cultural materialism have no such deductive or operational

38

status at the present time. The research strategy is
characterized by plausibility arguments and factional
disputes, rather than an active program of hypothesis
testing following standard scientific procedure (e.g.,
Sahlins 1976 vs. Ross 1980, or Sahlins 1978 vs. Harris
and Sahlins 1979). To be sure, the present situation
may reflect current research practices rather than the
inherent potential of cultural materialism. I simply
suggest that cultural materialists could further their
goal of explaining cultural variability by greater attention to both the content and the form of evolutionary
ecological theory (cf. Richerson and Boyd 1980).

Formal economic theory shares many analytical and
logical features with evolutionary ecology (Rapport and
Turner 1977). In particular, the study of optimal choice
or design is emerging as a major focus in evolutionary
research, and owes a great deal to similar research in
economics (Cody 1974; Maynard Smith 1978). However,
there is a fundamental difference between evolutionary
ecology and economic theory: the former deductively de-
rives its strategic analysis from the postulates of
natural selection, while the latter is forced to assume
that scarcity or maximization is an adequate foundation
for the deduction of theory. Therefore, it is reasonable
to argue that economic logic is a special case of adaptive logic, and that economic theory may in principle be
derivable from evolutionary theory (Richerson 1977; Etter
1978; Boyd and Richerson 1980); the converse scarcely
seems tenable. If that be so, we should not blithely assume that adaptive considerations are irrelevant to
ecological optimization models, nor that the interests
of anthropological explanation are best served by sev-
ering the connection between these models and the underlying neo-Darwinian theory. Neither the maximization of
profit nor the maximization of utility have the logical
status associated with the fitness criterion of evolutionary biology. Thus, while I agree that models in
evolutionary ecology and microeconomics exhibit formal
similarities, and may even lead to similar or identical
predictions (McCay 1981: 364, Orlove 1980: 257-58) there
are striking differences in explanatory depth and ability
to explain deviations from predicted optima. In other
words, territorial groups or optimal foragers (for example) may behave differently if maximizing a hierarchi-
cally-arranged set of long-term correlates of fitness
than if maximizing short-term economic variables.

If the occurrence of economic rationality is both
made possible by and ultimately constrained by natural
selection, the pursuit of economic goals should be highly
dependent on their contingent relationships with adaptive
outcomes--within certain bounds of indeterminism maintained by cultural modes of inheritance (Boyd and Richerson 1980). In other words, we should not expect individuals to engage in single-minded pursuit of profit

where this would reduce their expectations of survival
or reproductive success, nor should we expect economic
utilities to be independent of such Darwinian criteria.
Ecological variables are likely to play a major role in
generating and maintaining particular patterns of economic behavior under particular conditions. This may
help account for the variation in economic goals and
structures evident cross-culturally.

Conclusions

    Evolutionary ecology has developed theory in several
areas that appear to have relevance for analyses of human
social behavior. In this approach, mathematico-deductive
models are generated to represent variability in a set
of environmental and behavioral parameters. The models
represent ecological interactions in terms of hypothetically optimal solutions to adaptive problems, such as resource acquisition, competitive interactions, reproduction, and spatial organization. The underlying physiology and technology of the study species, and any unmodi-
fiable environmental characteristics, are taken as
"givens"--that is, as constraints on the optimal solution. Cost-benefit currencies employ operationally-defined correlates of fitness, such as net rate of energy
capture or reproductive output. Hence, the approach allows us to predict variation in behavior on the basis of
particular environmental features and associated adaptive
contingencies, and then to test these predictions with
empirical data. As with any research on human adaptation, including sociobiology evolutionary ecology has
limitations as well as strengths. We cannot examine directly the historical processes that have produced most
adaptive solutions, and we cannot directly test the
validity of the currency, constraints, and assumptions
built into each model. Furthermore, the optimization
bias inherent to "adaptationist" research programs can
become its own caricature if researchers are not careful
to maintain rigor and avoid plausibility arguments
(Lewontin 1977) . Nevertheless, evolutionary ecology
would seem to offer a necessary complement to sociobiological analysis whenever one is concerned with explaining the adaptive significance of unique human attributes,
or of variability in these attributes (Smith 1979).
    In the case of orthodox ecological anthropology and
cultural materialism, evolutionary ecology offers advantages primarily because of its reliance on hypothetico-
deductive methodology and its basis in neo-Darwinian
adaptation theory. The application of ecological and
materialist theory in anthropology has been vitiated by
several weaknesses, including over-emphasis on functionalism, use of inappropriate analogies, and failure
to state testable hypotheses, as discussed above. Theory
from evolutionary ecology is of course not immune to

being abused in this manner: the state can be compared
to a predator, or complex societies analyzed in terms of
community succession theory (both examples from Gall and
Saxe 1977). The studies summarized here are generally
free of these faults, however.

Finally, evolutionary ecology offers a more general
analytical framework than microeconomic theory. Although
microeconomic concepts and techniques have found much use
in ecological analysis, concepts of Darwinian adaptation
promise to greatly broaden the applicability of economic
logic in anthropology, and may conceivably replace its
arbitrary utilities with adaptive ones.

Evolutionary ecology provides a unique set of analytical tools for research on human social behavior.
Rather than threatening to replace other analytical approaches, evolutionary ecology offers a chance to improve
them in significant ways. Thus, one of the major attrac-
tions of this perspective is that it is at least partially compatible with these other approaches, and can
complement many existing anthropological research programs. While preliminary applications of the theory in
anthropology have been encouraging, only much further research will reveal to what extent evolutionary ecology
represents a real advance over extant approaches to explaining human behavioral diversity.

ACKNOWLEDGMENTS

I thank the following for comments and criticisms
(not always heeded) on this essay: R. Hames, J. Kurland,
G. Orians, and B. Winterhalder. Financial support from
the National Institute of Mental Health (predoctoral
fellowship No. 1 F31 MH05668) and the National Science
Foundation (postdoctoral fellowship No. SPI-8019913) is
gratefully acknowledged.

3
Nutrition and High Altitude Adaptation: An Example of Human Adaptability in a Multistress Environment

Jere D. Haas

Editors' Summary: In contrast to the previous two chapters which emphasize an evolutionary approach, Jere Haas takes a secular approach to attempt to demonstrate human biological adaptation to high altitudes through differential states of well-being as responses to environmental stress. He skillfully weaves together two theoretical approaches. The first is a research strategy designed to sort out the multiple stresses at high altitude (hypoxia, cold, limited food, intense UV radiation) and corresponding human responses (Baker 1976). The second approach involves an application of Mazess' (1975a,b, 1978) adaptive domains concept to structure the analysis of human responses to altitude. As Haas notes, individual adaptive domains such as child growth and neurological functioning can be studied in an interacting mode and evaluated in terms of whether individuals are conferred relative benefit within a stressful environment. The requirement that relative benefit be demonstrated before adaptation as a state is claimed requires individual sampling and population comparisons. It is rooted in Darwinian theory and avoids the weak judgments about adaptations made by cultural ecologists as cited by Dyson-Hudson and Smith in Chapters 1 and 2.

Haas stresses that proper evaluation of individual adaptive domains must take into account the interactions between environmental factors--particularly variations in diet--and biological factors that affect individual responses. Despite the fact that human responses to high altitude have been extensively studied by human biologists, a great deal more research is needed to document how these affect human adaptability and adaptation.

INTRODUCTION

For much of the fifties and sixties, research on human biological adaptation to the environment focused on simple stress-response observations which involved single environmental stresses such as heat, cold, high altitude hypoxia, disease and malnutrition. These early studies served to establish basic biological principles of human adaptation under rather controlled experimental conditions. However, with the advent of multidisciplin-

41

ary field-based projects of human adaptability in the
middle 1960s, it became apparent that much rethinking of
man-environment interactions had to take place. Specifically, the complexity of environmental stresses to
which a person is exposed is far greater than that examined previously under laboratory settings, and the complexity of biological and behavioral responses to these
multistress environments was recognized as being extensive. Because of their holistic approach to the study
of human adaptability, anthropologists recognized fairly
early that the laboratory studies of single stress-simple
response phenomena were inadequate to explain the evolutionary and population level adaptations that characterize our species. New research strategies had to be formulated to deal with the questions raised regarding complex adaptation patterns to complex environments.
      Two important methodological insights to this prob-
lem grew out of research conducted by Baker and colleagues (Baker and Little 1976) on human adaptation at
high altitude in the Peruvian Andes. The first is the
extension of the single stress-model of physiological
adaptation to the multistress models that more closely
approximate real conditions under which people adapt.
These various research models are discussed in some detail by Baker (1975) and Little and Baker (1976) in the
context of high altitude adaptation in the Peruvian
Andes. The second insightful contribution is Mazess'
formulation of the concept of adaptive domains for categorizing the complex of adaptive responses at different
levels of biological organization (Mazess 1975b). Mazess
also uses examples from high altitude research to document the utility of the concept. The purpose of this
paper is to present an example of a research strategy for
studying the complexity of environmental constraints and
adaptive responses using a research framework that em-
ploys a multistress approach to the environment and the
complexity of responses evaluated according to the criteria of the adaptive domains. The population to be examined will be the same high altitude Andean population
which served as the basis for the work of Baker, Mazess
and colleagues.

HIGH ALTITUDE ADAPTATION: THEORETICAL CONSIDERATIONS

      It would be pretentious to assume that all aspects
of adaptation to an environment can be comprehensively
examined within the confines of a single research
strategy. This is particularly apparent when one examines the state of knowledge regarding high altitude
adaptation. The impact of high altitude on the physical
well-being of native and non-native inhabitants has been
extensively studied (Baker and Little 1976; Baker 1978).
From these studies it is apparent that many aspects of
the physical environment at high altitude can limit human

performance. This has been documented for such stresses
as cold, malnutrition, and hypobaric hypoxia, all common
to populations living above 3000 meters altitude in the
South American Andes. Although our research into the
physiological responses to hypoxia, cold and malnutrition
have been extensive and research on the latter two
stresses not confined to high altitude, we are only now
at the threshold of understanding the complex biological
and social interactions which characterize the responses
to this multistress high altitude environment.

Of the above named stresses hypobaric hypoxia is the
most pervasive and the most systematically studied at
high altitude from the point of view of biological adaptations. Barometric pressure decreases with increasing
altitude above sea levels and the component of the total
atmospheric pressure that is oxygen decreases propor-
tionately. This results in a partial pressure of atmospheric oxygen at 3000 meters of 105 mmHg, or a 25 percent
reduction from normal sea level pressure of 159 mmHg.
At the mean altitude of the Peruvian-Bolivian Altiplano
(4000 m) the partial pressure of oxygen is 94 mmHg. This
limitation of oxygen available for respiration results
in numerous physiological responses along the oxygen
transport chain from pulmonary ventilation through oxygen
transport in the blood and cellular metabolism. Many of
these responses have been documented by Baker and Little
(1976); Frisancho (1975, 1979); Hurtado (1964); Little
(1981) and Mazess (1975b).

Models of Adaptation

Much of this knowledge was acquired over several decades of research that employed increasingly more sophisticated research designs. Baker (1975) summarizes these
basic approaches as: (1) one stress--one population
model, (2) multiple stress--one population model, (3) one
stress--multi-population model, and (4) multiple stress--
multiple population model. All of these approaches have
strengths and weaknesses which must be evaluated relative
to the specific research question being addressed.
Clearly a comprehensive assessment of adaptation by a
population of individuals living in a well defined environment such as the Quechua of the Peruvian altiplano,
must rely on a mixture of research strategies that examine interpopulation and intrapopulation variation and
the interaction of environmental stresses and biocultural
responses.

While the various research strategies described by
Baker (1975) compare and contrast a complex of single or
multiple stresses within a single population or between
several populations, the real subject of study in most
cases is the response of individuals within a population.
The complexity of responses is usually more difficult to
evaluate than the complexity of the stress.

In Mazess' (1975b) article he not only summarized much of our knowledge of high altitude adaptation but also presented a conceptual framework for examining the effectiveness of human adaptations in general. He suggested that for any biological response to be considered 'adaptive,' it must meet the criterion that it benefits the individual. This requires a re-evaluation of some earlier analyses, since many responses which were thought to be adaptations to high altitude have not been demonstrated to benefit the individual. The fact that biological variation exists between populations living in different environments does not necessarily mean that any unique characteristic of one population is in fact adaptive in the specific environment in which that population lives. It is the obligation of the scientist to document that those individuals who possess the characteristic actually benefit from it.

In order that benefit and hence adaptation can be assessed systematically for individuals, Mazess suggested a framework for categorizing areas or domains of adaptive importance. His "adaptive domains" include: (1) physical performance, (2) nervous system functioning, (3) growth and development, (4) nutrition, (5) reproduction, (6) health, (7) cross-tolerance and resistance, (8) affective functioning, and (9) intellectual ability (Mazess 1975a: 170).

While Mazess' adaptive domains pertain to the evaluation of individual adaptive responses, he cautions against the simple extrapolation of these individual responses to the assessment of population adaptations. Different adaptive domains characterize the population level responses such that the whole is not the sum of its parts. Also of importance is the observation that this is not an exclusive list of domains and that the responses in various domains may interact with each other. This is particularly true if you concede that benefit in the reproductive domain may be dependent upon an appropriate response during growth and development which in turn may depend upon adequate response in the nutrition domain. In this regard it is necessary to move beyond the documentation of benefit to any and all of the specific adaptive domains and examine the interactions between domains.

Both of the major approaches to adaptation thus far discussed--the single stress-simple response model of biological adaptation and the individual adaptive domains--are simplifications of natural conditions by which individuals adapt to the complex environments in which they live. They are essential concepts which are necessary steps to the more complete understanding of human adaptability, but they do not go far enough.

In this context Mazess (1975b) notes that the interpretation of "benefits" in any specific adaptive domain may be temporally, spatially and populationally specific

(p. 173). This adds further to the complexity if in interpreting high altitude adaptations, short and long term acclimatization as well as potential genetic adaptation must be considered as major factors in the phenotypic expression of adaptive responses. Different populations with different histories of previous altitude exposures or with different degrees and kinds of malnutrition and disease may respond differently to high altitude hypoxia. The population specificity and temporal specificity further complicates any assessment of genetic adaptations since the environmental conditions of nutrition and disease and the evolutionary forces associated with population structure have probably changed considerably since first human habitation of high altitude areas of the world. What we study today is the end result of a complex evolutionary process with virtual disregard for the changing selective pressures over several millenia.

Moreover, much of the inference about genetic adaptations has been based on research conducted on selected members of the high altitude populations. Subjects for most of the previous research were chosen either from the healthiest, best nourished segment of the population or with complete disregard for the potential variation in nutritional and health status that might distinguish high altitude from low altitude populations. This is a particularly important problem since undernutrition and disease often produce similar effects as hypoxia on individual performance (Haas and Harrison 1977). The U.S. National Academy of Sciences in its World Food and Nutrition Study (NAS 1977) has recognized the relationship between nutrition and certain areas of functional competence which closely resemble Mazess' adaptive domains. They call for additional research on the effects of mild-to-moderate malnutrition on reproductive performance, physical growth and behavioral development of children, disease resistance and physical work capacity.

The Interaction of Hypoxia and Malnutrition

Recognizing that hypoxia and malnutrition may interact in several ways to affect adaptation to high altitude, it seems reasonable that an investigation of this interaction might serve as a good test of a multistress-multiple-response model of human adaptation. Both stresses are pervasive in high altitude populations although malnutrition is more variable and complex. If we focus on energy, protein and iron malnutrition the problem is more clearly defined since they are more easily assessed and are the most prevalent forms of malnutrition in this part of the world. Also they are closely associated with simple food shortages which can be more easily documented than specific nutrient deficiencies. In this regard historical and archaelogical research on

food availability can be exploited to add temporal depth
to the research strategy.
When considering the biological responses to the
dual stress of hypoxia and malnutrition it is possible
to categorize the responses in several ways: (1) responses to hypoxia that are limited by malnutrition; (2)
responses to malnutrition that are limited by hypoxia;
(3) responses to hypoxia that are exacerbated by malnutrition; (4) responses to malnutrition that are exacerbated by hypoxia; (5) responses to hypoxia and malnutrition that are independent of each other. It should be
kept in mind that the responses to be documented must be
evaluated in terms of their being adaptive, neutral or
maladaptive with regard to relative benefit to specific
adaptive domains. This can be accomplished by investigating the various categories of observation of responses
within the adaptive domains as outlined in Table 3.1.
The adaptive domains listed by Mazess have been modified
slightly, partially to make them compatible with the NAS
recommendations for nutritional research.
It is not the purpose of this paper to evaluate the
evidence that pertains to each domain. Mazess (1975b)
has done this in regard to hypoxic effects and Baker and
Little (1976) organized their monograph along similar
lines. Although both publications do not consider nutritional constraints and interactions to the hypoxic responses within each domain, they do consider certain aspects of nutritional variation as a separate domain at
high altitude. Specifically, Picón-Reátegui (1976) documents the nutritional conditions of the Peruvian high
Andes, and Thomas (1976) and Little and Baker (1976) attempt to integrate certain components of the nutritional
environment into a general scheme for evaluating the
breadth of high altitude environmental variation. The
remainder of this paper will focus on several examples
of nutrition-high altitude interactions that have been
documented through continuing research in the Andes.
Much of these data have been published in more detailed
form elsewhere, while others represent only preliminary
analyses. The research that will be cited primarily represents the recent efforts of our research group at Cornell. Therefore, it is not a comprehensive review of the
state of research at high altitude. It is possible to
place this research into the broader context of other
research on high altitude adaptation by consulting the
review of Baker's <u>Biology of High Altitude Peoples</u> by
Haas (1980a).

HIGH ALTITUDE ADAPTATION: ADAPTIVE DOMAINS

The examples that follow fall into several areas of
functional competence which resemble Mazess' adaptive domains. The areas include (a) nutrition, (b) growth and

Table 3.1
Areas of Quantification for Several Adaptive Domains at High
Altitude

Adaptive Domains

Reproduction	Gametogenesis Fecundity Spontaneous abortion Fetal death Fertility	Obstetric pathology Fetal growth Neonatal death Congenital defects Lactation performance
Postnatal growth, development and maturation	Size-for-age Rates of growth Allometric growth Body proportions Age of maturity	Maturational rate Morbidity Pathology Mortality Developmental adapta- tions

Neurological func-
tioning and behavioral
development
	Neurological
	  maturity
	Cognitive devel-
	  opment
	Intelligence
		Motor development
		Learning
		Socialization
		Family-child inter-
		  action

Health and disease resistance	Morbidity Mortality Immunocompetence Parasitic infection	Infectious disease Chronic disease Degenerative disease Mental health Aging
Physical Performance	Endurance Strength Work efficiency	Maximum aerobic power Skill learning Specific oxygen trans- port responses Disability

Cross-tolerance and
stress resistance
	Cold tolerance
	Radiation tolerance
	Disease stress
	  response
	Nutritional stress
	  response
		Acculturation stress
		Acute psychological
		  stress response
		Responses to novel
		  stresses

development, (c) behavioral development, (d) physical
performance and (e) reproduction.

Human Nutrition

At this point it is important to briefly summarize
the nutritional conditions of the Peruvian-Bolivian altiplano. The traditional nutritional base of the high
Andes is subsistence agriculture with variable supple-
mental support from pastoralism. The economy is one that
relies to some degree on local and regional markets where
animal products and some staples change hands. Seasonal
variation in food supply greatly affects the nutritional
quantity and quality of the diet. Rural-urban differences in diet also exist that generally favor the more
monotonous but better balanced traditional rural diets
(Ferroni 1980). In general, however, the diets are marginal and the food supply is subject to periodic acute
disturbances.

The diet is generally high in carbohydrates, low in
fat and animal protein, but generally sufficient in total
protein, and most micro-nutrients. Dietary surveys suggest deficiencies of calcium and vitamin A. Limited data
are available on intrafamily food distribution patterns
which suggest that young children and mothers are at
greatest risk of nutritional deficiencies. Indian infants are breast fed until 22 months in the rural areas
and 14 months in the urban areas (Haas 1973). Surveys
of nutritional status using anthropometric, clinical and
biochemical methods of assessment are rare and difficult
to interpret without regard to other environmental factors that might affect these indicators (Haas 1981b).
In general these surveys also support the premise that
preschool children and women of reproductive age are the
most nutritionally vulnerable members of the population.
Protein energy undernutrition is common in preschool
children (Ferroni 1980; US AID, 1975) and iron deficiency
is prevalent among pregnant women, common among non-
pregnant women, but virtually non-existent among primary
school children (Haas 1981b; Haas et al. 1982b; Quinn
1982). In many ways the nutrition picture for the high-
lands is not much different from lowland rural areas in
other developing countries, although hypoxia and cold
may alter the requirements and metabolism of some nutrients. Of particular interest is the potential adaptive significance of alterations in carbohydrate, fat and
protein metabolism relative to their distribution in the
native diet (Mazess 1975b).

Growth and Development

For various reasons the study of growth and development of children has been used to assess the degree to
which a population is responding to specific environmen-

tal stresses. It has been shown that child growth is
particularly "eco-sensitive" in that only slight variation in diet and disease result in measurable changes in
attained growth and growth rate. For this reason, relative growth of children at all ages is a common indicator
of health and nutritional status. It is also important
to recognize that a major portion of the adult phenotypic
variation, which is the focus of much of the research in
human adaptability, and indeed several of the adaptive
domains listed above, results from a long period of interaction of genotype and environment during the first
20 years of life when that adult was growing and maturing. It is also a period of potentially active natural
selection when differential prereproductive mortality is
operating at its maximum. Finally, it is a critical time
of the life cycle when certain adaptive responses are established for specific environmental stresses. These
functional developmental adaptations which affect and are
affected by the rapidly growing and maturing morphology
of the child have been shown to be important aspects of
the acquisition of the adaptive repertoire in high altitude populations (Frisancho 1975; Little et al. 1971).
It should be apparent that the study of growth and maturation at high altitude may prove to be an important
integrating link between several of the environmental
stresses and the adaptive responses in various domains
that are the focus of specific studies of high altitude
adaptation.

The growth retarding effects of high altitude have
been extensively documented (Frisancho 1978). However,
two problems come to mind when evaluating the literature
on child growth at high altitude: (a) How much of the
retardation is due to hypoxia and how much is due to poor
nutrition and health? and (b) Is the pattern of growth
at high altitude adaptive? The evidence to answer the
first question is available in part for much of the life
cycle, the evidence to address the second question is
circumstantial but certainly intriguing.

The major factor that confounds our interpretation
of hypoxic effects on growth is the variation in diet
that also tends to distinguish highland from lowland
children. Attempts to control nutritional variation in
studying hypoxic effects on growth have employed three
research strategies: (a) examining growth of middle and
upper class children where nutritional problems are mini-
mized (Haas 1973, 1976; Haas et al. 1982a; Stinson 1981);
(b) statistically controlling for nutritional status differences between high and low altitude groups (Haas
1981b; Haas et al. 1982a), and (c) studying migrants from
high to low or low to high altitudes (Beall et al. 1977;
Mueller et al. 1978). In these studies it has been shown
that altitudinal effects on growth do exist independent
of the effects of undernutrition. This is true for fetal
growth (Haas 1980b; Haas et al. 1980), infant growth

(Haas 1976, 1981b; Haas et al. 1982a), and child and
adolescent growth (Beall et al. 1977; Mueller et al.
1978, 1980; Stinson 1981). However, for indigenous
children living at high altitude it is evident that many
factors including hypoxia, cold, chronic undernutrition,
and disease are all operating to varying degrees to reduce the achieved growth and rate of growth when compared
to lowland children (Little and Baker 1976). And if we
are to understand whether this pattern of growth is adaptive at high altitude we must keep in mind that the environment for growth at high altitude is complex.

The question whether small body size is adaptive
under conditions of limited food availability has been
widely debated. Much of the debate has focused on evidence from high altitude Peru (Frisancho et al. 1973b,
1975; Thomas 1976). During the period of growth, considerable food energy and protein are needed to support
maximal growth. It is clear that most poor children in
developing countries do not achieve this maximal growth.
However, it is valid to ask if they follow a growth pattern to achieve an optimal body size in light of environmental constraints on food. Since nutrient requirements
are directly and indirectly dependent on body size, a
smaller body should have lower requirements. Each child
may have a different optimum depending on specific conditions of acute or chronic food shortages, general health,
the stage of growth at which the shortage occurs and the
specific nutrients which tend to be deficient. Whether
cold and hypoxia also play a role in determining an optimum growth pattern for high altitude children is not
clearly known. However, we do have some idea what a well
adapted phenotype might look like at high altitude.

One striking aspect of growth in Andean populations
is the early appearance and persistent manifestation of
a large chest during growth (Beall et al. 1977; Frisancho
1969; Mueller et al. 1978, 1980). While linear growth
in stature may be depressed, lateral growth in the trunk
is not. This results in a slightly greater weight for
height in healthy high altitude children. These same
healthy well-nourished children also tend to be as fat
and muscular as lowland children even though they remain
shorter (Haas et al. 1982a; Stinson, 1981). Among highland children greater trunk growth may be compensated for
by a reduction in growth in the extremities. If food
scarcity leads to reduced energy and protein available
for total body growth, then an adaptive strategy could
have favored allocation of scarce nutrients for the ac-
celerated growth of the postulated adaptive characteristics of the chest; that is the lungs, heart and sternum.
Of course, central to this hypothesis is the assumption
that a large chest is indeed adaptive at high altitude.
The logic of the argument is compelling, but the evidence
is far from conclusive. While the chest dimensions have
been correlated with lung volume at high altitude (Fri-

sancho 1969), no evidence has been presented to my knowledge to show a benefit to work capacity that is associated with increasing lung or chest size.
   While the link between morphological growth and
function is weak, it is apparent that much of the physiological adaptation to hypobaric hypoxia that occurs at
high altitude depends on the individual being exposed to
hypoxic stress during the long period of growth and development (Frisancho 1975; Frisancho et al. 1973a; Mazess
1969). It is also apparent that not all children develop
a similar level of adaptation to hypoxia as they pass
through the growing years. It would be of greater interest to know to what degree nutritional factors affect
the child's ability to develop these adaptations which
are so important to later adult performance (Frisancho
1979). This question can be asked of low altitude populations as well, but seems to be particularly relevant
to physical work capacity at high altitude since developmental adaptations appear to play such an important role
in the rather extensive responses that are necessary for
adaptation to this environment. One could also ask to
what degree undernutrition affects other developmental
responses such as motor and intellectual maturation that
are so important for learning skills needed in adulthood.
This is yet another adaptive domain where nutrition may
interact with other high altitude stresses to affect individual adaptability.

Behavioral Development

   Research on neurological development and functioning
at high altitude is scarce. At extreme altitudes there
is clear documentation that mental and motor function is
impaired in selected adults (Van Liere and Stickney
1963), but at altitudes where most highland people reside
the results of these same tests do not indicate abnormal-
ities. This may suggest successful adaptation, the absence of sufficient stress to elicit a response, or the
select nature of the subjects thus far tested. What
limited research that has been done on young infants suggests no significant altitude effects on motor development (Haas 1976). However, reanalyses of these data indicated that when altitude differences in nutritional
status (as reflected by weight and height deviation from
appropriate high altitude growth standards) is taken into
account there are altitude differences in motor development for infants between 6 and 27 months of age. The
fact that poor nutritional status affects motor and cog-
nitive development is well documented for low altitude
populations (Brožek 1979; Latham 1974). Similar effects
can be expected in high altitude populations which would
confound the search for an altitude effect on behavioral
development.

52

It is difficult to predict what the long range effects of early disruption in motor development might mean
to later childhood and adult behavioral functioning. We
have virtually no information to even speculate, but can
safely assume that this is an important domain which warrants further study. And considering the evidence from
lowland populations, it is also clear that variation in
nutriture should be an important factor to consider in
these studies at high altitude.

Physical Performance

Of all the individual adaptive domains, physical
work capacity has been the most extensively studied at
high altitude. Hypobaric hypoxia severely limits the capacity to perform aerobic work as a result of reduced
oxygen pressure which exists throughout the oxygen transport system. Even in well adapted individuals the working muscles receive less oxygen than at sea level. Of
particular importance, however, is the fact that highland Peruvian Indians in their native environment perform
as well as lowlanders in their native environment in certain exercise tests that measure maximal aerobic capacity
or the overall efficiency to transport oxygen from the
ambient air to the metabolizing cell (Baker 1976). The
performance of these same highland natives is also similar to well trained lowland athletes who have been accli-
matized over a period of 4 weeks at high altitude (Baker
1969).
From studies of lowland men in Colombia and Vene-
zuela it has been shown that protein-energy undernutrition and iron deficiency anemia both significantly reduce
maximal work capacity (Barac-Nieto et al. 1978; Gardner
et al. 1975). Little effort has been made to account for
variation in nutritional status among the many subjects
tested at high altitude. Two recent studies on highland
natives in Bolivia have examined the relationship between
maximum and submaximum work capacity and either protein-
energy nutriture or iron deficiency anemia. Both studies
show a significant degree of nutritional variation.
Among 135 adult male aparapitas, or porters who carry
heavy loads in the La Paz markets, there are 20 percent
who could be considered low weight for height (Leatherman et al. n.d.). Among 600 male factory workers in La
Paz, 6.5 percent were iron deficient as judged by trans-
ferrin saturation below 15 percent (Tufts et al. 1981).
These factory workers are from a higher socioeconomic
stratum than the aparapitas, and also are represented to
a larger degree by men with European admixture. Nonetheless, both groups are lifelong natives to high altitude
and represent the manual working classes of the city.
Subsamples of each group were further studied for
physical work capacity relative to nutritional status.
Preliminary analysis indicates no relationship between

measures of protein or energy nutritional status and maximum oxygen uptake among the subsample of aparapitas.
However, Frisancho et al. (1975) have shown that native
highland men who are short in stature (often inferred as
an indication of chronic undernutrition during the growing years) actually have higher maximum oxygen uptakes
then men who are tall. Among a subsample of 60 factory
workers there is a relationship between indicators of
iron nutriture and maximum oxygen uptake (Tufts 1982).
Iron deficiency anemia (low hemoglobin and low transfer-
rin saturation) results in severe limitations to work capacity, while iron deficiency without anemia and anemia
without iron deficiency also limit oxygen uptake when
compared to normal controls. Considering the role of
iron in such components of oxygen transport as hemoglobin, myoglobin and the terminal oxydases it is not totally unexpected that iron deficiency and anemia together
and separately exert an influence on this domain.
We have great gaps in our knowledge of the extent
and degree of iron deficiency and protein-energy undernutrition that exists in the rural native population of the
high Andes. Considering the interaction of nutrition
with individual work capacity and the potential link between work capacity and economic livelihood (Spurr et al.
1977), it is essential that we document this variability
in nutritional status for all segments of the rural population engaged in economic activities. This includes
adult men, women and children, the latter two groups
being the most susceptible to undernutrition as well as
playing an important economic role in the highland society.

Reproduction

The ability of a population to reproduce and grow
has frequently been used as a criteria for successful
adaptation (Baker and Dutt 1972). Individual contributions to the population's reproductive capacity are known
to be variable and might reflect differential individual
adaptive responses to the specific environmental constraints which may be unique to each person. We have
considerable information on the effects of high altitude
on many of the areas of reproductive performance listed
in Table 1 (Clegg 1978). Moreover, many of these same
components have been shown to be affected by malnutrition. However, there has been limited effort to evaluate
the variation in reproductive performances at high altitude relative to variation of nutritional status that
exists in the general Andean population. Several relevant observations serve as examples.
Reduced completed female fertility and longer inter-
partum interval have been observed for high altitude Andean populations when compared to Peruvian lowlanders
(Abelson et al. 1974; Hoff and Abelson 1976). However,

there has been considerable debate on the extent to which
high altitude hypoxia may be responsible for these fertility patterns (Clegg 1978; Dutt 1976). One factor that
has not been considered is the effect of prolonged lactation in suppressing resumption of ovulation after child-
birth (Jelliffe and Jelliffe 1978; Delgado et al. 1977).
Traditional rural women in the Andes tend to breast-feed
their infants longer than urban highland women and lowland women (Haas 1973). The difference of 10-12 months
of additional lactation could contribute to a significant
reduction in female fertility. Also the nutritional
status of the lactating mother can affect her lactation
performance in such a way that duration of lactation and
the quantity of breast milk produced are both affected
(Jelliffe and Jelliffe 1978). These in turn can affect
infant health and nutritional status and ultimately,
survivorship. Subsequent capacity for effective child
bearing can also be affected by the nutritional status
of the women before and during a given pregnancy (Delgado
et al. 1977).

One important measure of reproductive performance
is infant birthweight. While fertility generally serves
to quantify the number of live born infants delivered to
a woman, birthweight tells us something about the quality
of the intrauterine environment as well as the potential
risk of early death during the immediate neonatal period.
Birthweights at high altitude are significantly lighter
than at low altitude (McClung 1969; Haas 1976; Haas et
al. 1980). However, the optimum birthweight at which infant mortality is the lowest is also lower for highland
Peruvian infants compared to lowland infants (Beall,
1981). All women at high altitude do not deliver infants of optimal weight and certainly maternal malnutrition is, at least, partially responsible for birthweights
below the optimum. Also, there is evidence that some
variation in birthweight at high altitude is associated
with maternal ethnic background and level of adaptation
to high altitude (Haas 1980b, 1981a; Haas et al. 1980).
Indian women in La Paz at 3600m deliver heavier and more
mature infants than women of European ancestry who were
themselves born and raised at high altitude. Moreover,
it appears that these Indian women deliver larger infants
despite their being less well-nourished and maintaining
a poorer state of iron nutriture (Haas et al. 1982b).
This is an interesting example of possible co-adaptation
to hypoxia and malnutrition which warrants further study
relative to several other domains.

The issue of small body size being adaptive surfaces
again in the context of reproductive performance. Frisancho et al. (1973b) have reported greater survivorship
of children born to smaller women versus taller women
living under poor socioeconomic conditions in Cuzco,
Peru (3400m). While far from conclusive in its implications, this observation provides yet another example of

the complex and at times conflicting pattern of interaction between hypoxia and nutrition.

CONCLUSIONS

In this article, I have discussed studies of high altitude adaptation in nutrition, growth and development, behavioral development, physical performance, and reproduction. Other adaptive domains such as health, cross tolerance and affective functioning have not been well studied at high altitude. Moreover, nutritional influences to the last two of these domains remains undocumented even at low altitude. It should be apparent by now that an evaluation of adaptation within the framework of identifying benefit to certain specific adaptive domains is a useful approach, but only to a point. The domains are reasonable categories which pertain to most individuals living under various types of environmental constraints. However, proper evaluation of individual adaptation within the specified domains must take into account the complexity of environmental and biological parameters that affect an individual's response. Of these environmental factors it is clear that variation in diet is extremely important. Other factors such as age, sex, general health, and genetic aptitudes that influence response to high altitude as well as poor nutrition must also be considered.

The examples presented above only serve to represent several areas where nutrition and high altitude adaptation may interact. One could probably present a similar argument for the role of infectious and parasitic diseases as limiting factors for successful high altitude adaptation or as a co-stressor along with malnutrition, hypoxia, and cold. Documentation along the lines presented here for nutritional effects at high altitude should be made for these other stresses if a clearer understanding of high altitude adaptation in populations of native individuals is to be achieved.

The ultimate goal of documenting genetic adaptation in the Andean population requires a series of quantum jumps from the demonstration of benefit in any or all of these individual adaptive domains. The first step is to move from the individual adaptive responses discussed here to the population level responses also discussed by Mazess (1975b). A clearer understanding of individual variation in responses and the many factors, such as variation in nutriture, that contribute to intrapopulation variation is an essential component to this first step. The second step is to assess the genetic component of these adaptive responses. This requires a different strategy as discussed by Mazess (1975a,b) of determining heritabilities for the presumed adaptive phenotypes. If any of this analysis should suggest that natural selection was or is active then reasonable selective mechan-

56

isms must be proposed. Only an understanding of the past
and present factors that might contribute to phenotypic
variation will permit construction of a reasonable genetic argument. It is unlikely that clear demonstration
of genetic adaptation to high altitude will be forthcom-
ing in the foreseeable future. This follows from the
complexity of these environmental and biological factors
and our dearth of information on how these factors interact at high altitude today, yet alone in the evolutionary
past. Clearly more research is needed.
   Many may feel that all that is to be known about
high altitude biology has already been documented. Indeed probably no other single population has been
studied from the point of view of adaptation to a unique
environment as the highland natives of the Peruvian-
Bolivian altiplano. However, from all of this knowledge
one thing is clear, the more questions we answer the more
questions we generate. This tremendous information base
we have for high altitude adaptation should serve as a
platform for further detailed research that certainly can
realize immediate practical benefits to the health and
well-being of the highland natives, and will lead to a
better understanding of human population level adaptations and perhaps even genetic adaptations.

ACKNOWLEDGMENTS

   Some of the research reported in this paper was supported by NSF Grants BNS-76-12312 and BNS-79-06270. This
is a report of research of the Cornell University Agricultural Experiment Station, Division of Nutritional Sciences.

4
Evolutionary Biology and the Human Secondary Sex Ratio: Sex Ratio Variation in the United States

Mary Jane Kellum

Editors' Summary: Mary Jane Kellum uses the sociobiological theory developed by Trivers and Willard (1973) in her discussion of the variations in secondary sex ratios (sex ratios at birth) in human groups. This theory suggests that parents 'manipulated' the sex ratios of their offspring in ways which maximize parental genetic contribution to the succeeding generation. Kellum examines United States census data and finds that it appears to conform with predictions based on this model. Obviously parental 'manipulation' of secondary sex ratios cannot be conscious, but must be based on physiological responses to environmental variables. Kellum discusses the proximate mechanisms which have been identified as contributing to variance in human sex ratios and concludes that only some of these would produce the effects predicted by the Trivers-Willard model. Some of these proximate mechanisms are also considered in the final chapter by Michael Little.

INTRODUCTION

This paper is concerned with the evolutionary significance of the human secondary sex ratio--the ratio of males to females at birth.[1] In particular, attempts are made to examine a recent theory proposed by evolutionary biologists who use parental investment theory to explain a sex ratio of 100 (equal numbers of males and females) as well as systematic deviations from this ratio (Trivers 1972).[2] Trivers and Willard (1973) propose that under certain well-defined conditions, a parent which can produce different proportions of males and females will have a selective advantage in terms of Darwinian fitness. According to their model, sex ratio manipulation will occur through the interaction of an organism's innate characteristics and particular environmental circumstances; there is not a strictly deterministic relationship between genes and behavior. The plan of this discussion is first, to outline Trivers and Willard's theory, discuss it in the context of its intellectual history, and make clear its significance to human social behavior; second, briefly to discuss related anthropological re-

search; and third, to examine whether in the United
States the special conditions prerequisite to sex ratio
manipulation exist, and present the evidence for sex
ratio variance. Fourth, possible immediate (proximate)
mechanisms which affect sex ratio will be discussed. The
final section will include conclusions and comments on
the usefulness to anthropologists of Trivers and Willard's model and other sociobiological models.

NATURAL SELECTION FOR A VARIABLE SEX RATIO

     Trivers and Willard (1973) contend that under cer-
tain conditions, variation from a 100 sex ratio at birth
can have adaptive significance. "Adaptive" in this sense
refers to reproductive success, an individual's success
in increasing his/her genetic representation in subsequent generations at the expense of other individuals in
the population. Trivers and Willard argue that natural
selection has favored a trait in many animal species including humans enabling a parent to adjust the sex ratio
at birth to optimize the reproductive success of offspring according to their anticipated condition at reproductive age. In circumstances where offspring can be
anticipated to be in good condition relative to other
individuals in the population, Trivers and Willard argue
that a parent should invest more in male offspring than
female. Under circumstances where offspring are likely
to be in poor condition relative to others, a parent
should invest in females. This prediction follows from
the observation that in populations where males compete
for females, a male in good condition can often mate with
a number of females, while the males in poor condition
may not mate at all. On the other hand, females commonly
do not display as much variance in mating success. The
number of offspring a female can bear is limited physio-
logically, by the length of gestation and of the period
of ovulation. Even females in poor condition tend to reproduce. Trivers and Willard argue:

     In short, natural selection favors the following re-
     productive strategy. As females deviate from the
     mean adult female condition they should show an in-
     creasing tendency to bias the production of their
     young toward one sex or the other. Whenever vari-
     ance around some mean condition is a predictable
     attribute of adults in a species, natural selection
     will arrange the deviations away from a 50/50 sex
     ratio at conception so that the deviations will tend
     to cancel out. Other things being equal, species
     showing especially high variance in male reproduc-
     tive success (compared to variance in female repro-
     ductive success) should show, as a function of dif-
     ferences in maternal condition, especially high
     variance in sex ratios produced. (1973: 90)

Trivers and Willard's model depends on three assumptions which they base on empirical data and theoretical arguments: (1) the conditions of the young at the end of parental investment will tend to be correlated with condition of the mother during parental investment, (2) difference in the condition of young at the end of the period of parental investment will tend to endure into adulthood, and (3) adult males will be differentially helped in reproductive success (compared to adult females) by slight advantages in condition.

Trivers and Willard indicate that their hypothesis might be tested in human populations, including the United States. The condition which must obtain for variation in sex ratio at birth to be advantageous is more variance in reproductive success (generally measured as relative fertility) among males in a population than among females. According to Trivers and Willard: "the model can be applied to humans differentiated on a socioeconomic scale, as long as the reproductive success of a male at the upper end of the scale exceeds his sister's, while that of a female at the lower end of the scale exceeds her brother's. A tendency for the female to marry a male whose socioeconomic status is higher than hers will, other things being equal, tend to bring about such a correlation and there is evidence of such a bias in female choice in the U.S." (Trivers and Willard 1973: 91). In other words, females marry up, leaving males at lower socioeconomic levels and females at higher levels without mates or with less desirable ones.

The trait that Trivers and Willard propose is manifested on an "if-then" basis. That is, sex ratio is reduced (there is a higher proportion of females) when maternal condition is poor and pregnancy is likely to result in low quality offspring, while sex ratio is increased (there is a higher proportion of males) when the mother is in better than average condition and likely to produce a high quality offspring. Trivers and Willard review studies where adverse environmental conditions for the mother are correlated with a reduced sex ratio at birth. Differential male mortality in utero seems to be the mechanism by which sex ratio at birth is manipulated, and elsewhere Trivers (1972) has suggested that some aspect of the mother's diet, possibly protein availability, is the immediate link between environmental quality and fetal mortality. (This will be discussed further in the section on proximate mechanisms.) As Trivers and Willard note, their model amounts in part to an adaptive interpretation of early differential male mortality: "That variations in sex ratio as large as those observed in nature should be a matter of indifference to the individuals producing them seems most unlikely" (Trivers and Willard 1973: 91). The significance of Trivers and Willard's hypothesis becomes most clear in the context of

60

the history of interest in sexual selection and parental
investment.

EVOLUTIONARY BIOLOGY AND THE SEX RATIO

The attention of evolutionists in the live birth sex
ratio can be traced at least to Darwin, who discussed it
in The Descent of Man and Selection in Relation to Sex
(1874). Darwin compiled data from the human birth records of several countries, from breeders of race horses,
pigeons, and livestock, as well as field data on fish,
insects, birds, and wild animals, and he found significant but inconsistent variations in sex ratio for some
species. Darwin attributed deviant sex ratios in some
cases to sexual selection, arguing that large males are
more successful than smaller males in competition for
females, passing on to their offspring a tendency to
produce large males. Since it seemed to Darwin that
large offspring are particularly vulnerable to injury
during parturition, and since male offspring tend to be
larger than females, he attributed a low live birth sex
ratio to birth trauma. He also tried to assess the effect of infanticide on a heritable sex ratio. Examining
data on the Todas of India and Maoris of New Zealand,
Darwin supposed that routine female infanticide reduced
the number of offspring left by parents who possessed a
trait for producing equal or low ratios (more female infants) and thereby increased the proportion of offspring
left in the population by parents who possessed the
ability to produce mostly male children. After extensive discussion, however, Darwin concluded: "I formerly
thought that when a tendency to produce the two sexes in
equal numbers was advantageous to the species, it would
follow natural selection, but now I see that the whole
problem is so intricate that it is safer to leave its
solution to the future" (Darwin 1874: 252).

The matter was again taken up in 1930 by R. A.
Fisher (1930) who discussed the influence of natural selection on the sex ratio in terms of the concept of
"reproductive value," that is, the present value of
future offspring (1930: 27) or the extent to which a
person of a given age on the average will contribute to
the ancestry of future generations. Fisher argued that
the total reproductive value of all males in a generation is equal to the total reproductive value of all females in a generation since each sex must supply half the
ancestry of future generations. Natural selection should
therefore favor an investment in the two sexes which
would result in equal parental expenditure at the age of
greatest reproductive value, about 18 1/2 for humans,
Fisher argues (1930: 28-29, 159). Unequal investment in
the sexes over many generations is evolutionarily unstable. Fisher notes:

From this it follows that the sex ratio will so adjust itself, under the influence of Natural Selection, that the total parental expenditure incurred
in respect of children of each sex, shall be equal;
for if this were not so and the total expenditure
incurred in producing males, for instance, were less
than the total expenditure incurred in producing females, then since the total reproductive value of
the males is equal to that of the females, it would
follow that those parents, the innate tendencies of
which caused them to produce males in excess, would,
for the same expenditure, produce a greater amount
of reproductive value; and in consequence would be
the progenitors of a larger fraction of future generations than would parents having a congenital bias
towards the production of females. Selection would
thus raise the sex-ratio until the expenditure upon
males became equal to that upon females. (1930:
159)

As for sex ratios in humans, Fisher states:

If, for example, as in man, the males suffered a
heavier mortality during the period of parental expenditure, this could cause them to be more expen-
sive to produce, for, for every hundred males successfully produced expenditure has been incurred,
not only for these during their whole period of dependence but for a certain number of others who have
perished prematurely before incurring the full complement of expenditure. The average expenditure is
therefore greater for each boy reared, but less for
each boy born, than it is for girls at the corresponding stages, and we may therefore infer that the
condition toward which Natural Selection will tend
will be one in which boys are the more numerous at
birth, but become less numerous, owing to their
higher death-rate, before the end of the period of
parental expenditure. The actual sex-ratio in man
seems to fulfill these conditions somewhat closely,
especially if we make allowance for the large recent
diminution in the deaths of infants and children;
and since this adjustment is brought about by a
somewhat large inequality in the sex ratio at conception, for which no a priori reason can be given,
it is difficult to avoid the conclusion that the
sex-ratio has really been adjusted by these means.
(1930: 159)

Thus sex ratio at the end of expenditure would depend on differential mortality during the period of parental investment, and if they exist, differential demands made by the offspring of different sexes during the
period of dependency.

Fisher concluded:

The numbers attaining sexual maturity may thus become unequal if sexual differentiation in form or habits if for other reasons advantageous, but any great and persistent inequality between the sexes at maturity should be found to be accompanied by sexual differentiations, having a very decided bionomic value. (1930: 160)

Since Fisher's work, interest in the sex ratio has increased. Some biologists have disagreed with Fisher's theory, maintaining that natural selection should always produce a 100 ratio. Kalmus and Smith (1960) maintain that chance encounters between males and females are maximized at a 100 sex ratio, a situation selectively advantageous since genetic variation in the population is maximized. Bodmer and Edwards (1960) propose that a 100 ratio would be favored since reproductive efficiency is optimized at a 50:50 phenotypic cost/genotypic benefit relation. These two theories argue a group or population benefit, and it is now generally accepted that group-benefit explanations should be avoided in favor of individual-benefit explanations (see Williams 1966; Pianka 1978). Evolutionary ecologists and biologists generally tend to agree with Fisher's formulation (Hamilton 1967; Trivers 1972).
It is important to note that Trivers and Willard's model does not contradict Fisher's theory: it is an extension of his basic model and applies to populations excluded in Fisher's original formulation. As Pianka (1978: 151-164) has pointed out, a number of specific population characteristics are assumed in Fisher's theory. First, and most significantly, Fisher assumes equal access to mates throughout the population, when in many cases there is variance in mating success among individuals. Secondly, Fisher assumes a randomly mating or panmictic population, and it is doubtful that any natural population is truly panmictic. Trivers and Willard's model deals specifically with populations where there is competition for mates within each of the sexes (the intrasexual component is sexual selection) and preference for some individuals over others (intersexual or epigamic sexual selection). It should also be noted that Fisher's argument was not that sex ratio did not vary, but that over many generations natural selection should not favor higher production of one sex. Trivers and Willard's model concerns only the advantage to the individual of contributing more of one sex to the next descending generation, a case which may in fact be covered by Fisher's note that sex ratio may be unequal if the inequality has some "decided bionomic value" (1930: 160). Further, as Trivers and Willard note, the deviations at

the population level will tend to cancel each other out
(1973: 90).

A study of variations in sex ratio is important because it relates to the concept of parental investment,
which Alexander (1974) has placed ("parental manipulation
of offspring" in his terms) as the most important of
three classes of evolutionary influences on social organization. These evolutionary influences are (1) reciprocal altruism (Trivers 1971) whereby altruistic acts are
performed toward non-kin when such acts may be returned,
enhancing both parties' reproductive success; (2) nepo-
tism, or kin altruism, whereby one's inclusive fitness--
"the sum of an individual's own fitness plus the sum of
all the effects it causes to the related parts of the
fitness of all its relatives" (Wilson 1975: 118)--is en-
hanced by altruistic acts performed towards kin; and (3)
parental manipulation of progeny whereby parents treat
offspring as reproductive investment (Alexander 1974).

According to sociobiologists, social organization
can be understood and even predicted with models based
on these three classes of behavior and knowledge of the
genetic and ecological parameters which exist for a population. Testing sociobiological hypotheses has proved
difficult since even the most basic of variables, such
as reproductive success, do not lend themselves to easy
measurement. Sex ratio is a variable that is, at least
potentially, measurable, enabling us to test an hypothesis derived from sociobiological theory. Thus it seems
worthwhile to test Trivers and Willard's model using
human populations, to gain some headway in evaluating the
body of sociobiological theory.

PREVIOUS RESEARCH

Anthropologists have had mixed success attempting
to test Trivers and Willard's model. Irons' (1976,
1979a) data on reproductive success and status among the
Yomut Turkmen, while not gathered to specifically test
Trivers and Willard's hypothesis, are consistent with it.
Irons differentiated his population on the basis of Yomut
criteria for status and wealth and found that in the
wealthier half of the population sex ratios at birth and
reproductive success of the males were higher than for
the poorer half (sex ratios were 119 and 106 respectively). The Yomut are polygynous and the greater access
to wives leads to higher reproductive success for the
wealthier males. Though limited (for instance, the reli-
ability of birth statistics is not clear), Irons' data
conform to the predictions of the model: the wealthier
half of the population had more offspring than the
poorer, and the sex ratio at birth for the wealthy half
was much higher than for the poorer half.

Chagnon, Flinn, and Melancon (1979) attempted to
apply Trivers and Willard's model to Yanomamo data but

were unable to find a positive relationship between sex ratio and status, although they did find status positively related to number of offspring (see also Chagnon 1979). They suggest that the absence of relationship as predicted by Trivers and Willard may be due to the difficulty in an egalitarian society of assessing the future success of unborn children, since that success is based partly on personal attributes such as charisma, beauty, or prowess. They further note that in Yanomamo society women have great value since kinsmen must have them to exchange for wives.

Dickemann (1979) has explored sex ratio manipulation at the cultural level, arguing that "human cultural history . . . is by no means independent of, but closely bound to, the biological history of human reproduction (p. 367). She follows Alexander (1974) in the argument that preferential female infanticide would be more likely in societies where women married higher-ranking men, the higher ranks disposing of females for whom mates were scarce and the lower ranks preserving females for marriage with higher classes. While Dickemann includes a wealth of data from feudal and post-feudal but pre-industrial northern India, China and Europe, the clearest associations between sex ratio manipulation and status exist for Indian subcastes, which tend to be exogamous within caste lines. In some states of India and among some castes, female infanticide in the upper subcastes approached 100 percent at the time of colonial census-taking. The lower subcastes sought to match their daughters with upper subcastes, providing often substantial dowries. This practice, combined with polygyny, meant a shortage of marriageable women for lower subcaste males who, if married at all, tended to marry widows, older women, handicapped women, or other less desirable women.

These studies can not clearly separate physiological from cultural sex ratio manipulation. Problems with accurate birth statistics and with the clandestine nature of infanticide make it difficult to do so. An argument can be made, as Dickemann has, that cultural manipulation is consistent and continuous with the biological model. However, since Trivers and Willard are primarily interested in physiological manipulation, and since the birth records in the United States are quite reliable, the present study will focus on the sex ratios which result from physiological mechanisms rather than cultural behavior.

REPRODUCTIVE SUCCESS IN THE UNITED STATES

Testing the model presented by Trivers and Willard is complicated by a number of human characteristics. Generally, unlike many other species, human males invest parental effort in their young, a trait associated with reduced variance in male reproductive success (Trivers 1972). Males tend to invest parental effort in offspring rather than relying on mating with numerous females to increase reproductive success; hence, male-male competition is reduced. However, the extent to which there is competition for females in a population varies among human groups. For the Trivers and Willard model to apply, reproductive success must vary among members of the population. Specifically, there must be more variance in reproductive success of males than of females. Males at the upper end of the socioeconomic scale must reproduce more than socially similar females, and females at the lower end must reproduce more than similar males. Thus measuring reproductive success and reproductive success variance is a prerequisite for predicting sex ratio variance.

Reproductive success in human populations has been measured as the number of offspring produced (cf. Barkow 1977; Chagnon 1979; Irons 1976, 1977, 1979a). Measuring reproductive success in some human populations may appear to be complicated by the deliberate limiting of family size which seems to contradict the notion of maximizing reproductive success. There are two reasons why the contradictions may be more apparent than real. First, there is evidence that many species produce offspring in numbers below their maximum capacity to bear young (Stearns 1976; Horn 1978). The optimal reproductive strategy is often to maximize quantity without sacrificing quality of offspring. Second, although the current two-child average in the United States seems to leave little room for competitive reproduction, it is important to note that it is not the absolute number of offspring but the differential contributions of individuals to generations which is important in selection. Crow (1966) has proposed an Index of Opportunity for Selection, defined as V/x^2, where V is the variance and x the mean number of progeny per parent. The Index (I) can be separated into components due to mortality and to fertility differences, and the changes in the two components within a changed environment can be striking. The Index of Opportunity for Selection due to deaths decreases as the death rate lowers. In the United States, the pattern has changed from uniform high fertility (x large, I_f small) through low fertility with considerable variability from family to family (x small, I_f large) to the most recent situation where the family size is more uniform and I_f is again small. The Index due to mortality has dropped from about 1 for those born 100 years ago to less than 0.1 for current death rates, so that most selection is due to differential fertility. The opportunity for selection for even small differences in fertility (1 to 2 children) is large enough so that a considerable amount of selection could be occurring.

A very real obstacle, however, to measuring reproductive success is that we need data on the relative fertility of women and men differentiated socioeconomically.
The fertility data which exist almost exclusively pertain to women. Not only are data concerning the fertility of males difficult to obtain, for obvious reasons,
but demographers who work with fertility data consider
females "the breeders" in a population and males simply
"accessories" (cf. Teitelbaum 1972: 91) and do not rou-
tinely try to obtain such information. We can therefore
compute reproductive success of women only and must find
indirect evidence for male reproductive rates.

Variance in Reproductive Success Among Females

For females in the United States it is fairly clear
that there is an inverse relationship between socioeconomic status and fertility. The group with lowest fertility (see Table 4.1) are women with incomes over
$15,000 and 4 or more years of college (Nam and Gustavus
1976: 118-119). The marriage and divorce statistics in

Table 4.1
Average Number of Children Born to Women Aged 35 to 44 by
Color and Socioeconomic Status (for Women ever Repro-
ducing) (Nam and Gustavus 1976: 118-119)

| | | Average Number of Children Born | |
| | | White 1972 | Black 1972 |
Socioeconomic Status Measure			
Educational Attainment			
Elementary:	less than 8 years	3.7	4.8
	8 years	3.4	4.8
High School:	1 to 3 years	3.4	4.5
	4 years	3.0	3.6
College:	1 to 3 years	2.9	2.6
	4 years or more	2.6	2.6
Family Income			
Under $3,000		3.2	4.4
$ 3,000 to 4,999		3.5	4.4
$ 5,000 to 7,499		3.5	4.4
$ 7,500 to 9,999		3.3	3.4
$10,000 to 14,999		3.1	3.4
$15,000 and over		3.0	3.4

Table 4.2 show that the highest status group, white women with 5 or more years of college, are less likely to be married than any other group of persons. Women at this level are also more likely to be divorced, non-white women more so than white. This association between higher socioeconomic status and low fertility and marriage rates among women is consistent with the Trivers and Willard model and establishes part of the necessary conditions for sex ratio manipulation advantages.

Male Variance in Reproductive Success

It seems reasonable to assume that men who have access to women through marriage tend to father more children than men who do not and that men who spend more time married are likely to have more children than those married less.[3] There is ample data on marital status of men and women in the United States, and so it is possible to use information about trends in marriage and divorce as an indicator of access to mates and of reproductive success.

Several sources suggest that United States males do not have equal access to females for marriage. An analysis of the sex ratio of the United States population by age in 1970 (Table 4.3) shows that from 15 years of age on, there were fewer males than females in every age group (Nam and Gustavus 1976: 197). The fact that there were fewer males than females over 15 years old, and that approximately 7 percent of males never marry, compared with 4 percent of females, suggests that all males do not have equal access to mates. When the male population of the United States between 45 and 54 years of age is broken down by socioeconomic status (Table 4.4), men with high status and income were more likely to be married and less likely to be divorced or single than men with low status and income. Only 2 percent of the white men with high status were unmarried compared to 13.4 for white men with low status. The relationship is similar for non-whites but not so extreme. Married men had higher earnings than any other category, and of men known to have been divorced, those remarried had higher earnings than those still divorced.

Variance Between the Sexes in Reproductive Success

In a strictly monogamous mating system, reproductive success would be equal for the sexes, but the United States system has more accurately been described as serial polygamy. One third of all marriages in the United States now end in divorce (Carter and Glick 1976: 385) and most occur during the peak reproductive years of the women involved (between the ages of 20 and 29). Three out of five of these marriages involve children

Table 4.2
Percent Married and Percent Divorced, for Persons 35 to 44 years old, by Years of School Completed, Color, and Sex, 1960 (Carter and Glick 1976: 72)

Year or Period and Years of School Completed	Percent Married				Percent Divorced			
	Men		Women		Men		Women	
	White	Nonwhite	White	Nonwhite	White	Nonwhite	White	Nonwhite
Total: 35-44	89.3	83.5	87.9	80.4	2.5	3.5	3.6	5.7
Elementary:								
0-4 years	76.9	82.4	76.9	76.6	2.5	2.4	3.2	3.6
5-8 years	87.3	84.1	88.0	80.7	2.9	3.1	3.5	4.8
High School:								
1-3 years	90.2	83.6	89.4	80.8	2.8	4.4	4.0	7.0
4 years	90.5	83.1	89.1	81.9	2.3	4.5	3.3	6.8
College:								
1-3 years	91.0	83.2	87.1	80.9	2.5	4.8	4.2	7.6
4+ years	90.4	85.0	80.5	78.1	1.5	2.6	3.3	6.6
4 years	91.3	84.3	85.6	80.3	1.5	2.8	2.8	6.4
5+ years	89.3	85.6	68.1	74.7	1.5	2.4	4.6	6.8

Table 4.3
Sex Ratios for the United States Population by Age for 1970
(Nam and Gustavus 1976: 197)

Date and Age	Sex Ratio, Males / 100 Females
1970 Total	95
0-4 years	104
5-14	104
15-24	98
25-34	96
35-44	95
45-54	93
55-64	90
65-74	78
75+	64

Table 4.4
Percent Distribution by Marital Status for White and Black Men 45-54
Years Old of High and Low Socioeconomic Level: U.S. 1970 (Carter
and Glick 1976: 405)

	White Men		Black Men	
Marital Status	High SES	Low SES	High SES	Low SES
Total, 45-54 years old	584,054	107,799	6,353	70,388
Percent	100.0	100.0	100.0	100.0
Single	2.2	13.4	4.5	10.6
Married	95.4	76.8	91.6	79.5
Widowed	0.6	2.6	0.9	5.3
Divorced	1.8	7.1	3.0	4.6
Married Once, Wife Present	84.2	57.7	68.5	49.8
Known to Have Been Divorced	10.0	18.9	22.0	18.6

under 18 years old. Since more males than females re-
marry (3/4 of all women and 5/6 of all men), there is the
possibility that the number of children fathered per reproducing male could differ from the number born to each
reproducing female. The age gap is wider at second mar-
riages--a male is more likely to marry a woman younger
than his first wife by 3 to 6 years--so that a remarry-
ing male will once again be married to a woman in her
peak reproductive years if he is in his mid-thirties (the
age at which divorce rates are highest for males) (Carter
and Glick 1976: 409). At any status level, men between
the ages of 35 and 44 are more likely to be married than
women (Table 4.2) although black men are somewhat less
likely to be married than white. Apparently, men are
spending more time married than women.

On the basis of limited and circumstantial data, the
special conditions proposed by Trivers and Willard which
make sex ratio manipulation advantageous do appear to
exist. First, if women of higher status are not marrying
at the same high rates as men of higher status, then it
appears that higher status men are marrying women of
lower status. Therefore, women seem to be moving up in
the system, necessarily leaving lower status men without
mates or with less desirable ones. Men of lower status
at least seem to have less opportunity to reproduce than
men of higher status, even though fertility data are not
available. Second, using the amount of time spent married or divorced as an indicator, men have more opportunity to reproduce than women. Sex ratio in the United
States, then, should vary in the following manner: high
status persons should produce more males than females
since high status males are more likely to mate than high
status females. Low status persons, however, should produce more females, since females may move up in the system, mating successfully, and low status males may not.

SEX RATIO IN THE UNITED STATES

Whereas there are considerable data relating to the
human secondary sex ratio, the data are sometimes contra-
dictory and confusing. Factors which seem to have received sustained attention and exhibit the most consistent results are race, birth order, maternal age, and
socioeconomic status. These variables are all associated
with the physiological condition of the mother (Peterson
1975). To be consistent with Trivers and Willard's
model, variables which indicate poorer condition (minor-
ity race, high birth order, high maternal age, low socioeconomic status) should be associated with lower sex
ratio, and variables which indicate better maternal condition (Caucasian race, high socioeconomic status, low
birth order, low maternal age) should be associated with
higher sex ratio. Some research has treated each of

these variables separately, but other studies use a multi-variable approach.

A relationship between socioeconomic status and sex ratio has long been suspected. Bernstein (1948) compared the sex ratios of offspring of persons in the higher social strata to that for the U.S. population in general. Using a sample of 3898 completed white families drawn from Who's Who in Commerce and Industry, she found a secondary sex ratio of 125 as opposed to 106 for the total white population. She attributed the difference to reduced spontaneous abortion and stillbirth among the healthier upper class. Winston (1931) obtained similar results with a sample of 15,763 children of upper class families; he found a ratio of 112 compared to 105.8 for the United States as a whole. He also attributed the difference to fewer stillbirths and abortions. One of the most extraordinary sex ratios reported was by Woods (1939) who found a sex ratio of 137 for the twenty-one royal families of Europe, about 900 individuals born during the 19th and 20th centuries. Apparently Woods attributed the sex ratio to an inherited trait. These studies are not entirely reliable due to problems with accuracy in the data base, especially Woods (1939), but they do indicate the long-standing interest in the relationship between socioeconomic status and sex ratio.

Much of the work associating several factors with the sex ratio has been confusing or ambiguous. In Australia, Pollard (1969) found a negative relationship between sex ratio and maternal and paternal ages, but no relationship at all with birth order. Greenberg and White (1968) found a negative relationship between sex ratio and the birth order (higher sex ratios with early birth order). Novitski and Kimball (1958) found negative correlations between birth order and sex ratio in a study of almost 4 million live births in the U.S. It seemed that paternal age was in some way associated with the sex ratio, but the relationship decreased with increasing age. There seemed to be no association with maternal age.

Teitelbaum (1972), using a different statistical technique in analyzing Novitski and Kimball's data, found a highly significant effect for the birth order on sex ratio. The odds for a male child for birth 5 or above were about 2.6 percent lower than at the first birth. Neither paternal nor maternal age seemed involved when adjustments were made for the birth order effect. The apparent effect of paternal age in Novitski and Kimball's data disappeared when Teitelbaum controlled for a disproportionate number of large families with young fathers who were overwhelmingly in the lowest socioeconomic categories. Looking at census data for that time period, he found a highly significant difference between the sex ratios of whites and blacks after adjusting for the birth order effect: probability of a male child was 3 percent lower for blacks than whites. Using data for some 40,000 live births, Teitelbaum and Mantel (1971) found a significant positive effect of socioeconomic status (using an index based on education, income and occupation) on the sex ratio after adjusting for race and birth order. Children in the lowest socioeconomic levels had 6 to 9 percent lower probability of being male than those born to families in the moderate and higher categories. There seemed to be a "diminishing return curve" where there were big increases in sex ratio from low to middle socioeconomic status, but none between middle and high status families. Even after controlling for socioeconomic status, Teitelbaum found a small racial effect which he attributed to the possibility that blacks, even in middle socioeconomic status may have more health problems than whites.

Erickson (1976), like Teitelbaum, found that maternal and paternal age effects on the sex ratio disappeared when the data were controlled for birth order. He also found a racial effect when birth order was controlled. Garfinkel and Selvin (1976), using data from 1.4 million single live white births in New York State, found a significant association between the sex ratio and birth order. They concluded, however, that the association, complicated by associations with parental age, was produced by some third factor and suggest socioeconomic status.

The data associating live birth ratio with socioeconomic status, parental age, birth order, and race reveal several relationships significant to Trivers and Willard's hypothesis. It is probable that there are variances in sex ratio, small but consistent, in subgroups of the United States population. Although the differences in sex ratio are not great, the magnitude of variance can significantly affect the growth rate of a population (Teitelbaum 1972) and marriage patterns (Hirschman and Matras 1971). The variances observed seem especially related to factors affecting physical condition of mother. As predicted by Trivers and Willard's model, there is a positive relation between socioeconomic status and sex ratio.

PROXIMATE FACTORS AFFECTING SECONDARY SEX RATIO

While there are few theories which challenge Fisher's or Trivers and Willard's evolutionary models of sex ratio, there are a number of hypotheses for the immediate cause, or proximate mechanism, which affects the sex ratio at birth. Trivers and Willard argue that the mechanism for sex ratio manipulation is differential male fetal mortality. Manipulation does not occur at fertilization but during fetal development when the fetus is affected by maternal condition. Therefore the proximate mechanisms examined here relate to fetal mortality.

A major hypothesis accounting for the difference in sex ratio at birth is that males, being hemizygous for the X-chromosome, are susceptible to X-linked lethal recessive traits. Consequently, more male fetuses than females are expected to be defective and are aborted disproportionately. Trivers and Willard argue this is not the reason for male fetal mortality. Evidence to support their argument exists. Stevenson and Bobrow (1967) have shown that X-linked recessives can make no appreciable contribution to fetal loss, since such traits in males behave as dominant lethals and are rapidly eliminated from a population. New detrimental mutations would have to occur in extraordinary number to account for all male fetal loss observed. Further, as Trivers (1972) argues, in homogametic fish and moths, where there is not the problem of an unguarded X-chromosome, male mortality remains higher than female. Further, since males generally outnumber females at birth, the X-linkage hypothesis assumes a very high sex ratio at conception, with considerable male fetal loss. While at one time this possibility was widely accepted, there is now evidence that extensive male fetal loss observed in past years may actually be due to difficulties in sexing very young fetuses as, for example, when XO individuals are mistaken for XY individuals (Teitelbaum and Mantel 1971). With new methods for sexing, it seems that spontaneous abortions in the first weeks of pregnancy involve a disproportionate number of female fetuses, and at later stages, males predominate (Stern 1973). Stern (1973) suggests that the losses per sex even out over the prenatal period.

Other possible mechanisms not mentioned by Trivers and Willard, however, confound their argument. Another mechanism for disproportionate male fetal loss may be an incompatibility reaction between mother and fetus. Stern (1973) suggests that the mother's system responds to the presence of the Y chromosome carried by the male fetus. Golovachev (1970) found very low sex ratios (88) correlating with high incidence of toxaemia (nausea) in the first half of pregnancy in 27,500 births. He attributes the association to an incompatibility reaction between the mother and fetus, but not due to the presence of the Y-chromosome as has sometimes been thought. Rather, the reaction of the mother's system is to the differences in the amount of chromatin (3 to 4 percent) present in the female and male genomes contributed by the father. This difference in chromatin content is due to the difference in the size of the X and Y chromosomes.

Stern (1973) suggests that there may be an immunological mother-fetal reaction in ABO blood groups since AB mothers seem to produce more males than females, and the sex ratio is higher among O children than A. Hesser, Blumberg, and Drew (1976) found that the Hepatitis B Surface Antigen (HBsAg) is associated with the live birth

sex ratio. In Greek populations and Melanesian populations, carriers of HBsAg (persons who can affect others
but who are not themselves ill) make up between 9 and 11
percent of the populations. In Papua, New Guinea,
families with mothers positive for HBsAg and fathers
negative had lower sex ratios than other types of
matings (77 and 108 respectively). In Greek populations
tested, matings with one positive parent and one
negative produced sex ratios of 85. Where both parents
were negative, the sex ratio was 112.

Besides the problem of diverse mechanisms for sex
ratio difference, there is reason to doubt Trivers' proposed proximate mechanism. Trivers (1972: 163-64) suggests the proximate cause for sex ratio variation is the
presence of protein in the diet. He cites laboratory
studies with rats which indicate males excrete 4 times
more protein than females. Males suffer more from protein deficient diets as well, gaining less weight and
surviving less well than females on similar diets. A
protein-deficient environment, Trivers argues, will affect the health of individuals reaching maturity and
serve as the mechanism which affects the sex ratio.
There is reason, however, to be cautious in generalizing
from small laboratory animals to higher mammals. Riopelle and Favrat (1977) experimentally investigated the
effects of protein deprivation on pregnant rhesus monkeys. They found that no significant difference could
be detected between the offspring of protein-deprived and
those of normal mothers. The mother fed low protein during pregnancy is apparently able to adjust her metabolic
processes to accommodate the infant's requirements at a
heavy loss to her own. Riopelle and Favrat explain this
as an adaptation to long gestation periods, when the
season of conception is quite likely to be different from
the season of birth. Primates have developed adequate
adjustment mechanisms to sustain them through seasons of
poor food supply and are able to produce an infant with
a high probability of surviving.

The relation between nutrition and pregnancy is complex. Nutritional stress in general may "reduce fertility by retarding growth rates and slowing or preventing
sexual maturation; reducing the ovulation rate including
precipitation of anovulatory phases; reducing sperm
count, motility, longevity; causing resorption of the
fetus(es); causing lactational failure; or increasing the
risk of infant death from various causes associated with
low birth weight" (Gaulin and Konner 1977: 4). Sex ratio
may be affected by substances in the diet other than proteins. Lyster and Bishop (1965) found seasonal variations in secondary sex ratio apparently related to seasonal variations in rainfall in Perth, Adelaide, and
Brisbane, Australia. Elevated sex ratios were found
where conceptions would have been six to ten weeks after
the onset of rains. For this reason, Lyster and Bishop

suggest that the ratios are elevated not through increased male fetus viability, but during the period of
spermatogenesis in the male, possibility through an increase in the numbers or effectiveness of spermatozoa
bearing Y chromosomes. Lyster (1970) found further
evidence when the area near Canberra, Australia, was examined. He associates the changing sex ratio with
changes in the ratio between magnesium and calcium in the
area's drinking water due to the onset of rainy seasons,
and he speculates that the condition may be loosely
analogous to hypomagnesaemia in cattle grazing on pas-
tures over-rich in potassium or nitrogen. Although
Lyster's work concerns the primary sex ratio, or sex
ratio at fertilization, and is therefore not the central
interest of this paper, it does indicate the sensitivity
of sex ratio to substances other than protein in the
environment.

Evidently the relationship between sex ratio and
environment is more complex than argued by Trivers and
Willard. It seems impossible to single out one
proximate mechanism for sex ratio variation: it is
likely that the sex ratio is affected by the variables
described above, and by others (cf. Edwards 1970;
Teitelbaum 1972). While some of the associations
described here are consistent with Trivers and Willard's
model, others are not easily reconciled with the model.
The literature documenting the relationship between
maternal condition and sex ratio is so extensive that it
seems probable that a portion of the sex ratio variance
is attributable to mechanisms such as Trivers (1972)
proposes. However, there probably are also proximate
causes of sex ratio variance which have little to do
with maternal condition (for example blood group and
incompatibility reactions) and this presents a problem
for evaluating Trivers and Willard's theory. Information
on how much variance is due to each factor seems necessary to completely evaluate the hypothesis presented
here.

CONCLUSIONS

In this paper, Trivers and Willard's (1973) hypothesis of sex ratio variation has been examined in the
light of research on sex ratio at birth in the United
States. They propose that variance from a 100 sex ratio
at birth can be advantageous for parents in terms of reproductive fitness. The condition prerequisite for the
advantages of sex ratio manipulation is inequality in reproductive success within and between the sexes. Parents
should invest in the sex which will be most reproduc-
tively successful, e.g. males if they can compete well,
females if they cannot. Measuring reproductive success
in the United States is difficult, since there are few
records of male fertility. For females there is a clear

correlation between high socioeconomic status and low
fertility and high socioeconomic status and low marriage
rates. For males there is some evidence that unequal access to mates exists in the United States, with men of
higher socioeconomic status spending more time married
than men of low socioeconomic status. Consistent with
these findings, as predicted by Trivers and Willard's
model, there is apparent systematic but small sex ratio
variance in the United States, with higher sex ratios at
birth for the offspring of higher socioeconomic status
parents. The problem of proximate mechanism responsible
for sex ratio variance is a major unresolved problem in
the Trivers and Willard argument; sex ratio may be related to many factors including nutrition, the presence
of trace elements in the diet, incompatibility reactions
between fetus and mother, and blood group. No factor can
be identified as the single cause, and it seems likely
that several are responsible with condition of mother
being significant.

Leaving aside the problem of proximate mechanisms,
there are other more important issues concerning the usefulness of Trivers and Willard's model in anthropological
research and the usefulness of sociobiological models in
general. Two of the most common charges are that sociobiological models are too deterministic and simplistic
to be applied to human groups. Is the Trivers and Willard model deterministic? On this point, the model fares
rather better than many sociobiological models. Trivers
and Willard make it quite clear that the expression of
the behavior (sex ratio manipulation) is facultative, depending upon condition of the mother which depends upon
environmental quality and depending upon the behavior of
other members of a population. The model may be faulted
in that the range of responses other than differential
male mortality possible to a parent is not considered.
Trivers and Willard do note that manipulation can take
place at any time prior to the end of the period of parental investment, but the earlier the manipulation, the
less costly termination will be. Their model does not
rule out cultural manipulation, but does not discuss it.
Dickemann (1979) has shown how sex ratio manipulation can
take place, using a number of cultural mechanisms including enforced celibacy, sale of children, infanticide,
suicide, and infant abandonment.

Another criticism of Trivers and Willard concerns
the nature of status in human societies. They assume
that the condition of young at the end of parental investment will tend to endure into adulthood, which is not
the case in all human societies. However, they do point
out that predictions of condition of offspring must be
high if sex ratio is to be manipulated advantageously.
This condition may help to account for the diverse findings of other anthropologists reviewed above. While
Yomut society (Irons 1976, 1979a) and the societies of

feudal and post-feudal or pre-industrial Europe, China
and India (Dickemann 1979) were found to have high variation in sex ratio along status lines, United States society, and the Yanomamo (Chagnon et al. 1979), were
found to have some variation and none, respectively. The
difference in rigidity of status distinctions is marked.
The groups with a high variance in sex ratios (Yomut,
pre-industrial Europe, China and India) had more rigid
status distinctions than do those with low or no variance
in sex ratio (United States, Yanomamo), which fits
Trivers and Willard's condition.

The result of the present study suggests that some
sociobiological models applied to human groups can raise
interesting questions about adaptation. The physiological manipulation of sex ratio proposed by Trivers and
Willard may help to explain the variance in secondary sex
ratio in the United States. However, humans with their
uniquely long period of parental investment and varied
social organization have many more opportunities and
means to effect similar ends through cultural means. In
the United States an interesting question would be if or
how parents manipulate sex ratio after birth.

Research using evolutionary models will be most productive if it includes the possibility of human response
at biological and cultural levels. The advantage of parental manipulation of the sex ratio and of human behavior will depend upon specific environmental, including cultural, circumstances. Behavior of organisms cannot be predicted without reference to a unique configuration of circumstance and even then there is a wide range
of possible responses.

ACKNOWLEDGMENTS

I would like to thank Bruce Winterhalder and William
Pollitzer for reading early drafts of this paper and for
their helpful comments. Parts of this paper were written
under a traineeship grant from the Carolina Population
Center, Population Studies Training Grant from NICHD,
HD07168, Richard Udry, Director.

NOTES

1. There are three conventional measures of sex
ratio. The primary sex ratio is the sex ratio at fertilization. There has been a great deal of research on the
primary sex ratio since there is interest in sex prede-
termination. The secondary sex ratio is the ratio at
birth, sometimes referred to as the live birth ratio.
The tertiary sex ratio applies to specific age levels at
any time after birth and varies at different ages. Unless otherwise noted, "sex ratio" here will refer to the
live birth sex ratio, the secondary sex ratio.

2. Sex ratio is conventionally presented as the ratio of the number of males per 100 females in a population, and will be so presented here. The sex ratio 110 means there are 110 males per 100 females.

3. This assumption is strengthened somewhat by the fact that only 6 percent of white births occur outside marriage. However, for nonwhites, 40 percent of births occur outside marriage. Therefore, the data for whites presented here are probably more reliable (Moore and Caldwell 1976).

5
Noble Family Structure and Expansionist Warfare in the Late Middle Ages: A Socioecological Approach

James L. Boone

Editors' Summary: *James Boone, in this chapter, develops a model for the origin of complex and hierarchical societies and competitive warfare which takes as its fundamental premise that social behavior of groups is best explained as the aggregate consequence of individual behavior strategies. For example, Boone argues that warfare in complex societies is really the result of individual adaptive strategies to maximize political and economic position or control over resources. This is in marked contrast to the cultural evolutionary theories of, for example, Harris (1979) and White (1975) which view societies and cultures as functionally integrated, self-maintaining systems, and warfare as a population control mechanism (Divale and Harris 1976). Boone then analyzes historical data from France and the Iberian Peninsula and shows that they better fit the predictions of his model, which is compatible with Darwinian theory, than those developed by cultural ecologists, which are not.*

INTRODUCTION

Because states are so often conceived of as entities unto themselves, it is easy to forget that they are created by and maintained as organized groups of individuals. The view of the state as a "social organism" dates back to antiquity and has often characterized Western political and social theory throughout history. In recent decades the "organismic analogy" has become prominent in cultural ecological theory, where it has been tied with the concept of adaptation borrowed from evolutionary theory. Here, the analogy carries with it the idea that social groups operate as functionally integrated adaptive systems wherein various social behaviors arise as adaptive strategies that promote the survival of the group ("the society" or "social organism") even at the expense of individuals within the group.

Nowhere has the functional-adaptive viewpoint been so apparent as in theories of the evolution of hierarchical societies. In looking back over the ever increasing spectrum of inequality that has characterized human societies from the development of agriculture, many cultural evolutionists seem to have come to the conclusion that since inequality exists, it must have some "purpose" in the maintenance of society. In adopting this point of view, they implicitly advance the notion of a kind of "benevolent despotism," in which controlling elites, in maintaining exclusive access to most or all of the re- sources available to a polity, perform services for the population at large that would be beyond the means of an egalitarian society. Such services entail more efficient information processing which helps to solve organiza- tional problems associated with production arrangements, to integrate socially or ecologically diverse populations or environments, and to act as a buffer against local re- source production failures (cf. Peebles and Kus 1977: 427-431 and 445 for a review of this viewpoint).

There is no doubt that hierarchically arranged deci- sion making systems are more efficient at solving complex organizational problems, that decision making hierarchies are key features of state organizations, and that studies of such systems are basic to our understanding of states (cf. Wright 1977). It is questionable, however, whether the functional aspects of administrative organizations really account for the ontogeny of social hierarchies. They might more properly be thought of as part of the system of control imposed by controlling elites in situ- ations where unequal access to resources is already a condition of the society. In the following pages, I will present an alternate view of the development of hierar- chical societies which will emphasize group formation and resource competition rather than efficiency in problem solving as the principal condition under which hierar- chical societies develop. In doing so, I will focus on one major aspect of state maintenance, warfare associated with the acquisition of territory, because it has been clearly associated with system-maintaining functions of the state in previous literature.

In their recent paper, "Population, Warfare and the Male Supremacist Complex," Divale and Harris (1976) have succinctly stated a common cultural ecological position on the adaptive significance of warfare in both primitive and state-level societies. According to these authors, among primitive societies, warfare represents a "systemic attempt to achieve stationary or near stationary popula- tions," whereas among state-level societies, expansionist warfare is a "systemic attempt to solve production defi- ciencies through perpetual territorial and demographic expansion" (Divale and Harris 1976: 531). In both primi- tive and state-level societies warfare is seen as confer- ring an adaptive advantage on populations that practice it by regulating population density in relation to re- sources.

The unlikelihood of population self-regulation in view of the problems with the group selection theory on which it depends has been extensively reviewed by biol-

ogists (Williams 1966) and more recently in relation to
anthropological theory (Irons 1979a; Lees and Bates
1979). Durham (1976b) and Lees and Bates (1979) have
specifically criticized group-level adaptive explanations
of primitive warfare such as Divale and Harris. In the
discussion below, I shall present an alternative theory
of expansionist warfare among state-level societies from
a similar point of view. I argue that territorial expansion does not necessarily arise as an adaptive response
on the part of a polity to expand its resource base or
to solve productive deficiencies facing the population
at large: expansionist warfare often results from attempts by individuals or coalitions to maintain control
by directing the competition of their immediate subordinates away from themselves and against neighboring
territories. These strategies may have little to do with
expanding the resource base to the benefit of the majority of the populace and, as will be shown in the case
study presented at the end of this discussion, may be
maintained at a considerable resource deficit seen from
the point of view of the general population. The explanatory framework adopted here, presented in contrast to
those explanations which seek a group or "system" benefit, is that social forms, rather than having a "function" or "adaptive significance" in and of themselves,
may instead be the result of the aggregate consequences
of individual adaptive strategies.
   In the discussion below some general factors contributing to organized aggression, particularly concen-
trating on the relationships of within- and between-group
competition will be outlined. I shall review some of the
recent thinking on the ecological determinants of competition with respect to the formation of groups and the
formation and maintenance of dominance systems. I discuss the special characteristics of dominance-submission
behavior among relatives, particularly siblings, and the
role of parental manipulation in channeling offspring
into alternative social roles. Finally, a case study is
presented in which parental manipulation in the form of
restrictive inheritance is suggested as an important
generative factor in the pattern of institutionalized
aggression and expansion that took the form of Crusade
warfare during the later Middle Ages.

COMPETITION AND GROUP FORMATION

   The theoretical view fundamental to the approach to
intergroup aggression developed here is that social behavior of groups is best explained in terms of the aggregate consequences of individual behavioral strategies
aimed at maximizing access to or control over limiting
resources through competitive and cooperative interaction
with other individuals. Such strategies involve the investment of time, energy, and under some conditions,

bodily risk, and as such are understandable and analyz-
able in cost-benefit terms.

Viewed in cost-benefit terms, cooperation in groups
arises from mutual self interest: individuals can generally be expected to carry out group-maintaining activities only insofar as such activities serve their own
interests as well (cf. Alexander 1974). Since individual
benefits are often highly contingent upon continued group
functioning, complex cooperative activities may emerge,
particularly among human groups, such that group behavior
may take on the outward appearance of functional "adaptive" organization at the group level. Nevertheless,
life in social groups necessarily incurs at least two
distinct disadvantages to the individual: intensified
competition for limiting resources and increased exposure
to disease. Thus individuals will remain in groups only
as long as they continue to benefit relative to emigra-
ting to an unoccupied territory or affiliating with
another group (Alexander 1974: 327-337). The lack of
alternative strategies is likely to be a strong factor
in promoting continued group membership, even in the face
of extreme disadvantage, in a situation where there is
strong competition among groups, strong sanctions against
individuals changing their group affiliation, or no unoccupied territory.

In evaluating how group size and complexity are influenced by intergroup competition, two important considerations emerge: first, the relationship between
competition and aggression and second, the ecological
conditions under which intergroup competition and aggression are most likely to occur. All evidence indicates
that aggression is not a "given" in human behavior but
instead is a highly elastic behavioral trait subject to
a wide range of forms and intensity of expression under
varying conditions of the social and natural environment
(Wilson 1971). Direct aggression is favored when there
are fewer resources than competitors and when a group or
an individual can achieve an immediate gain by forcibly
appropriating resources controlled by another. Thus it
follows that direct aggression further depends on the
potential yield of the resources at stake and the relative fighting and defensive capability of the competitors
(Durham 1976b: 390; Parker 1974: 224).

Like territoriality (Dyson-Hudson and Smith 1978)
direct aggression is most intensely favored among groups
controlling highly predictable resources which are relatively densely distributed. This follows since resources
distributed in this way will yield the highest immediate
gain to the successful aggressor. Since these resources
are also economically the easiest to defend, a positive
feedback effect may emerge involving intensifying aggressive and defensive strategies among groups competing for
highly predictable densely distributed resources.

Groups size is itself an important factor bearing on successful defense against aggression. Group size will tend to increase with the intensity of intergroup competition. As suggested above, group size will continue to increase as long as all the individuals in the group benefit relative to the alternate strategies of emigration or alternate affiliation. Under competitive pressure from outside the group, individuals within the group will tend to share resources more freely as a defense strategy in itself. By the same token, however, it is among strongly exclusive, mutually hostile, or competitive groups that the disadvantages arising from the lack of the alternative strategies listed above are likely to provide leverage for individuals or coalitions to gain control over resources within a group at the expense of others, particularly "late comers." This leads to formation of within-group hierarchical organization based on differential access to critical resources. Thus it follows that while resource availability within a defended territory is theoretically the limiting factor in population increase, population density is contingent upon competitive pressure from outside the group. Hierarchical organization is similarly influenced by competition with neighboring groups and in turn has an important effect on the number of individuals who are willing to or forced to remain in affiliation with a given territorial group. These intermediary factors help to explain why "carrying capacity" based on a simple per capita resource relationship has proved such an elusive concept in demonstrating "population pressure" as a force in social-cultural change.

Increasing group size and territorial accretion among competing human groups often take the form of alliances and forced or voluntary affiliation among smaller, previously sovereign territorial groups. These alliances and affiliations may be facilitated by a central individual, kin-group or coalition. For all the many causal factors that have been cited for the development of states, it appears that the underlying mechanisms in the formation of large territorial state-level societies may be no more mysterious than the ones outlined here (cf. Carneiro 1970a). In reviewing the relationship between resource distribution, competition and group size, Alexander's (1974) position is that today's complex societies are the result of a long history of intergroup competition and warfare. This position takes on more weight when one considers the rapid acceleration in the development of group size and complexity that throughout prehistory has followed the advent of intensive crop agriculture, a resource characterized by high predictability and density (cf. Alexander 1974, 1979; Carneiro 1970a; Dyson-Hudson 1979).

DOMINANCE HIERARCHIES AND "FLOATERS"

In further considering how intergroup competition
is generated, I turn now to group organization resulting
from competition within a defended territory. Dominance
hierarchies consist of a system of asymmetric compromises
resulting from competition among individuals within a
group over rights of access to limiting resources (Williams 1966: 218). Dominant individuals control resources
which they share within a group in return for some benefit they accrue in the way of services. Such services
include aid in defense and/or accumulation or production
of resources. Subordinate individuals will accept a less
advantageous position in the hierarchy as long as they
benefit relative either to the costs of attempting to
oust the dominant individual(s) or to the cost of emigra-
ting from the group entirely. Thus, the dominant individual's strategy is to attempt to persuade lower ranking
individuals to maintain noncompetitive affiliative roles,
either through force or through rewards involving sharing
of resources. However, dominant-subordinate transactions
may not entail actual resources, but may instead take the
form of deception or ideological manipulations involving
the passing of "artificial currency" having little or no
resource value at all (Clutton-Brock and Harvey 1978:
300).
Social hierarchies in human societies are very complex systems composed of dominant-subordinate relations
among individuals, kin groups, coalitions of non-related
individuals, or any combination thereof. Complex hierarchies can be "nested" or "stratified." This is an aspect
of organization which is of more than passing significance, since it is within these sub-groups that expectations regarding access to resources are circulated.
These expectations, which correspond to "values," form
the basis for competition for positions in the hierarchy.
The intensity of competition, along with the potential
for mutualism leading to the formation of controlling
coalitions, increases towards the top of the hierarchy
(cf. Dickemann 1979: 324-325 for a similar point). The
form and content of values or expectations regarding
rights to resources at any given time are dependent upon
the history of social interactions within the group and
with other groups, and are therefore not directly redu-
cible to considerations of population size or density,
resource availability or other ecological conditions.
Some behavioral ecologists have noted that social
hierarchical organization is a significant force for
population dispersion (Brown 1975: 97-123; Christian
1970). As Brown (1975: 113) has stated, "A natural response of an individual living in a state of forced subordination is to try to find an area where he can be
dominant." In the same sense that dominance behavior is
the social analog of territoriality (Wilson 1971: 196),

individuals in groups who disperse as a result of subordination effects are analogous to "floaters" produced by
exclusion effects in single individual territorial systems. Like "floaters," individuals dispersing as a result of subordination effects are often characterized by
relatively higher mortality rates and lowered reproduction rates (Brown 1975: 98). Among competitive human
groups, dispersion resulting from subordination effects
can take the form of direct aggression against neighboring groups. Controlling individuals or coalitions can
be expected to encourage subordinates in this activity
when the alternative is having the competition directed
against themselves. In this sense, expansion would not
be due directly to a desire by controllers to accommodate
general population pressure per se, but rather to direct
the competition of close subordinates against other
groups. I suggest that this is an important factor in
generating expansionist warfare among early states. In
these cases subordinates who conquered neighboring lands
might remain affiliated with the parent state (depending,
again, on considerations of defense), leading to the formation of "empires."
     Although the probability of cooperation and aid-
giving behavior is much higher among relatives than among
non-related individuals, relatives may also become each
other's closest competitors under conditions where resources are scarce and/or expectations are high. Such
is often the case, for example, within kin-groups that
form the ruling elites of highly stratified societies.
Among societies where power relationships are based on
kinship, the family is likely to constitute the link between basic demographic processes and larger institu-
tional forms like warfare. West Eberhard (1975: 15-18)
has suggested a special case of dominance-submission behavior among relatives, particularly siblings, where an
individual might increase his/her inclusive fitness by
adopting a subordinate role involving aid-giving or defense behavior towards a dominant relative. This altruism may be imposed through parental manipulation of offspring, in which parents manipulate some offspring into
less advantageous roles in favor of others, if such a
strategy increases their own inclusive fitness (Alexander
1974: 337; Trivers 1974; West Eberhard 1975).
     Within the context of the case studies which I now
present, this general theory suggests an explanation for
the activities of religious military orders among the nobility of feudal Europe, particularly with respect to the
membership of "younger sons" of noble families, who,
denied rights to land through restrictive inheritance,
were channeled into less advantageous, albeit highly es-
teemed military roles.
     It will not be possible, with the kind of data that
is now available to me, to investigate directly the
specific interactions which occur at the family level in

medieval Europe other than to describe some of their
general characteristics. In any case, an extended
analysis of the very complex issue of parental manipulation and competition among siblings is beyond the scope
of this chapter, since I am more generally concerned with
the effects of these interactions on expansionist warfare
among state-level societies. The material presented below is intended to test several general aspects of the
model of within- and between-group competition that I
have outlined above: (1) that increased competition contributes to the development of hierarchical organization
of territorial groups, which leads to (2) intensified
competition within the polity, particularly among the
controlling elite, (3) this competition generates a certain number of subordinates who exhibit the characteristics of "floaters" predicted by the model, and that (4)
competition between "floaters" and the controlling elites
results in episodes of territorial expansion (Figure
5.1). The case studies presented below attempt to place
within the context of the model outlined above a social
phenomenon from the medieval period already recognized
by many historians.

YOUNGER SONS IN MEDIEVAL FRANCE

> The second and third born sons, and others, who by
> the custom of the land have little or no portion in
> the inheritance of their fathers, and who by poverty
> are often constrained to follow wars that are unjust
> and tyrannical so as to sustain their estate of
> noblesse, since they know no other calling but arms;
> and therein they commit so much ill that it would
> be frightening to tell of all the pillaging and
> crimes with which they oppress the poor people.
>
>   Phillipe de Mézières (cited
>   in Keen 1976: 43)

Feudal society in medieval western Europe developed
during the 8th and 9th centuries around a basic dominant-
subordinate social arrangement in which members of the
landholding elite granted land and other material recom-
pense to lower ranking males in return for loyalty and
military service. From the beginning, the ruling nobility justified their noble status not only specifically
in terms of their lineage, but more generally in terms
of their role as defenders of society at large, since it
was only they who could support the warrior class required in defense against outside invaders. Some historians argue that feudal society, with its proximate
beginnings in the Carolingian empire, developed as a defensive response by landholding elites to protect their
lands and agricultural labor forces against the incur-
sions of steppe nomads from the east, the Viking raids

Figure 5.1. A model illustrating some of the relationships discussed in this chapter

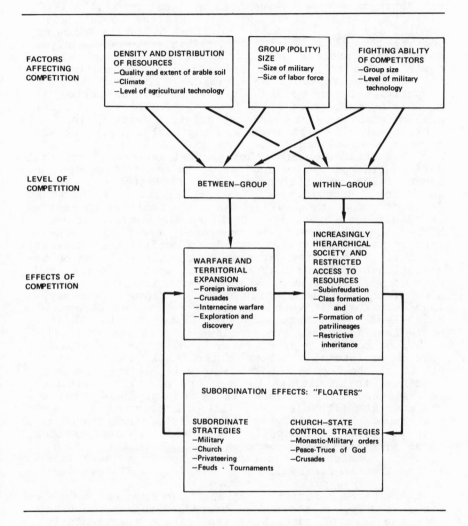

from the western coasts, and the Arab invasions from
across the Pyrenees to the south (cf. for example Reynolds 1961: 158-164). To the extent to which this interpretation can be supported, the underlying mechanisms of
state formation during that period can be understood in
terms of the model of competition and group formation
outlined in above sections of the discussion.

With the subsidence of external threats and with the
proliferation of lineages claiming descent from Charle-
magne and other rival houses, the Carolingian empire,

having lasted only a few generations, broke up into
smaller warring states. With all the available lands in
the heart of Europe having been at least nominally laid
claim to by these rival parties, internal competition
predictably led to increased vertical differentiation of
society throughout the region. This occurred mainly
through the process of subinfeudation, in which the
basic dyadic relationship of vassalage was continued
through several levels of hierarchy. In areas where
competition began to stabilize later in the period,
increasing numbers of fiefs became hereditary, and there
was increasing status differentiation within the
nobility itself, with lower ranking nobles paying homage
to more powerful regional lords.

Subinfeudation and other general aspects of vertical
differentiation can be understood in terms of gradually
intensifying competition among the nobility over lands
and labor. However, a closer consideration of the effects of competition within the noble families themselves
is required in order to understand why warfare at the
higher level of the state presented itself as a constantly regenerating and amplifying condition of medieval
society. Such a consideration must begin with the observation that while reproductive success may be correlated
with economic success (a stated assumption at the beginning of this chapter), high rates of reproduction may,
in highly competitive social contests, almost paradoxi-
cally lead to downward social mobility (Herlihy 1973).
Noble families faced two problems in this respect: (1)
allowing too many sons to marry resulted in the proliferation of lateral branches of the family and the dissi-
pation of the "house," particularly if (2) the patrimony
continued to be divided between the offspring through
several generations. Thus, it is not surprising that by
at least the 11th century social practices began to appear among the nobility which restricted inheritance to
a single male line, usually the eldest. In many regions,
these practices began before the 11th century among
wealthy and high-ranking families, but began much later
in the Iberian Peninsula, for example, as discussed below.

Practices restricting access to resources, which began at the top of the social hierarchy and spread down,
took the form of outright primogeniture (particularly
with entailed lands) or practices which restricted marriage to the eldest son. These practices may be seen as
family strategies which attempted to strike a balance between the economic advantage presented in maintaining
family assets intact and the clear disadvantage of reducing the survival value or even eliminating entirely
its younger male and female offspring.

In a detailed and closely documented series of articles on noble family structure and the origin of
knighthood, Duby (1977) has traced the shift to patri-

liny and restricted inheritance in France during the
10th through the 12th centuries, particularly in the region of Macon. Here, de facto primogeniture took the
form of restriction of marriage to the oldest son: "all
brothers had the same rights of inheritance on their
father's death. Only one of them married and begot legitimate sons. The latter, thanks to the practices of
prolonged joint ownership, would collect without difficulty the rights of their uncles" (Duby 1977: 74). Outright primogeniture may have been more commonly associated with entailed lands (this was clearly true in the
case of the Iberian Peninsula, see below discussion),
where the rule was connected with feudal law which prevented the subdivision of fiefs. Younger brothers may
have received small inheritances (particularly new lands
acquired by the father, in contrast to the patrimony itself), but possession in such cases "was precarious, and
fragments such as these bred discord between brothers and
encouraged cupidity and sharpened the temptation of other
brothers or nephews to seize whatever they could by
force" (Duby 1977: 117-118). It seems likely that the
most extreme inheritance occurred where the rules of succession were imposed through entailment, and that more
flexible, reversible strategies were practiced by families who controlled their own inheritance, since the more
extreme the restriction of investment to one offspring,
the greater the danger that the family line might,
through accident or barren marriage, become extinct altogether (Duby makes this point in a different context,
cf. 1977: 110 and 120).

Duby further explores the ramifications of the problem of succession in a chapter devoted to aristocratic
"youths." Here, the term "youth" (juvenis), rather than
having a strict chronological connotation, referred instead to noble males who had not yet married and established an estate. Following adolescence, a period of
vagabondage was considered a necessary element in an
aristocratic male's development. Vagabondage was not
usually solitary, and often bands of "youths" lived and
travelled together: a newly dubbed "youth" might arm and
take with him the sons of his father's vassals who were
his own age. Arms and money were provided by the house
to which the young nobles and vassals were attached. The
period of vagabondage was de rigueur for the eldest sons
as well and apparently functioned to delay the young
heir's marriage and accession to his patrimony: "The
eldest son who as a 'youth' was surrounded by 'young'
companions . . . began to struggle openly against the old
lord. . . . His father would give him leave to depart
with some relief, and he would not recall his son until
his own powers waned" (1977: 117). This is an interesting point in itself in that it indicates considerable
parent-offspring conflict and competitive interaction
even in the case of the rightful heir, much more so for

the younger sons who were destined to remain "youths"
far into middle age or indefinitely. Their usual
recourse was to enter the Church or military service.
   Thus, Duby argues that it was this expanding group
of "youths" who constituted the "spearhead of feudal aggression" (1977: 115). As such, these bands of armed
"youths," whose class expectations and military
expertise were quite high, represented a significant
disruptive potential within the noble families
themselves, within the organization of the state or
principality as a whole, and for the system of alliances
that developed between states. And, with primogeniture
spreading lower into the ranks of the nobility, these
landless "youths" were increasing in numbers. It is
certainly within the context of this growing problem
that the Church began to take an increasing role in the
affairs of the Christian states, particularly through
the role it played in territorial integration and in
rechanneling aggression. Early manifestations of this
role in France are exemplified in the peace of God
movement of the 10th and 11th centuries. Duby outlines
a variety of complex features of this movement and I
will recount only a few of them here.
   With the strengthening of the power of regional
lords and the virtual collapse of monarchial power, the
peace of God movement was a response to "conditions in
an enclosed agrarian society, no longer nourished by the
profits of war which had formerly been put into circulation by the sovereign" (Duby 1977: 86). Warfare up until
and during that time was not simply a pastime for
"youths," it could and often did lead to palpable gain
on the part of young men who had been denied inheritance
through their families. (The Norman conquest of Sicily
is a case in point.) It also provided a means by which
the ruling elite could relieve themselves of the demands
of these landless nobles, as the above quotation suggests, for fathers to provide directly for their own
younger sons through acquisitions. The paix de Dieu
shifted the emphasis on warfare as an institution for
personal gain (at least within Christendom) to an institution for the glorification of Christianity. As such
it paved the way for the segregation of "youths" into
religious military orders under the control of the Church
and to their deployment in Crusades outside the Continent. Duby (1977: 120) writes: "It is obvious that it
was the bands of 'youths' excluded by so many social
prohibitions from the main body of settled men, fathers
of families and heads of houses, with their prolonged
spells of turbulent behavior making them an unstable
fringe of society, who created and sustained the crusades."

INDIVIDUAL ADAPTIVE STRATEGIES AND "FLOATERS"

It becomes clear from the above discussion that the landless younger sons, subordinated at the family level by the rules of restrictive inheritance, fit rather well the "floater" profile predicted by the model outlined in the beginning of this chapter in terms of social origin, mortality and reproductive rates, and dispersing tendencies. Duby (1977: 115-116) reports that the most frequent references to "youths" in his research were in connection with their violent deaths, resulting from tournaments, hunting accidents, and warfare. Reproductive rates of younger males were also lowered through restriction from marriage and delayed marriage. While these individuals undoubtedly produced illegitimate children, the survival and reproduction rates of the majority of these should have been inferior to those of the eldest sons, since only the most powerful could afford, both politically and economically, to maintain and confer status on their bastard children. Equally significant was the monastic character of the religious military orders into which many younger sons were channeled. While the family may have restricted marriage, the Church ideology attempted to restrict nonmarital sexual intercourse altogether. The rule of lifelong celibacy was widespread, although not universal, among monastic orders throughout the period.

Among the Latin Christian states, the Church had a crucial integrative role in reducing the warfare and local chaos resulting from the increasing organizational problems that faced the ruling elites. Principal among these problems was the intensifying competition for land and other means of support among the lower nobility, as attested by the Church's role in rechanneling aggression away from the European political arena and against non-Christian lands. This regulatory role, and many other 'functions' the Church performed relating to family structure and other aspects of society (cf. Dickemann 1979), brings to mind the "ritual regulation" theory put forward by Rappaport (1971a). I argue here that the regulatory role of the Church should not be viewed as a self-organizing aspect of the social system as a whole, but as a specialized creation of the actors involved, who sought to maintain their own interests. The nobility tolerated the Church because it provided them with a legitimacy to power, allowed them to solve complex political problems at the "international" level, and gave them a very powerful means of controlling the population at large. The nobility not only tolerated the Church, it helped create it: the membership of the ecclesiastical hierarchy was drawn largely from the nobility, particularly younger sons (and daughters), who in turn were able to assist their families in various ways.

Even at that level, the Church and its role in or-
ganizing Crusades should not be viewed as a vast "conspiracy" directed against the less fortunate. As I have
already pointed out, warfare up until that time had been,
and in some cases continued to be, a profitable venture
for landless nobles, who gained the ransom, booty and
land that could be forcibly expropriated from neighboring
polities. (Particularly in the later Middle Ages when
new lands were "discovered," the courts of the European
nobility abounded with travellers and chroniclers who
presented oral and written accounts-- often highly exag-
gerated--of riches to be had in foreign lands. These
individuals were not pawns in a conspiracy, they simply
told the landless nobles what they wanted to hear.)
Moreover, state organizations needed armies in time of
danger, both in cases of civil unrest and foreign invasions, and they rewarded their soldiers, noble and com-
moner, for their services. Feudal society was based
largely on that arrangement. The institution of religious warfare could never have existed if this tradition, which gave rise to a whole value system referred
to as "chivalry," had not existed before it. With the
Crusades, however, we do see a manipulative pattern
emerging, in which the high esteem with which military
service in knighthood was imbued (through a complex in-
terplay of secular personal gain, family honor and ecclesiastical patronage) can be viewed as a form of
reward--"artificial currency"--"paid" to the landless
nobles for maintaining a non-aggressive role within the
ruling power structure.

"UN-ECONOMIC WARFARE": PORTUGUESE EXPANSION IN
NORTH AFRICA

While the Crusades against Palestine and Syria
ended, by and large, by the end of the 13th century, a
similar pattern of warfare continued on the Iberian
Peninsula with the Reconquista. Here the Papacy also
assumed a role in territorial integration of the Iberian
Christian kingdoms by attempting (chiefly through arbi-
tration of secular treaties) to control which Muslim
lands were available for conquest by the respective
monarchies of Portugal, Castile, and Aragon. As a
general rule, each kingdom could take only land directly
south of its borders. Even by the 15th century, the ideological content of Papal Bulls obtained by Portuguese
monarchs in order to conduct conquests in North Africa,
still place this southward extension of the Reconquista
firmly within the tradition of the Crusades (Oliveira
Marques 1972: 140-141) although there were secular aspects as well (cf. Godinho 1962: 83-109 and passim). The
Portuguese conquests, in fact, constituted something of
an historical link between the medieval tradition of Crusade warfare and the more familiar pattern of colonial

expansion which, with the development of gunpowder warfare, transoceanic sailing vessels, and the rise of mer-
cantilism as an alternate means of accumulating wealth,
led, almost incidentally, to the dispersion of European
populations over much of the Earth (cf. Wallerstein 1974:
46-47). In the discussion below, I present this pattern
of warfare in more detail because it will illustrate more
clearly two important points with which this paper is
concerned: (1) that there is a relationship between intensifying competition for lands among the expanding nobility, the shift to patriliny and restricted inheritance, and the generation of expansionist warfare; and
(2) that expansionist warfare does not necessarily arise
as a system-maintaining institution designed to solve
production deficiencies pertaining to the whole population.

The Reconquista, the reconquest of the Iberian
Peninsula from Muslim invaders, had a number of
important effects on the development of state
organization among the Iberian Christian kingdom. With
the disintegration of Ummayad control over the Peninsula
into rival taifa kingdoms, the lands to the south
presented a relatively easy means (both ideologically
and militarily) for the Christian monarchs to put into
circulation new territories to satisfy the demands of
their noble underlings. In the case of Portugal, this
process resulted in the monarch's direct control over
much of the lands within the expanding state, with the
majority of the nobility remaining either in direct
vassalage to the king or to a few powerful regional
lords, often his sons. Thus throughout the medieval
period Portugal remained a much more highly centralized
state than the feudal states of France and England. By
the 13th and 14th centuries the Portuguese monarchs were
able to "nationalize" most of the religious military
orders and usually appointed the masterships of these
powerful estates to their own younger and/or
illegitimate sons. Portugal rarely, if ever,
participated in the eastern Crusades.

The availability of "new" lands for conquests next
to Portugal's own borders explains why we do not see the
development of subinfeudation or institutionalized primogeniture associated with entailed estates until after the
middle of the 13th century, when the Reconquista was
"completed" in the Algarve region of the Iberian Peninsula (in 1249). With this source of territory used up,
intensifying competition within the state led to the institution of morgados, or entailed estates which carried
the stipulation of primogeniture (Gama Barros 1945: v.
8, pp. 227-253; Oliveira Marques 1975: 386-387; these
were similar to mayorazgos in Spain, cf. Cooper 1978).

The existence of a class of cavalaria, composed of
males of noble origin, who were considered lower in
status than the fidalguia or nobility (Gama Barros 1945:

v. 3, 345-491; Oliveira Marques 1975: 386-387) is the
principal evidence that some system of restricted
marriage/inheritance, perhaps similar to the French example cited above, existed even before the end of the Reconquista. This cavalaria appears to have consisted of
nobility who, being poorer in land, sought homage to the
king or other powerful houses. In any case, the institution of primogeniture in the 13th and 14th centuries
hastened the appearance of landless younger sons whose
only recourse was to join the Church, military service,
or the ranks of the rising burguesas or commercial class
(Oliveira Marques 1975: 387; Mattoso 1975).

The Portuguese extension of the Reconquista into the
Maghreb region of North Africa began with the reign of
João I (reigned 1385-1433). His rise to power is an in-
structive case study in the disruptive potential of the
younger sons. He was the illegitimate son of the reign-
ing Portuguese monarch, and had been appointed the mas-
tership of the Order of Avis (a military order) by his
father. When the king's only legitimate male heir died
in youth, the throne was left to his daughter whom he had
given in marriage alliance to the king of Castile. Thus
Portugal was threatened with the loss of its sovereignty
under Castile. João took advantage of the dissatisfac-
tion of some of the nobility to seize the throne in a war
of succession which lasted two years. Among his principal supporters, Oliveira Marques writes, were the
"younger sons who were eager to get land and positions
belonging to the powerful feudal lords" (1972: 128; cf.
also Mattoso 1981: 26-27). This "revolution" resulted
in a general turnover in the older, established nobility.

Since the king was the principal holder of wealth
and land, he was obliged to support the nobility, as a
form of redistribution, with not only land but yearly
monetary allowances. With the great monetary crisis that
occurred between 1350 and 1435 (Oliveira Marques 1972:
v. 1, pp. 113-114), these fixed incomes of the nobility
became worth less and less. This caused particular hard-
ship among the cavalaria, who had little else in the way
of support (Godinho 1962: 80). Many of them turned to
piracy and robbery, while others were kept busy with the
raids against neighboring Castile, raids that produced
considerable booty and ransom. When a general peace was
signed with Castile in 1411, João I was left with a vola-
tile situation. Malowist (1964: 15-16, author's translation) writes with respect to this period: "the chron-
icler speaks clearly that it was above all the cadets,
who lacked land and other sources of revenue within the
country (who) desired war, which would permit them to ac-
cede to a situation of social and material indepen-
dence." It is under these circumstances that João I
appears to have taken advantage of the Crusading tradition by obtaining Papal authorization to attack Ceuta,
an Islamic coastal entrepot on the Moroccan coast, in

1415. This pattern of warfare against the coastal
cities of Morocco continued for over 100 years under
much the same circumstances.

It is sometimes argued that the primary motive for
Portuguese expansion was a desire to control the wheat
of the Moroccan interior, as the Romans had done a mil-
lenium before. However, throughout the period of conquest, Newitt writes, "the kings poured more men, money
and ships into Morocco than they ever invested in their
Indian enterprises, yet the Moroccan conquests never
yielded any return (Newitt 1973: 5). The Portuguese
North African campaign was maintained on a wheat
deficit, and great amounts of wheat had to be imported
from the Azores, Portugal and Andalusia to maintain the
Moroccan colonies (Oliveira Marques 1968: 242). This
expansion only served to exacerbate the serious wheat
shortages that periodically existed in the often
famine-stricken Portuguese countryside. Throughout the
late medieval period, production deficiencies were
caused not by overpopulation but under-population and a
shortage of labor (cf. Boserup 1965: 95-98). At the
same time the Portuguese monarchs were planning
expansionist campaigns in Africa, they were also
attempting to enforce ordinances (such as the Lei de
Sesmarias, cf. Newitt 1973: 2-3) designed to legislate
cultivators back onto the land already controlled by the
nobility. These policies actually worked against each
other since the foot soldiers required in expansion were
drawn from the potential agricultural labor force. Thus
it appears in this case, as doubtless in many others,
that expansionist warfare actually represented a
controlling strategy undertaken by elites to direct the
competition of close subordinates away from their own
political positions, a pattern of competition which
occurs when population numbers are far above the
"carrying capacity" of the land and had little to do
with production deficiencies associated with it.

CONCLUSIONS

The case studies and discussion presented above have
argued against the use of the interpretive framework
which views states, societies and "cultures" as functionally integrated, self-maintaining, "adaptive" systems
based on the organismic model in which each component of
a system has its function in the maintenance of the whole
(for example White 1975; Gall and Saxe 1977; Harris 1979;
among many others). There was clearly a lot of regulating and controlling going on in the medieval period, but
little of it was carried on in the interests of the majority of the population that made up these societies.
The framework adopted here views societies as interactive
systems in which social forms develop as aggregations of
individuals, kin-groups and controlling coalitions co-

operating and competing to maintain their self-interests within the social and natural environment. While the model is based ultimately on the principal of natural selection, it views human behavior within the context of an "open genetic system" which emphasizes phenotypic plasticity and the role of the environment, and makes minimal assumptions regarding the connections between genes and behavior (Dyson-Hudson 1979; Smith, Chapter 2). Far from validating the "status quo," a criticism often directed at sociobiology, the case studies I have presented here merely illustrate that the rich and powerful often constitute as serious a "social problem" as the poor. Far from viewing warfare as "adaptive" (as population control, or other modest proposals), this approach places a destructive and complex institution back where it belongs with the other three "Horsemen of the Apocalypse": disease, famine, and greed. Finally, in the rather brief space in which I have presented these case studies, I have attempted to show that rather than being "reductionist," this approach to human behavior presupposes that an anthropologist must use an integrative model, taking into account the ecological circumstances, the particular historical developments, and the social-cultural practices of a society, before the concept of adaptation can be applied to his or her research.

ACKNOWLEDGMENTS

Part of the research for this paper was supported by NSF grant SPI-7913993.

6
Woman Capture as a Motivation for Warfare: A Comparative Analysis of Intra-Cultural Variation and a Critique of the "Male Supremacist Complex"

James Dow

    Editors' Summary: *James Dow challenges the Divale and Harris (1976) assertion that the male supremacist complex of warfare, female infanticide and male dominance serves to regulate population with respect to resources--a functional explanation which is incompatible with Darwinian theory. He summarizes the previous criticisms of Divale and Harris' theory. He then makes predictions about what the demographic structures of populations should be if the male supremacist complex were operating as specified. An analysis of the demographic data demonstrates that in general they do not fit the predictions. Thus Divale and Harris' theory must be rejected on empirical as well as theoretical grounds.*

INTRODUCTION

    Cultural ecologists have proposed group level explanations to account for patterns of human social interactions. For example, Divale and Harris (1976) propose that warfare, female infanticide, and male dominance, a complex of traits they call the male supremacist complex, adapt band and village societies to low environmental potentials and function to regulate population. This chapter challenges their assertion that these traits work together as the adaptive system they describe. The chapter first reviews published critiques of the male supremacist hypothesis to establish its present status among other researchers. It then presents a new critique directed at the lack of evidence that the capture of women provides a motivation for warfare. In total these critiques show that the male supremacist complex as Divale and Harris have described it does not exist in most band and village societies.

THE MALE SUPREMACIST COMPLEX

    The male supremacist hypothesis states that a high value placed on men causes mothers practicing infanticide to do away with newborn girls more often than with boys. Divale and Harris write:

> Warfare functions in this system to sustain the male
> supremacist complex and thereby to provide the prac-
> tical exigencies and ideological imperatives for
> postpartum cultural selection against female in-
> fants. (Divale and Harris 1976: 527)

If fewer women survive childhood, then fewer children
will be born. Thus Divale and Harris see intensive warfare in these band and village societies as regulating
population not by battle casualties but rather by the
encouragement of preferential female infanticide. The
capture of scarce females is an important part of their
hypothetical system. They regard it as an ideal motivation for stimulating warfare:

> Sex, rather than other forms of reinforcement such
> as food or shelter, is used to condition warlike be-
> havior because sexual deprivation does not lead to
> the impairment of physical fitness, whereas depriva-
> tion of food and shelter would cripple fighting
> capacity. (1976: 526)

The shortage of women created by the female infanticide
exacerbates the warfare; more raids have to be conducted
to capture women. The increasing warfare again leads to
a higher rate of female infanticide in order to produce
more warriors. Thus they see the system perpetuating itself.

As validation of their hypothesis, Divale and Harris
offer a cross-cultural survey showing an association between warfare and high child sex ratios (the ratios of
boys per 100 girls) in a sample of 112 band and village
societies. This is supposed to prove that warfare leads
to preferential female infanticide in the way they describe.

PREVIOUS CRITICISMS

There have been many published criticisms of Divale
and Harris's theory. Chagnon, Flinn, and Melancon (1979:
291) and Fjellman (1979: 195) note that the child sex
ratio is not a perfect indicator of preferential female
infanticide, yet Divale and Harris use it as their measure. Differential fertilization, fetal wastage, and differential patterns of postnatal care are some of the
other factors that affect child sex ratios (Chagnon,
Flinn, and Melancon 1979: 291).

Other critiques attack the statistical methods used
by Divale and Harris. Hirschfeld, Howe, and Levin (1978)
and Fjellman (1979: 92) challenge the use of the t-test
for differences between sample means to test the association between child sex ratio and warfare. They claim
that, for this statistical procedure to produce valid results, the sex ratios in the populations being compared

must have normal distributions with equal variances. However, variances can be changed by Divale and Harris's method of averaging sex ratios when cultures are represented by several populations.

Blalock (1972: 226-228) reports a version of the t-test that does not require the assumption of equal variance, but one does not know which t-test Divale and Harris used. One can also ask, what was the universe and what was the sample? Apparently the universes were all band and village societies with certain characteristics, and the samples were those societies on which Divale and Harris managed to get information. The random sample assumption for the t-test was therefore violated, but it is often so violated in cross-cultural research. Nevertheless, Hirschfeld, Howe, and Levin (1978) seem to be mistaken in assuming that the human populations themselves were sampled and that equal variance in them were required.

Divale, Harris, and Williams (1978) respond to Hirschfeld, Howe, and Levin's criticism by noting, after the fact that not the actual populations but an estimate of their child sex ratios were sampled; therefore the t-test was appropriate. They also write that in their view the estimates of the child sex ratios "appear to be normally distributed" (1978: 381), thus filling this other requirement for the t-test. Since the significance of the association between warfare and child sex ratios is basically what is at issue, they deal with the problem by offering another more valid test, a sophisticated analysis of variance, which confirms their original conclusion that there is a significant connection between warfare and high child sex ratios. Later replies by Howe (1978) and Hirschfeld (1979) justify their right to disagree with Divale and Harris but do not present further arguments.

The confusion over statistical tests could have been avoided by a clearer description of them in the original article. To have also published the data, or to have made it more readily available would have made a resolution of such controversies much easier. After all the real issue is not what test you use but whether or not the data support what you say.

Kang, Horan, and Reis (1979) criticize Divale and Harris for a lack of full consideration of all possible combinations of variables in the statistical tables. The problem manifests itself particularly in Divale and Harris's Table VI (1976: 528) where all combinations of infanticide and warfare were not tabulated. This table, therefore, cannot show a direct association between infanticide and warfare independent of child sex ratios. Kang, Horan, and Reis (1979: 207) also feel that Divale and Harris's definition of "warfare" is too broad and imprecise. Kang, Horan, and Reis code infanticide separately in a cross-cultural sample of 66 cultures, find

100

no association of it with warfare, and conclude that
"infanticide is an adaptive method of population control
among primitive people which occurs independently of warfare."
Other criticisms question the validity of the cross-
cultural sample. Kang, Horan, and Reis (1979) criticize
the non-randomness of the sample, the non-independence
of many cases in it (Galton's problem), and the existence
of regional biases. Norton (1978) claims that the male
supremacy argument is invalid because Divale and Harris
drop and add cases from an earlier sample (Divale 1972).
When the dropped cases are restored she claims that the
data do not support the association between warfare and
female infanticide. Divale and Harris point out that it
is their right to use a different sample if it meets a
justifiable sampling criterion (Divale and Harris 1978b)
and admonish Norton for not noticing that the allegedly
dropped !Kung societies were not dropped at all and that
the other societies that were dropped still support the
hypothesis. Norton's minor and inaccurate recalculations
are no challenge to Divale and Harris' theory.
Others object to the emphatic way in which Divale
and Harris describe male dominance in human cultures.
Lancaster and Lancaster (1978) think Divale and Harris
see more male dominance than really exists. In a similar
vein Kang, Horan, and Reis (1979: 205-297) accuse them
of making "a number of gross and false assumptions" about
male dominance. Poewe (1980: 113) accuses them of posi-
tivistic hierarchical thought which constrains them to
see men as central to society. Her impassioned radical
critique seems to regard any empirical approach to the
question as biased and non-essential. Some of the institutions Divale and Harris adduce as indicators of male
dominance, such as polygyny, can also be associated with
female power. However, the colorful description of male
dominance with which Divale and Harris introduce their
article is not essential to providing their more modest
hypothesis. Divale and Harris respond to the Lancasters'
criticism by pointing out that there is really no substantial disagreement between them over the nature of the
basic hypothesis (Divale and Harris 1978a: 117-118).
A recent criticism of the male supremacist hypothesis is that it is based on a theory of group selection
rather than on a theory of individual selection (Irons
1979a: 81; Chagnon, Flinn, and Melancon 1979: 273). Divale and Harris propose that bands and villages that do
not control their populations by means of the complex
will be replaced by those that do. They write:

   Band and village societies which failed to attain
   stationary populations suffered cuts in their standard of living and were threatened by hunger and
   disease. Societies which achieved stationary populations by means other than the male supremacist-

warfare complex were routed and destroyed by their
more aggressive neighbors. (Divale and Harris
1976: 531)

They see selection as resulting from competition between
groups. The entire theory of group selection of genetic
traits is strongly criticized by biologists, anthropologists, and others who believe that it rarely occurs
(Irons 1979b; Bates and Lees 1979: 278). The individual
selection process resulting from continual selective
pressure for the behavior of individuals whose differential reproductivity or influence is high (Irons 1979b:
10-13) is more in accord with theory and data. The
theory of individual selection is usually phrased in
terms of genetic adaptation, but Durham (1979) attempts
to modify it to deal with non-genetic cultural behavior.
    Strongly favoring the individual selection process,
Bates and Lees (1979) point out that Divale and Harris
make the unwarranted assumption that any social institution reducing population growth is ipso facto a population stabilizing mechanism. Divale and Harris do not
show evidence that preferential female infanticide is
regulating population, that it is a response to environmental degradation, or that it has led to a stable population in any of the societies considered by them.
    A major, often unstated, source of support for the
male supremacist hypothesis is ethnographic data from the
Yanomamo, a warlike tribe in the Amazonian area (Chagnon
1974, 1977). However, there is serious doubt that, even
among the Yanomamo, the system of population regulation
proposed by Divale and Harris exists. Chagnon, Flinn,
and Melancon (1979) have recently shown that the high
child sex ratios among the Yanomamo probably exist at
birth. Therefore they can be explained without invoking
preferential female infanticide and without the male
supremacist complex. They find that the sex ratio at
birth favors males and suggest that biological adaptation
could contribute to a skewed sex ratio. Fisher (1930)
and Kolman (1960) have shown that genetic evolution tends
to drift toward equal parental expenditures on the two
sexes. Chagnon, Flinn, and Melancon (1979) suggest that
cultural practices that kill off males before full parental expenditure has been made could result in biological
evolution toward sex ratios favoring more males at birth.
A similar process operating as obligate or facultative
adaptation could explain the entire cross-cultural association between high child sex ratios and warfare in
small populations. However, the theory of sex ratio selection is complicated and needs further specification
to show how such a biological evolution might proceed.
One concrete mathematical model (Leigh 1970) shows that
secondary sex ratios (at birth) should not be affected
by differential mortality between the sexes.

After reviewing it and its detractors, one can see
that the male supremacist complex is essentially a systems model of cultural adaptation. It has two parts:
(1) a system for regulating population growth based on
the interactions of warfare, male dominance, and female
infanticide, and (2) a theory that such systems evolve
because they confer selective advantage on groups. The
cross-cultural association adduced by Divale and Harris
does not prove that this system exists in any particular
case nor in a significant number of cases in the sample
because it does not present evidence that the systems
variables interact as they are supposed to in any one
culture. Although there is an association between child
sex ratio and warfare cross-culturally, there is no proof
that this association is due to the systemic interaction
proposed by Divale and Harris. It could be due to other
types of interactions or to joint associations with many
other variables. Male dominance need not have any relationship to child sex ratios or warfare. According to
Fjellman (1979: 199): "Whatever the merits of their
theory, it cannot be tested on the data as presented by
them."

Nevertheless, the cross-cultural association between warfare, as Divale and Harris choose to define it,
and child sex ratio holds up in spite of the attack that
has been made on their statistical tests. Although their
sampling is not up to the highest statistical standards,
this association in their sample is due to some real cultural phenomena and not to a biased selection of cases,
as some critics have implied (Kang, Horan, and Reis 1979:
204). If the male supremacist hypothesis were true, it
would explain the existence of the association between
child sex ratios and warfare. However, the existence of
this association does not prove the male supremacist hypothesis. An association between two variables does not
demonstrate cause and effect. As the critics have amply
demonstrated, the hypothesis needs other confirmation if
it is to be accepted.

The remainder of this chapter is devoted to presenting and analyzing data that disproves the existence of
the male supremacist complex in some band and village societies. It is based on the quantitative analysis of intracultural variations in another association implied by
the male supremacist hypothesis, which so far has not
been considered by the critics--the connection between
shortages of women and the frequency of warfare. If the
system operates as Divale and Harris postulate and the
capture of scarce females provides a motivation for warfare, then societies with a high frequency of warfare
should also exhibit a shortage of women.

AN INTRA-CULTURAL METHOD

When a connection between a shortage of women and
increased raiding in warlike band and village societies
is being considered, it is important to note the difference between ideological and material connections. An
ideological connection exists when capturing women is a
legitimate goal of warfare. In this case an actual
shortage of women may have no effect on the frequency of
raiding. A material connection exists when the shortage
of women governs the frequency of raiding. A material
connection implies demographic feedback to military activity which could be part of an important population
regulation mechanism.

The cross-cultural method used by Divale and Harris
led them to propose a single system found to a greater
or a lesser extent in all band and village societies.
This method attempted to validate a single hypothesis
with the whole cultural sample and not with individual
cultures of the sample. On the other hand the method of
intra-cultural variation introduced here, looks for evidence of the system separately in each culture of the
sample. It is based on the idea that a particular adaptive system is much more likely to be found in separate
units of a single culture than in separate cultures.
Each unit in a culture is taken as a case of the same
adaptive system in a different state. Comparisons between the units allow one to see the different states of
the system and to examine the correlation of variables
that are functionally interrelated. A further advantage
of this method is that it requires similar data gathering
methods only for units within a culture. One of the
first applications of the idea of studying intra-cultural
variations was made by Leach (1965), who used it to analyze political transformation in Highland Burma. As
Pelto and Pelto (1975) have pointed out, intra-cultural
diversity provides a great opportunity for theoretical
breakthroughs in anthropology. The method presented in
this chapter involves a quantitative approach to the
analysis of intra-cultural variation.

As it was employed here, the method used census population data from each of a number of warlike band and
village societies. All of these societies engaged in
some sort of warfare close to the time of the census.
Published censuses provided the data on a number of
separate populations in each culture. The populations
were divided into age groups, adult and child, and into
male and female. The four age-sex groups were male children (BOYS), female children (GIRLS), male adults (MEN),
and female adults (WOMEN). Four ratios were calculated
for each unit in the cultural sample in order to measure
mortality and the ratio of the sexes.[1]

male loss ratio (MLOSSRA)   = BOYS / MEN

```
female loss ratio (FLOSSRA)    = GIRLS / WOMEN
child sex ratio (CHSEXRA)      = BOYS / GIRLS
adult sex ratio (ADSEXRA)      = MEN / WOMEN
```

Partial correlations between the mortality ratios and the sex ratios were calculated over the population samples from each cultural group.

Age was divided into just two categories, adult and child, because published population data on primitive societies often does not make fine divisions of age. It is difficult to make precise estimates of age in pre-literate cultures (Howell 1979: 24-25). Population data that were more refined were aggregated into these two age categories to permit uniform statistical processing. Thus, by using the rough categories, more cultures were included in the study, and the data were processed in a uniform manner. The use of ratios and correlations made the analysis independent of the absolute values of the quantities. Thus, for example, the worldwide tendency to underreport females 10 to 14 years old (Fjellman 1979: 189) would not affect the correlations. A positive correlation between child sex ratio and male loss ratio would remain, even if females were uniformly underreported.

Ideally one should have had figures on the amount of warfare in each unit, but again quantitative data of this sort are practically never gathered and published by ethnographers. Although many factors contribute to male mortality, it does reflect changes in the amount of warfare when other causes remain the same. The method did not require that an indicator actually measure a phenomenon such as raiding frequency but just that it vary systematically with that phenomenon. Thus male mortality is correlated with anything that is correlated with the amount of warfare, although it is not a direct measure of the amount of warfare. Other factors affecting male mortality and not linked to the lack of women vary differently and reduce the significance of the correlation with the sex ratio but may not obscure it. The ratio of male children to male adults was used as a secondary indicator of overall male adult mortality because accurate mortality statistics for simple cultures are hardly ever recorded. It was assumed therefore that the processes being measured were operating for at least two generations.

Partial rather than raw correlations were calculated because the use of ratios instead of population counts introduced mathematical dependencies that could have been confused with real effects. For example, a fluctuation in women and boys would cause the male loss ratio (BOYS/-MEN) to increase automatically as the adult sex ratio (MEN/WOMEN) went down. To remove these dependencies partial correlations controlling for the common term in each of the two ratios were used.

The sources of the population data are shown in
Table 6.1. Divale's (1972) earlier article on warfare
and infanticide provided a valuable bibliography of

Table 6.1
Sources of Population Data

Data	Culture	No. of Units	Source
1	Yanomamo: central villages	11	Chagnon 1973: 137
2	Yanomamo: peripheral villages	12	Chagnon 1973: 138
3	Andaman Islands	10	Radcliffe-Brown 1948: 16
4	Yanomamo: Sierra Parima	3	Smole 1976: 72
5	Yanomamo	1	Lizot 1971: 42
7	Onges	4	Sarkar 1960: 561
8	Kutchin	3	Osgood 1936: 13ff
12	Siriono	2	Holmberg 1960: 51
13	Yir Yoront: 1933 (a)	2	Sharp 1940: 486
14	Yir Yoront: 1935 (a)	2	Sharp 1940: 486
17	Eskimo	11	Weyer 1962: 134-135
18	Eskimo: Tree River	1	Jenness 1922: 42
19	San	2	Lebzelter 1934: 19
20	Aborigines: North Terr. Walbiri, Pintubi, and Yangman	3	Meggitt 1968: 182-184
21	Totones	12	Schoolcraft 1857: 702
22	Eskimo: Central	9	Boas 1888: 18

(a) These samples include 4 linguistic groups of aborigines: the
Yir Yoront, Yir Mel, Taior, and Ngentjin. Because of the peculiar-
ities of the census which ignored encampments as a unit, the Yir
Yoront and Yir Mel population is aggregated as one case and the
Taior and Ngentjin population as another. I have aggregated "mis-
sion" and "bush" populations because Sharp reports a selective female movement between the two that could skew the sex ratios. The
two census years were taken as separate cases of a system in different states. The aboriginal age categorization of pre- and post-
puberty was used instead of the census age estimates to divide the
age groups.

sources on band and village societies practicing warfare.
In spite of this aid it was not easy to find usable population statistics. Thus the intracultural method could
not be applied to a wide sample of cultures. Some of the
data gathered by different field workers were taken from
the same culture and could be grouped to make the statistical tests more significant. Table 6.2 shows how the
data were grouped for the correlational analysis.

Table 6.2.
Data with Aggregations

Data Group	File Code	Culture	Groups Aggregated	No. of Units
1	yacc	Yanomamo: central villages	1	11
2	yacp	Yanomamo: peripheral villages	2	12
3	anr	Andaman Islands	3	10
7	onge	Onges	7	4
8	kutch	Kutchin	8	3
9	eskw	Eskimo	17,18	12
12	sirio	Siriono	12	2
19	bush	San	19	2
20	abom	Aborigines: North Terr.	20	3
21	totones	Totones	21	12
22	centesk	Eskimo: central	22	9
23	yanal	Yanomamo: aggregated	1,2,3,5	27
24	yyap	Yir Yoront	13,14	4

RESULTS

Table 6.3 shows partial correlations between male loss ratio and adult sex ratio. Only four of the cultures had significant correlations at the 0.07 level.[2] They were Yanomamo (S = .012) and its sub sample the Yanomamo-peripheral villages (S = .065), Eskimo (S = .051), and the Central Eskimo (S = .019). S is the probability of the data set sampling a population in which the correlation is zero. The lack of significance in the other data groups is due to their small size and/or their failure to show a distinct linear relationship leading to a correlation other than zero. It was important to have these less significant data groups in the data pool to check the significance and to have the data available to combine at a later date with other data.

The surprising thing about the four significant correlations in Table 6.3 is that three of them are negative: Yanomamo-peripheral, Eskimo, and the Yanomamo-aggregated (Group 23). This means that the male loss ratio goes down as the adult sex ratio goes up. Figure 6.1 shows a scattergram illustrating this relationship in the Yanomamo-aggregated data group.

One would expect a positive, not a negative, correlation if the lack of sexually available women stimulated raiding. The negative correlations in Table 6.3 suggest that there is a rapid reduction of the adult sex ratio by warfare. Most likely this is the result of battle

Table 6.3
Partial Correlations Male Loss Ratio vs. Adult Sex Ratio Controlling
for Men

Group No.	Culture	Partial Correlation Coefficient	Significance Level for P=0
1	Yanomamo: central	-0.242	0.251
2	Yanomamo: peripheral	-0.487	0.065*
3	Andaman Islands	-0.115	0.385
7	Onges	+0.941	0.500
8	Kutchin	-1.000	0.500
9	Eskimo	-0.549	0.051*
12	Siriono	--	--
19	San	--	--
20	Aborigines: North Terr.	-1.000	0.500
21	Totones	+0.019	0.478
22	Eskimo: Central	+0.734	0.019*
23	Yanomamo: aggregated	-0.443	0.012*
24	Yir Yoront	-0.581	0.500

*Significant at the 0.07 level of probability.

--Too few units.

casualties, which can be heavy according to ethnogra-
phies. Chagnon reports that 24 percent of male deaths
in a sample from the Yanomamo were due to warfare (1968:
140). The effect of battle casualties can be seen in
Table 6.4 which shows the change in sex ratios from
childhood to adulthood.[3]
     If male battle losses reduce the sex ratios, then
one cannot use adult sex ratio as a measure of the lack
of women before raiding. Women capture as a motivation
for warfare implies a time lag: first, there is a shortage of women, then there is raiding to capture women.
The indicator of the lack of women must belong to an
earlier time than the indicator of warfare in order to
test the existence of a material connection. Since a
census samples the population at a single time, it cannot measure both prior and current conditions.
     The measurement problem can be overcome if we as-
sume that the cultural system does not change radically.
Then child sex ratios indicate the lack of women in a
unit, because male children are not lost more rapidly
than females by raiding. The children grow up, so that
their sex ratio indicates the availability of women in
the unit before a period of raiding may begin. If the
units go through cycles of raiding motivated by the lack
of women there should be a positive correlation between
the male loss ratio and the child sex ratio, and a negative correlation between male loss ratio and adult sex

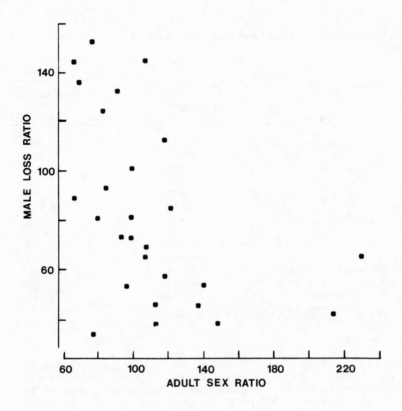

Figure 6.1. Yanomamo (data group 23) male loss ratio vs. adult sex ratio

ratio. The amount of raiding will go down as adult sex ratios are reduced by male casualties but will be stimulated again by a lack of women maturing from childhood.

Table 6.5 shows the partial correlations between child sex ratios and male loss ratios. Two groups have significant positive correlations at the $p < 0.05$ level, the Yanomamo-peripheral villages (S = 0.026) and the central Eskimo (S = 0.018). Three other groups have correlations close to zero: the Andaman Islanders, the Eskimo, and the Totones.

The Yanomamo exhibit correlations that can be interpreted as the material stimulation of warfare by a shortage of women. The effect is due to what is happening in the peripheral villages of the sample and not to what is happening in the central villages, which do not have a significant correlation when taken alone. The Central

Table 6.4
Change in Sex Ratios: Adult Sex Ratio Minus Child Sex Ratio

Group	Culture	Sex Child	Adult	Change
1	Yanomamo: central	157	115	-42
2	Yanomamo: peripheral	121	111	-10
3	Andaman Islands	132	112	-20
7	Onges	142	169	+27
8	Kutchin	157	112	-45
9	Eskimo	156	88	-68
12	Siriono	85	86	+1
19	San	85	46	-39
20	Aborigines: North Terr.	116	90	-26
21	Totones	122	83	-39
22	Eskimo: central	105	94	-11
23	Yanomamo: aggregated	130	108	-22
24	Yir Yoront	130	96	-34

Table 6.5
Partial Correlations of Male Loss Ratio vs. Child Sex Ratio Controlling for Boys

Group	Culture	Partial Corrl. Coeff.	Sig. Level, S for P=0	Lower Limit for P accept.	Upper Limit for P accept.
1	Yanomamo: central	+0.215	0.276	-0.383	+0.686
2	Yanomamo: peripheral	+0.599	0.026*	+0.109	+0.855
3	Andaman Islands	+0.086	0.413	-0.526	+0.640
7	Onges	+0.973	0.501	--	--
8	Kutchin	--	--	--	--
9	Eskimo	-0.150	0.340	-0.625	+0.406
12	Siriono	--	--	--	--
19	San	--	--	--	--
20	Aborigines: North Terr.	+1.000	0.500	--	--
21	Totones	-0.054	0.438	-0.562	+0.484
22	Eskimo: central	+0.738	0.018*	+0.208	+0.933
23	Yanomamo: aggregated	+0.296	0.071	-0.038	+0.570
24	Yir Yoront	+0.426	0.500	--	--

*Significant at the 0.05 level of probability.
--Too few units.

Eskimo (Group 22) have a positive correlation but this
must be interpreted differently because its correlation
in Table 6.3 was also positive. These Eskimos and the
significance of the correlations will be discussed later.
The Andaman Islanders, the Eskimo (Group 9), and the Totones have small correlations indicating that women capture could not materially stimulate warfare.

This analysis indicates that shortages of women
stimulate raiding in the Yanomamo-peripheral villages but
not significantly in the Yanomamo-central villages, or
rather, that there is a greater tendency for women shortages to stimulate raiding in the peripheral villages.
This result is surprising because the intensity of warfare and the lack of women is greater in the central villages. About the central-peripheral difference Chagnon
writes:

> Compared to the periphery, warfare is considerably
> more intense at the center and an elaborate alliance
> system has developed that enables the members of the
> independent villages to establish peaceful, but ten-
> uous, social ties whose functions are to reduce the
> possibility of warfare between the allied groups.
> (1973: 130)

> First the intensity of female infanticide is ap-
> parently much higher at the center where greater em-
> phasis on masculinity and warfare exists. For the
> age category 0-14 years, there is a 21 percent ex-
> cess of males at the periphery compared to 57 per-
> cent at the center. The overall shortage of fe-
> males in the two areas is also revealing: for all
> age categories combined there is a 15 percent ex-
> cess of males at the periphery compared to 30 per-
> cent at the center. (1973: 134)

The change from child to adult sex ratios in Table 6.4,
which measures the intensity of male mortality, show the
central villages with a change of -0.421 and the peripheral villages with a change of only -0.102. Thus, there
is demographic evidence of more warfare in the central
villages. The villages at the periphery are smaller and
more isolated. Their average size is 53.2 people as compared to 76.4 people at the center. The central villages
have a more elaborate complex of alliances based on formal reciprocal trading and feasting (Chagnon 1968: 114),
and a more elaborate system of fighting which includes
chest-pounding duels, side-slapping duels, club fights,
spear fights, raiding, and treacherous feasts (Chagnon
1973: 135). About sex and violence in the central and
peripheral villages, Chagnon reports:

> At the center, trysts inevitably lead to fighting
> and often to killing and village fissioning. At the

periphery, the affairs are tolerated if not institutionalized. A corollary of this is the surprisingly
high incidence of polyandry in some villages at the
periphery, all of which may be summarized by concluding that there is a more equitable distribution of
the sexual services of women at the periphery and,
therefore a great reduction in one of the major
causes of Yanomamo disputes. (Chagnon 1973: 135)

The peripheral villages are involved in a different
demographic and cultural system. Analysis of the data
indicates that the more elaborate system of higher violence is associated with decreasing, not increasing,
material effects of women shortages on warfare. The relationship between women shortages and warfare is probably ideological in the central villages. We cannot
demonstrate a material relationship in the demographic
data. In the central villages, more formal political
ideologies such as vengeance and fierceness could be re-
placing direct personal motivation for warfare, such as
capturing a wife when one does not have one.
The only other data group that has a significant
positive correlation between male loss ratio and child
sex ratio is the Central Eskimo group. This data comes
from a census made by Boas (1888) in 1883 of the bands
living on the southeast side of Baffin Island. The group
was fairly homogeneous culturally and had an average band
size of 32 persons. There is no mention in the ethnography of extensive raiding to capture women, although the
groups did have feuding (Boas 1888: 174) which is sufficient for Divale to categorize them as a culture in which
warfare is present (Divale 1972, Cases 53 to 61). Divale
and Harris (1976: 533, Case 24) classify them as a cultural group commonly practicing infanticide and with war
present at the time of the census or stopped with five
years.
The positive correlation between adult sex ratio and
male loss ratio in Table 6.3 sets this group apart from
the other cultures with positive correlations between
child sex ratio and male loss ratio in Table 6.5. That
both ratios are positive suggests a different relationship between the presence of women and male mortality.
This culture apparently is one in which having women is
associated with male longevity. The presence of women,
either adults or children, seems to have a positive connection with male survival. Or we can say conversely
that the absence of women is associated with a higher
male death rate. However, this does not occur through
the raiding complex we have outlined since the effects
of male battle losses are not seen in the correlation between adult sex ratio and male loss ratio.
One can speculate about the reason for the positive
influence of women in this culture. The Eskimo nuclear

family is a group that depends on the labor of women as much as that of men. The safety of Eskimo men depends on the skill of women in fashioning protective clothing (Briggs 1974: 288). Briggs notes that Eskimo men need the affection of women (1974: 283). Female support and concern may help men face the hazards of hunting. An alternate explanation is that there were radical enough ecological differences between the bands to promote both female infanticide and male accidents in environmentally endangered groups (Balikci 1970: 153). One environmental theory proposes that females threaten an endangered group because they attract outside hunters who cannot be supported by the game resources (Riches 1976).

The Andaman Islanders, the Eskimo (Group 9), and the Totones all show partial correlations between male loss ratio and child sex ratio that are close to zero. Although these cultures have high child sex ratios possibly indicating preferential female infanticide and high relative male mortality, they do not clearly show women capture as a material stimulus to warfare. In these three cases the data allow a range of null hypotheses of a positive correlation to be accepted at a 0.05 level. If one assumes that a material effect will manifest itself with a partial correlation no lower than +0.5, which is lower than that in the Yanomamo peripheral villages (P = +0.599), then the Eskimo and the Totone data show the significant absence of women capture as a material stimulation of warfare.

CONCLUSIONS

So far we have determined that only the Yanomamo show the demographic effects which result in women capture as a motivation for warfare. The following conclusions about the whole male supremacist complex can be drawn from the summary of relevant data in Table 6.6. Out of the eleven cultures the Siriono and the San do not seem to have the demographic effects of female infanticide (Column A). In the remaining nine cultures the Onges do not show a male mortality high enough to have resulted from warfare (Column B). (However their census figures may not be correct [Sen 1962: 70-72].) The Andaman Islanders, the Eskimo (Group 9), and the Totones have a low correlation between male loss ratio and child sex ratio indicating that women capture could not be materially connected to warfare. This element of the male supremacist complex is lacking in these three cultures. Among the Yanomamo-central villages, the Kutchin, the Aborigines of the North Territory, and the Yir Yoront, nothing definite appears concerning a material effect of women shortages on warfare. The effect, if it exists, is too small to be revealed or denied by the data and method being used. Finally the Central Eskimo show the demographic effects of a system probably quite dif-

Table 6.6
Various Indicators of the Male Supremacy Complex

Group	Culture	A	B	C	D(a)
1	Yanomamo: central	157	-42	ns	ns
2	Yanomamo: peripheral	121	-10	-0.487	+0.599
3	Andaman Islands	132	-20	ns	small
7	Onges	142	+27	ns	ns
8	Kutchin	157	-45	ns	ns
9	Eskimo	156	-68	-0.549	small
12	Siriono	85	+1	ns	ns
19	San	85	-39	ns	ns
20	Aborigines: North Terr.	116	-26	ns	ns
21	Totones	122	-39	ns	small
22	Eskimo: central	105	-11	+0.734	+0.738
23	Yanomamo: aggregated	130	-22	-0.443	+0.296
24	Yir Yoront	130	-34	ns	ns

(a) A=Child sex ratio in total population. Increases with prefer-
ential female infanticide.
B=Adult sex ratio minus child sex ratio in total population.
Decreases with increasing relative adult male mortality.
C=Partial correlation coefficient of male loss ratio with adult
sex ratio.
D=Partial correlation coefficient of male loss ratio with child
sex ratio.

ferent from the male supremacist complex. Apparently in
the face of preferential female infanticide and a high
relative male mortality the presence of more women of all
ages is correlated with male survival. However, the correlation may be explained as the result of a third variable, ecological stress.

Thus, one aspect of the male supremacist complex,
women capture as a motivation for warfare, is not demonstrated materially in the cultures tested except for the
Yanomamo, and even there it is demonstrable only in one
of the groups, the peripheral villages. If the secondary
sex ratio is close to 129, as Chagnon, Flinn, and Melancon suggest (1979: 309), then the infanticide component
of the male supremacist complex may be lacking there.

One must conclude that the association between high
child sex ratios and warfare, which has been found generally in band and village societies by Divale and Harris
(1976), is due to a variety of systems that work differently. In view of the criticism of group selection as a
viable process in human evolution, it is unlikely that
the association will be explained as the parallel evolution of the same population control mechanism. Although
it is true that both warfare and female infanticide lower
the rate of population growth, they may be totally sepa-

114

rate adaptive strategies rather than part of a single
adaptive complex.

From the point of view of cultural evolution, female
infanticide might be explained as an effort of parents
to compensate for the high mortality of males. This behavior would have to be cultural, since an adequate genetic or quasi-genetic mechanism has yet to be demonstrated. Since the high mortality of males would not
theoretically alter investment strategies according to
the more sophisticated genetic model of adaptation (Leigh
1970), the idea that high secondary sex ratios are due
to high male mortality during the period of parental investment (Chagnon, Flinn, and Melancon 1979: 297) needs
more sophisticated mathematical proof. An alternate explanation of male-favoring strategies from a sociobiological point of view might focus on a possible high reproductive potential of males vis-a-vis females in these
particular societies. This seems highly unlikely at
first glance because, when polygyny exists, high male
mortality does not alter the relative reproductive
potential of males at birth. The key may lie in the
effect that males may have on the reproductive power of
females (Chagnon, Flinn, and Melancon 1979: 299). Some
explanation of high secondary sex ratios may be possible
if males multiply the reproductive power of females in
these cultures by providing something like food, shelter,
or protection for them. Then the association between
high child sex ratios and warfare might simply be a consequence of greater mate competition. It would be well
for researchers to focus on this question, for it appears
as a possible explanation for data among the Yanomamo and
the Eskimo. The adaptive systems that could be involved
are not simple nor intuitively obvious and one can only
conclude that an explanation of the association between
warfare and high child sex ratios requires a new level
of data analysis and theory.

ACKNOWLEDGMENTS

I wish to thank Raymond Hames for his reading of the
manuscript and his helpful comments, and Peter Bertocci
for his suggestions and encouragement. This work has
been supported by a Faculty Research Grant from Oakland
University.

NOTES

1. Note that the actual mathematical sex ratios
(number of males divided by the number of females) were
employed in this chapter for mathematical analysis because such ratios are more appropriate for the mathematical techniques used here. Following the analysis,
the ratios were converted back to the more common value

of males per 100 females for ease of understanding by
the reader.
2. Tests of significance were performed by the SPSS
partial correlation program and were based on a one-
tailed Student's "t" distribution with

$$t = r[\frac{N - 3}{1 - r^2}]^{1/2}$$

S is the probability of the data set sampling a
population in which the correlation is zero. The use of
"S=" figures rather than "P<" is an acceptable way of
dealing with the results of a hypothesis test. S is the
probability of getting this correlation if the null hypothesis were true. A 0.07 level for rejecting the null
hypothesis was taken because two correlations were hover-
ing around the .05 level and needed to be considered
theoretically. In view of the extensive theorizing that
sometimes takes place in cultural anthropology from data
that have been obtained from a small non-random sampling
of cases we feel that opening our discussion to correlations that are significant between the 0.05 and 0.07
levels is not out of line.
3. The peculiar high adult sex ratio among the
Onges is an unresolved problem. Sen feels that the overall Onge sex ratio is much more balanced than indicated
in the census (1962: 70-72).

7
Mobility as a Negative Factor in Human Adaptability: The Case of South American Tropical Forest Populations

Emilio F. Moran

    Editors' Summary: *Emilio Moran argues that we cannot assume that observed behaviors are necessarily adaptive. His concerns are with agricultural productivity in the Amazonian rain forest. He argues, very persuasively, that shifting cultivation as practiced by Amazonian lowland natives is not an adaptive response to absolutely poor soils, as is commonly believed from environmentally deterministic approaches. Rather, noncircular forms of shifting cultivation result from the interaction of mobility (required to maintain the productivity of hunting), of adaptation to species-specific rather than site-specific resources, and of the need to select agricultural practices that were relatively reliable. Manioc fulfills these conditions exceedingly well but its low-protein content favors reliance on animal protein provided by hunting. Moran makes the important assertion that some tropical forest soils can support a sedentary population of cultivators, and challenges the generalization that all humid tropical soils are poor. The identification of the scarce high fertility soils presents a problem for local populations that is resolved by favoring adaptation to the more frequent nutrient-poor soils in combination with precise adaptations to the behavior of specific faunal resources. The reader should note that the emphasis on mobility is not an effort to replace one form of determinism (soil nutrient depletion) with another (animal protein depletion). Rather, Moran proposes an interactive model for explaining human adaptive strategies in the Lowlands of Amazonia. The relative influence of single factors will depend on site-specific conditions, both environmental and historical.*

    One of the most often cited adaptive responses of human populations to a variety of constraints is mobility. Among hunter/gatherer societies, mobility helps in locating dispersed resources and is also implicated in reducing fertility and, thus, pressure on available resources (Lee and DeVore 1976; Frish and McArthur 1974; Howell 1976). Mobility makes it possible for East African pastoral populations inhabiting arid and semi-arid lands to exploit the environment by following a migratory cycle adjusted to the availability of water and pasture (Gulliver 1955; Spencer 1973). Mobility has also been

118

cited as an important adaptive response of South
American tropical forest populations through patterns of
shifting cultivation.
   Amazonian tropical forest peoples move in response
to a variety of environmental constraints presented by
their environment: declining soil fertility after the
first year of cropping (Meggers 1954; Meggers and Evans
1957), weed infestation (Carneiro 1970a), population
growth in villages (Chagnon 1977) and declining yields
from hunting effort (Gross 1975). While one or more of
the above factors may reduce the efficiency of the system
of domestic production of native Amazonians, thereby mo-
tivating populations to move to new sites, it is a serious oversight to see mobility purely as a positive response that enhances the adaptability of human populations to the Amazonian environment.
   The purely positive role assigned to spatial mobility reflects a tendency to view all human behavior as
adaptive. This is particularly true for the behavior of
non-modern peoples. The assumption has been that if a
population has occupied an environment without destroying
it, or itself, then it must have achieved adaptation to
its habitat. This may, in fact, hold, but given the relatively few studies of human ecological adaptation in
tropical rain forest ecosystems such an assumption is
premature. It is the contention of this paper that the
assumption is not always valid and that it should be put
to the test in the field.
   The assumption of the adaptiveness of mobility has
tended to support deterministic models and explanations.
Despite the apparent discrediting of environmental determinism in this century, explanations of human/habitat interactions, in the rain forest still suggest that the environment is responsible for particular forms of human
behavior or social organization. So pervasive is the environmental determination implied, that there have been
difficulties in integrating recent research, research un-
covering the great variety of ecological conditions in
the Amazon Basin into the existing conceptual framework.
The reasons for these difficulties must be found in the
assumptions that posit behaviors such as mobility as un-
qualifiedly adaptive--as a positive response to environmental limiting factors such as poor soils, pest and weed
infestation, or decline in yields. In this paper I begin
by defining criteria with which to determine the adaptability of a population to its habitat. An examination
of the deterministic model suggests the conditions under
which the assumptions are unwarranted. The paper concludes with hypotheses that offer more dynamic approaches
to explanation in tropical forest human ecology, which
emphasize interactions between variables and the considerable role played by choices made by individuals in a
social aggregate.

It is important at the outset to define the criteria for assessing the adaptability of a population to its habitat. Adaptability refers to non-genetic adjustments made by a population to the multiple constraints they encounter (Moran 1982). It includes physiological adjustments, such as differential heart rates, and social/cultural adjustments, such as dietary and organizational features. In turn, these adjustments modify the habitat itself, thereby creating conditions requiring constant readjustment (Bennett 1976).

There is no currently available, single index by which adaptability is measured, but various measures may be used as approximations. Energetic efficiency is an important indicator of how well a population allocates its labor inputs into the production process. Since the populations in question in this paper grow crops for most of their calories, one approximation of efficiency is yield per unit of land. Yield per unit of land is associated with the intensity of labor inputs and/or overall knowledge of cropping systems, as well as shifts from one crop to another. Crop shifts, for example, can radically change the efficiencies without altering any other features of the system (Miracle 1973). Yield per unit of labor is also useful in that it implies experience or familiarity with the environment, as well as being an index that most individuals use to assess their labor allocation (Gross et al. 1979). No less useful as an indicator is the complexity and accuracy of ethnoecological knowledge in predicting the agricultural potential of an area to be cultivated (Moran 1981; Conklin 1957). Nutrition and health indicators may also be used to determine the well-being of a population.

The term "mobility" in this paper refers to non-cyclical changes in the location of settlement by either households or communities. It does not include the mere shifting of cultivated areas near a settlement. As Carneiro (1957) pointed out, it is possible to have relatively sedentary settlement in the Amazon and sizable communities. He emphasized the role of manioc in making such large sedentary settlements possible, whereas Roosevelt (1980) emphasized the role of riverine settlement and their switch from manioc to maize cultivation. While I agree that these factors may play a part in the process, the multiple interactive factors that appear to have been responsible for the frequency of small and highly mobile settlements have been overlooked due to the dominance of a deterministic model emphasizing environmental deficiencies.

DEVELOPMENT OF THE DETERMINISTIC MODEL

The tendency to view the Amazon Basin as a relatively homogeneous habitat has had a profound impact on theories of the social evolution of tropical rain forest societies. Anthropologists have relied heavily on the classification used in the Handbook of South American Indians (Steward 1939-1946) in describing the cultural and social adaptations of native peoples to the Amazonian habitat, most of the people of the Amazon falling into Steward's "Tropical Forest Culture" type. This typology treated the Amazon as a broad habitat type, across which the population could move with familiarity and with a set of cultural ecological adaptations.

The Amazon peoples were said to be characterized by: (1) small settlement size, (2) low population densities, (3) frequent movement of settlements, (4) local political autonomy, and (5) warfare/witchcraft complexes. Low population densities were maintained by practices that included warfare, female infanticide, and village fissioning. The ease and frequency of village fissioning among Amazonian aboriginal peoples is striking. As population increased in villages, stresses and strains increased and the lack of internal political controls and weak chieftainship failed to discourage a village faction from splitting off (Carneiro 1974: 78). Explanations for the high frequency of village fissioning have suggested that tribal politics (Chagnon 1977), exhaustion of suitable land within proximity of the village (Carneiro 1957: 198), declines in protein supply (Lathrap 1968; Gross 1975), and availability of unoccupied land (Carneiro 1970b) may also be implicated.

The dominant interpretation of the ecology of tropical forest populations is that presented by Meggers (1954, 1971). According to this view the Amazon Basin can be divided into two ecological zones: the terra firme (upland) and the varzea (floodplain). Populations inhabiting the varzea zone were able to develop more stable settlement and larger population aggregations due to the richer resources in the riverine environment and due to the seasonal enrichment of the floodplain by sediments carried downriver from the Andes. The uplands, which make up 98 percent of the Amazon rain forest, are said to be regions of absolute low agricultural potential and thus of low potential for the development of cultures (Meggers 1954; 1971: 14). The acidic, nutrient poor soils cannot sustain prolonged cultivation (Meggers 1971: 14). Shifting cultivation is therefore required by the poverty of the environment and populations are forced to move settlements, and to develop cultural practices to maintain low population numbers (Meggers 1971: 23).

Despite a persuasive response by Ferdon (1959) which emphasized the impact of cultural knowledge and technology on agricultural potential, the dominant view as described by Meggers (1971) has persisted. Meggers' model posits a relationship between agricultural potential and development of civilizations (see Figure 7.1). The Amazonian environment is rated as low in agricultural poten-

Figure 7.1. A deterministic model of the Amazon Basin

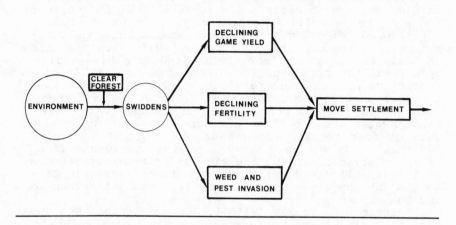

tial and the region's people adjusted to this limited
potential by the adaptive response of shifting
cultivation. Attempts to introduce more advanced
techniques, according to this deterministic view, were
doomed to failure. Shifting cultivation is seen as a
response to poor soils and a climate that leaches out
whatever organic matter accumulates on the ground.

The state of knowledge of Amazon ecology was limited
at the time the deterministic model was first presented.
What we had were a few surveys carried out along river-
banks (cf. Sombroek 1966; Gourou 1953), naturalists' ac-
counts (Bates 1892; Wallace 1895; inter al.), and some
limnological research which noted that few nutrients were
found in rivers fed by terra firme (Sioli 1951). Meggers
and Evans (1957) were among the pioneers in Amazonian research and deserve credit for leading the way in this
area. The current state of Amazonian studies has come a
long way from the 1950's (cf. Moran 1981, Scazzocchio
1980; UNESCO 1978; Wagley 1974) but even now the number
of studies addressing the major questions in human ecological adjustment are limited in number. The merit of
several recent studies lies in beginning a trend towards
micro-ecological research which had been sorely absent.
In the section that follows I will review the recent research which forms the basis for rethinking the appro-
priateness of seeing mobility and shifting cultivation
as necessary and positive adjustments to the absolute
poverty of the Amazonian environment for anything other
than small and dispersed human aggregates.

RESEARCH ON SOILS OF THE HUMID TROPICS

Tropical soils are commonly said to be leached,
acidic, lacking in horizon development, poor in nutrients
and able to be cultivated for only a couple of years
after forest clearing (cf. Gourou 1953). This generali-
zation, and the one that rain forest soils are lateritic
(McNeil 1964), result from the limited data base available until the decade of the 1970's. Gourou (1953) presented the dominant deterministic view when he described
tropical shifting agriculture as "remarkably in harmony
with the health and pedological conditions. . . . Any
other system would be liable to give poor yields to the
acre or poor returns for the labor involved" (Gourou
1953: 32). Only 4 to 8 percent of the cultivable land
is in cultivation at any one time under traditional forms
of forest fallow and this low proportion of land in production at any given time assured that densities were low
and that human settlements remained small.
Research by Conklin (1957), Popenoe (1960), Nye and
Greenland (1960) and Watters (1971) among others showed
that the practice of shifting cultivation was highly variable in response to a variety of factors. Clarke (1966)
demonstrated for New Guinea that variations in shifting
agricultural management appear to be more associated with
population pressure on land than with environmentally deficient areas. The independent research of these and
many other investigators was synthesized in a review of
pedological research (Sanchez 1972). In that review
shifting cultivation emerged as a dominant agricultural
system for people lacking access to capital inputs. Its
presence was independent of the fertility status of the
soils.
That same year a publication from the National
Academy of Sciences reviewed the state of knowledge of
soils of the humid tropics (NAS, 1972). While the summary reaffirms that soils are generally poor, the individual papers raise many questions as to the adequacy of
current knowledge on soils of the region. Moorman (1972)
emphasized the unusual degree of microvariability in
humid tropical soils. The variability within relatively
small distances is based on a number of factors: pedoge-
netic (common also in temperate zones), biogenetic (such
as the presence of given native species of trees), ter-
mite mounds, and human activities such as <u>citemene</u>
(wherein vegetation is piled and burned, thereby concen-
trating nutrients). Moorman (1972: 48) also raised questions of the adequacy of standard sampling techniques.
He argued that new techniques may need to be developed
to accurately measure the microvariability typical of
humid tropical soils and to adequately address the region's soil management variables.
Agronomic research in the past decade has shown that
soils under tropical rain forests and cultivated by

shifting cultivation tend to be varied and much like the
soils of the non-glaciated temperate zone (Sanchez and
Buol 1975). Any agricultural system consists not merely
of a static soil potential but is a dynamic system that
integrates biotic and abiotic factors with human management considerations such as crop combinations, soil
cover, weeding, treatments to replenish lost nutrients,
and demands from the social/cultural systems for food,
fiber and alternative labor allocation.

Three major soil types predominate in the humid
tropics: oxisols (also called latosols), ultisols
(podzols) and alfisols (terra roxa estruturada). The
most extensive are the oxisols, characterized by an "oxic
horizon" that consists of hydrated oxides of iron and/or
aluminum. Laterite, or, more accurately, plinthite, develops when the conditions that create an oxic horizon
are accompanied by a fluctuating water table--a phenomenon that affects only about 2 percent of the Amazon Basin (Wambecke 1978). Whereas oxisols are indeed acidic,
poor in organic matter, low in exchangeable bases and
poor in horizon development, they have excellent structural characteristics. Alfisols and ultisols are less
weathered, commonly result from basic rock parent material, and have medium to high fertility. In addition,
there are significant pockets of other soils as well,
including young entisols and inceptisols created by
alluvial deposition. However, generalizing about the the
soil types presents does not provide a sense of the site-
specific variability of soils in the Amazon.

The only maps of soils for the Amazon until recently
were region-wide maps in the scale of 1:100,000 to
1:500,000. At this scale not only does the patchy
character of soils fail to emerge but even the extent of
each soil type may be misjudged. A technologically sophisticated aerial photographic survey of the Amazon
(RADAM 1974), for instance, at a scale of 1:100,000 observed that the dominant soil type in an area of Maraba
was the ultisols. A localized study by Ranzani (1978),
on the other hand, developed a map at a scale of 1:10,000
that demonstrated that oxisols constituted 65 percent of
the soils, entisols 22 percent, and ultisols only 13 percent of the area in question. Almost kilometer to kilometer changes in soil type were noted by Ranzani (1978).
Studies by Moran (1975), Smith (1976), Fearnside (1978),
and Furley (1980) in other areas of the Amazon confirmed
this great variability.

Whereas even poor soils can be made productive for
a short period by slash and burn cultivation--because of
the addition of nutrient-rich ash--there is a clear association between the rate of yield decline with cultivation and the initial pH of the soil. Soils with a pH of
6.0 took as much as fifteen years for yields to drop 50
percent below those of the first cropping season (Sanchez
1976: 375), but soils with lower pH, ranging from 3.5 to

5.0, often dropped below the 50 percent rate by the second year of cultivation. However, in both types of studies the crop combinations, frequency of weeding, and length of fallow significantly altered the results. Nutrient demanding cereals such as rice and corn led to more rapid declines in yields and soil fertility than the cultivation of crops such as manioc and cowpeas (Sanchez 1976: 376).

The argument that soil fertility depletion is the chief cause of field abandonment remains undemonstrated. Very little correlation has been shown between declines in yield and measurable soil changes before and after cropping (Sanchez 1976: 377). Although in the poorer soils it is clear that soil depletion and low yields may be primarily responsible for field abandonment, Falesi et al. (1980) have demonstrated that soils are not significantly impoverished by most agricultural practices in the Amazon--using virgin forests as a baseline to assess soil degradation.

Probably more significant factors in forcing farmers to shift fields are weed infestation, pests and diseases. Following the burning of fields the land is relatively free of weeds and if the burn was well carried out (which is not always the case) weeds do not constitute a severe problem during the first cropping season. However, by the second crop weeds become a problem and require high labor inputs. Nye and Greenland (1960) and Jurion and Henry (1969) assert that weeding labor costs are the primary reason why cultivators shift fields in Africa. They suggested that cultivators may decide on shifting when the labor costs of clearing new forest are lower than those of weeding cultivated fields. However, native American grasses are not as aggressive colonizers as African grasses. Pests and diseases also increase over time as fields are kept in continuous cultivation. The multiple cropping of traditional farming systems reduced the incidence of damage from these and it is unlikely that under those conditions pests were primarily responsible for shifting of fields (Sanchez 1976: 379).

Soil erosion can also bring about soil deterioration, reduce yields and lead to shifting of fields. But most native Amazonians practice a multi-stored approach to agriculture and minimum tillage practices reduce the danger of soil damage. The damage has become more common as natives and peasants are forced into increasingly steep areas and are encouraged to produce monocrops for the market rather than maintain diversified multi-storied cropping systems that reduce soil exposure to the elements (Scazzocchio 1980).

Social and cultural factors are also relevant in the maintenance of a productive farming system. Decisions on how much time to allocate to farming operations are affected by other, often conflicting, demands on the time available to the persons responsible for the farming tasks. Decisions to abandon fields are affected by enemy raids (Lizot 1977), witchcraft accusations (Vickers 1976), death of chiefs, and symbolic associations built into the folk culture of the population (Chirif 1978). The careful collection of data on the work effort in a variety of subsistence activities and the collection of ecological data by Gross et al. (1979) is a fine example of the type of research likely to integrate through time the relative influence of ideological, ecological, and economic variables.

In short, shifting cultivation can be a highly so-phisticated system of agriculture, or it can be a de-structive and low-yielding system. Conklin (1957) con-trasts these two systems by the terms "integral" and "pioneering" shifting agriculture. Whereas the low pop-ulation densities of Amazonian populations reduced the danger of ecological devastation, only in a few cases are high yields sustained (e.g. the Kuikuru). Are the reasons for the infrequency of sustained-yield agro-ecosystems in Amazonia determined by an absolute "low agricultural potential" (Meggers 1954, 1971) or is it in product of complex interactions between Amazonian popula-tions and the diverse habitat?

SOIL SELECTION AND FOLK CRITERIA

In order to obtain good yields from agricultural ef-forts, a cultivator must accurately identify soils with above average initial fertility. To make such choices requires either precise ethnoecological criteria capable of distinguishing between soil types and predicting crop responses or a soil map at a scale of 1:10,000. The classic case of such cultural categorization is the shifting agricultural system of the Philippine Hanunoo (Conklin 1957). The Hanunoo, who inhabit an isolated montane valley, distinguish between ten basic and thirty derivative soils. Effects on soil quality of erosion, exposure, and over-cultivation are well understood and frequently discussed. Because they practice their swid-den agriculture within a restricted territory, their knowledge of the area's soils is precise and highly complex--incorporating not only vegetational criteria, but also previous use, terrain characteristics, soil firmness, soil color, and religious criteria.

There are few other published cases of how native cultivators choose soils for farming, but the criteria used in the Amazon contrasts by its simplicity with that of the territorially-restricted Hanunoo. Selection of land for gardens in Amazonia is rarely based on the ap-plication of precise criteria but includes a number of non-agronomic considerations that enhance the potential for choosing inappropriate areas. The Siona-Secoya of lowland Ecuador use color and texture in distinguishing

soils but they temper such knowledge with a preference
for sites near the rivers, to ease the burden of carrying manioc tubers back to the village (Vickers 1976).
It is areas near a river bank which experience periodic
wetting and drying--a circumstance conducive to the formation of plinthite or laterite. Because the populations
often prefer to settle on or near old habitation sites,
it is likely that these people regularly choose to live
in areas which have soils poor for agriculture.

The criteria for selecting soils and village sites
are even less specific among the Tapirape of central
Brazil (Wagley 1977: 51). Village land had to be free
from flooding during the rainy season, within close proximity to a stream, not too far from savanna areas for
ease in hunting, and with "high forest suitable for gardens." The main criterion of suitability was that the
forest should have lain fallow for at least twenty years.
Villages were relocated every five to seven years, probably not an unusual rate for most non-floodplain native
Amazonians.

The acculturated Bare and Curripaco population of
the upper Rio Negro in the Venezuelan Amazon distinguish
between only three soil types. One is the white sand
podzolics covered by caatinga scrub forest ("bana") which
are not cultivated. The other two soils, which are
cleared for agriculture, are clay soils distinguished by
color criteria only--yellow clay and black clay (probably
oxisols) (Moran, field notes, 1979). Informants were unable to indicate any differences in vegetation between
the two clay soils but indicated that only black clay
soils would support banana plantings (cf. Smole 1976).

Most ethnographers who have noted criteria for
choosing village sites rarely mention soils for agriculture as a major consideration used by native Amazonians
in choosing village or garden location. Rather, availability of white clay for rituals, declining yields from
hunting (Holmberg 1960; Harner 1972), protected location
from enemy raids (Chagnon 1977), and proximity to a major
river predominate as criteria for village location. The
Campa in the Gran Pajonal locate their swiddens immed-
iately adjacent to their houses on the upper slopes, even
though the most fertile and moist soils tend to be on the
lower slopes (Denevan 1976, personal communication).
Whether this reflects the lack of interest in ethnoecol-
ogy on the part of most Amnazonian ethnographers, a cur-
ious lack of specific soils knowledge on the part of native peoples or deculturation due to decimation by disease and dispersion resulting from colonial occupation
of the floodplain, is a major research question.

SPECIES-SPECIFIC KNOWLEDGE

In contrast to this simplicity in identifying the
variable soils present in the Amazon, native peoples have

been noted to have complex ethnobotanical and ethnozoological taxonomies (Taylor 1974; Berlin 1978; Berlin
and Berlin 1979; among others). Hunting and gathering
are important elements in the nutritional well-being of
native Amazonians and involve species-specific knowledge
that allows them to know when and where to take advantage
of the productivity of these plants and animals (Chirif
1978, 1979). As with soils, some scholars have suggested
that the productivity of hunting limits the size and per-
manence of settlements in the Amazon (Lathrap 1968; Gross
1975). This view has come under attack recently on the
grounds that it is too deterministic and fails to consider the differential productivity of hunting (Chagnon
and Hames 1979; Hames 1980; Beckerman 1979; Vickers
1976).

Most of the evidence concerning the scarcity of animal protein in the Amazon has been based on occasional
observation and acceptance of the natives' point of view
rather than on extensive data gathering. Although among
tropical forest peoples "hunger for meat" is a constant
concern (cf. Holmberg 1960; Siskind 1973), this does not
mean that this is based on a real dietary lack. What it
does express is the uncertainty associated with hunting
effort. The problems of obtaining protein result as much
from its dispersed nature and the nocturnal or arboreal
habits of the animals as much as from its absolute scarcity. Among the Siona-Secoya inhabiting an upland forest
area in Ecuador, even the least successful hunter managed
a mean kill of 13.08 kg of butchered meat per hunt--with
an average for all hunters of 21.35 kg (Vickers 1976).
This translated to 80.7 g of protein per person per day,
an amount well above protein needs. Even in an area in-
habited continuously for thirty two years the mean kill
was 5.67 kg per hunt per hunter. However, given the nocturnal habits of the game, the high canopy habits of the
birds and monkeys, and the aggressiveness of the pec-
caries, it is not surprising to see a great deal of cultural attention given to hunter/animal relations even if
there is sufficient protein present in the habitat. Of
all the subsistence activities, hunting is the least
secure and the first to decline in yield due to the es-
cape of animals into less hunted refuges.

Gathering forest products is subject, too, to the
peculiar periodicities of the tropical forest. The collection of forest products involves work by men, women
and children and even greater mobility than does hunting.
Both activities involve a dispersed resource base characterized by few individuals of a given species per unit
area, microecological seasonal availability, and easy depletion of the resource if intensively used.

Mobility in order to exploit wild plants and animals
would not have the same impact on the development of ethnoagronomic knowledge if the environment were more homogeneous and the soils less varied. It is precisely

this assumption of homogeneity and poor soils which is
at the basis of the deterministic model. It is only in
this past decade that evidence has begun to be generated
to document the presence of many more habitats than had
been recognized before.

Denevan (1976: 208) correctly noted that the traditional ecological division of the Amazon into floodplain
and upland is inadequate. He showed that historically
populations of the Amazon differed greatly in density as
a response to the diverse resource base (see Table 7.1).

Table 7.1
Population Estimates of Amazon Native Peoples Per Habitat Types

Habitat	in kilometers	Estimated Density per km^2 in 1492	Estimated Total Population in 1492
Floodplain	102,814	14.6	1,501,084
Coastal	105,000	9.5	997,500
Upland Forest	1,472,800	0.8	1,211,000
Lowland Forest*	5,037,886	0.2	1,007,577
Central Savannas	2,178,000	0.5	1,089,000
Northern Savannas	395,000	1.3	513,500

*Both wet and moist forest, as well as Rio Negro caatingas are in-
cluded. These are areas about which the demographic history is
quite obscure.

The coast probably offered the earliest human habitat,
as evidenced by the Marajo sites at the mouth of the Amazon (Meggers and Evans 1957). The floodplain formed a
natural extension of the coastal adaptations--both being
characterized by rich aquatic resources and high agricultural productivity resulting from the silt-enriched soils
on the levees (Meggers 1971). Lowland savannas are semi-
aquatic, periodically inundated zones with poor soil resources (Denevan 1966). A transitional form are caatingas or scrub forests of the upper Rio Negro (Herrera et
al. 1978) which are characterized by white sand and pod-
zolic soils, nutrient-conserving mechanisms, and criss-
crossed by black-water rivers. Upland forests (montaña)
which begin at about 700 meters or a mean annual temperature of 24°C., should be distinguished from lowland forests but this distinction has been suggested only in the
past decade and is still seldom made. The cooler temper-
atures and gently sloping land provide a less leached environment for agriculture but the productivity of game
is apparently lower. Fishing is poor due to the lack of
major streams and the absence of lagoons. The lowland
interfluvial forest is not as uniform as many writers
would have us believe. Rainfall varies between 100 and

200 cm, and elevations vary between sea level and 600
meters. Soils are patchy with soils of medium to high
fertility occupying small areas throughout up to 10 or
20 percent of the Basin (Wambecke 1978). The potential
of this vast habitat, making up 95 percent of the Basin,
relains largely unexplored. A portion of the Amazon
Basin is upland savanna, covering areas in Central
Brazil and the Guianas. Soils are leached and there is
a prolonged dry season, leading to less successful agriculture and greater emphasis on trekking to hunt and
gather than in the other habitats (Maybury-Lewis 1968;
Werner 1979).

What this habitat variability teaches us is that
considerable variation in human/habitat interactions can
be expected to exist within each of these types reflec-
ting: soil variability, the complexity of the river
basins drained, seasonality, knowledge of specific resources in an area, and the accuracy of cultural knowledge of specific species and sites. Given the tendency,
particularly among older ethnographers, to record as completely as possible the culture of the people studied, I
suggest that the simplicity of the ethnoagronomic taxonomies, side-by-side with the complexity of ethnobotanical
and ethnozoological taxonomies, indicates that aboriginal
Amazonians followed a typically hunter/gatherer adaptive
strategy to habitat diversity. Unlike many other anthropologists, I view this strategy as a result not of poor
soils or lack of protein resulting from a homogeneously
poor habitat, but as a consequence of the systemic interactions between chronic mobility, dependence on hunting,
subsistence reliant on protein-poor manioc due to its
trustworthiness in yield regardless of soil conditions,
and inadequate ethnoagronomic criteria for soil selection.

Thus far the evidence for the relationship between
mobility and the complexity of soil selection criteria
comes either from New Guinea (Conklin 1957), Africa
(Colson 1971), or from Amazonian studies of colonization
(Moran 1975; 1979; 1981). These studies provide inferen-
tial evidence that mobility influences agricultural productivity. Figure 7.2 summarizes the association between
rate of household mobility and productivity, i.e., yield
per unit of land. The data from this one study clearly
suggest that farm management is seriously affected by
chronic residential mobility. Such limited evidence
should not be taken uncritically as proof of the hypothesis that chronic mobility prevents the development of
site-specific ethno-agronomic knowledge necessary to develop complex and stable agricultural systems. It simply
suggests that the hypothesis is worth testing in a variety of settings and that it offers a more complete and
satisfactory explanation for the frequency of small settlements in Amazonia than the deterministic model currently in vogue.

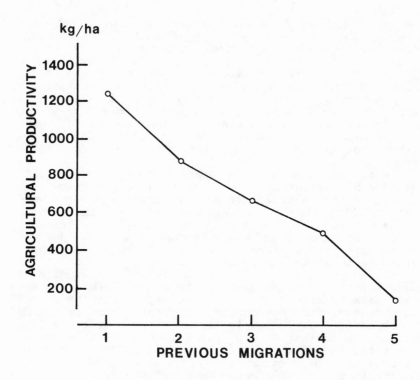

kg/ha

Figure 7.2. Relationship between Agricultural Productivity and Frequency of Mobility (n = 25)

In short, mobility strategies noted in human adaptations to tropical rain forests constitute an effective hunter/gatherer response to habitat diversity. Hunting knowledge is extensive, emphasizing knowledge of animal ethology and conservation practices that reduce the likelihood of depleting the resource too quickly (Reichel-Dolmatoff 1971; Taylor 1974; Moran 1974). Gathering involves close observation of the forest's periodicities and is frequently associated with hunting or with seasonal trekking (Werner 1979; Maybury-Lewis 1968). It is when one comes to farming that mobility becomes a negative rather than a positive factor. Farming in a diverse habitat requires identification of appropriate soils; location of fields that cut down on labor costs and reduces pest/pathogen damage; selection of crops appropriate to the climatic and soil conditions; and management that provides a satisfactory balance between needs and available resources. Unlike hunting and gathering which re-

quire species-specific knowledge, farming requires site-
specific knowledge and it takes no less than four years
to acquire such knowledge from scratch--and perhaps as
much as ten years (Colson 1971; Scudder personal communication; Moran 1975, 1979, 1981). This means that the mobility required for dependence on wild game as a major
protein source inhibits the development of complex agricultural systems capable of producing vegetable protein
on a regular basis.

DISCUSSION

At least two different subsistence strategies can
be identified in the Amazon basin. Some native Amazonians moved cyclically among a restricted number of areas.
Posey (1982) has found that the southern Kayapo exploit
"islands" within the forest/savanna environment. They
keep a restricted number of areas constantly in cultivation and visit them regularly to harvest the produce.
By maintaining constant contact and reducing the number
of sites encountered they have, in effect eliminated the
need to confront the heterogeniety of the tropical rain
forest and reduced the system complexity to a small number of intimately known resource islands. This is the
first case of such a strategy in Amazonia to come to my
attention but it may have been more extensive than commonly recognized by researchers (cf. Smith 1978). The
strategy is similar to the exploitation of "islands of
resources" in the Andes--an adaptation to the zonal distribution of resources across a vertically-structured
habitat (Murra 1972; Baker and Little 1976). Such a
strategy requires mobility of individuals among the
islands but it need not be associated with settlement
mobility.
Other native Amazonians resorted to a subsistence
strategy that combined hunting/gathering/fishing with
agriculture. These people had a high rate of settlement
mobility, complex ethnobotanical and ethnozoological
taxonomies, dependence on manioc in subsistence agriculture, simple ethnoagronomic taxonomies, and small settlements. Agriculture was dominated by manioc (Manihot
esculenta), a hardy crop that provides reliable and remarkably high yields even in poor soils (Moran 1973,
1976a, 1976b). Of all the available crops, manioc is the
most resistant to pest/pathogen damage; is the least affected by nutrient and pH variation in soils; and gives
the highest yields--five to ten tons/hectare--with minimal inputs and is one of the easiest to transport and
replant due to lightweight stem-cuttings used in vegeta-
tive reproduction. On the negative side is its low protein content, the high labor cost of processing to ex-
tract prussic acid, and the need to place gardens at some
distance from the village to prevent accidental poisoning
by the children. Other crops having higher nutrient de-

mands and high protein value (such as corn and beans) were planted but most ethnographers comment that they were insignificant proportions of total area planted and total food consumed yearly in most of the Amazon Basin. Although some crops such as sweet potatoes (Ipomea batatas), yams (Xanthossoma ssp.) and (in post-Columbian times) bananas (Musa ssp.) are comparable to manioc in yield and are less costly to process, they are less easily transportable from one site to another and are more sensitive to soil conditions than is manioc. Corn and beans are particularly sensitive to nutrient deficiencies and form a more important element of agriculture only in the rich volcanic soils of the Central American rain forests (Popenoe 1960; Moran 1975), and the alluvial varzeas of the Amazon in pre-Columbian times (Roosevelt 1980).

Dependence on manioc placed the burden for the provisioning of proteins on hunting or fishing. The relative weight assigned to either of these two activities depended on environmental factors. Fishing was not a reliable source of protein, except along the clear water rivers, such as the Xingu and the Tapajos; along the main channel of the Amazon with its rich fauna of turtle, manatee, and other large prey; and in some areas of the upper Amazon. Hunting dominated areas away from the major clear water rivers, but required frequent movement of villages, as the area within a reasonable distance of the villages was hunted, and game fled into other areas. A village had to evaluate the economy of hunting in its present territory versus its cost in relocating. The conscious motive for moving villages in the upper Amazon has been and is still decline in hunting yields and distance required to obtain game (Lathrap 1968; Denevan 1973; Stocks personal communication). This dependence on a low-protein manioc agriculture supplemented by hunting helps maintain a pattern of chronic mobility.

The relationships here are interactive and systemic (see summary in Figure 7.3). It is difficult to try to establish the origins of the subsistence strategy of mobility, manioc dependence, and dependence on hunting for protein. However, it seems likely that the requirement of mobility imposed by hunting locked the population into that pattern once it was chosen and prevented the development of more complex ethnoagronomic, site-specific knowledge applicable to agriculture; for example, of soils capable of sustained cultivation and of crop choices that would reduce dependency upon hunting for needed protein (e.g., the corn/beans complex). This, in turn, precluded the development of sustained yield agroecosystems capable of supporting either stable or larger populations, which would in turn allow for the possibility for that development of more complex forms of social organization.

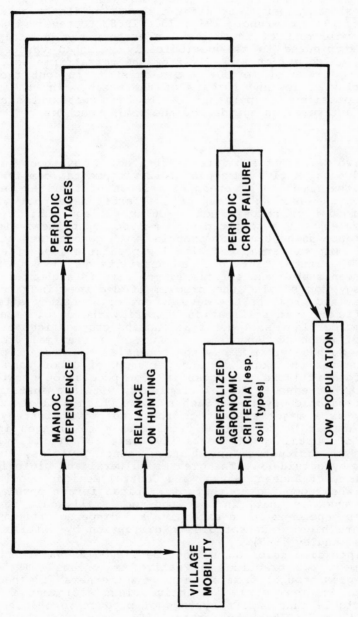

Figure 7.3. An interactive model of the Amazon Basin

Complex agricultural systems have only been found
along restricted areas of the Amazonian floodplain
(varzea) and major clear water tributaries (Lathrap 1968;
Meggers 1971; Sternberg 1973; Eden 1978; Roosevelt 1980).
The development of these complex systems has commonly
been attributed to the periodically enriched varzea
soils, which differ markedly from the terra firme soils.
However, areas of fertile soils exist throughout the
interfluvial lowland forests of the Basin. Why these
were not sites for permanent settlement constitutes an
important research agenda for the coming decades.

CONCLUSIONS

Two different subsistence strategies have been identified among native Amazonians. Environmental complexity
was either reduced by creating islands of familiar resources and using the rest of the forest as a pool of
wild foods; or chronic non-circular village mobility
strategies were associated with manioc dependence, with
a reliance on hunting for protein, with generalized ethnoagronomic criteria, and with low population densities.
While the latter pattern of adaptability can be said to
have been stable and efficient, mobility is a short-term
strategy for solving the problem of declines in game
yields, and prevents the development of necessary site-
specific soil identification criteria, the development
of complex plant-soil associations and crop choices capable of reducing dependence on hunting for animal protein. Such a system lacks the potential to increase production per unit of time and per unit of labor, and
therefore it lacks the potential for population growth
and for increase in social complexity within a sustain-
able production system. Such systems which utilize mobility as a major element in their adaptive strategy
would appear to be extremely vulnerable to changes in
rates of mortality and morbidity, rates of fertility,
levels of agricultural production, hunting yields, and
attack by outsiders. The greater cultural and biological
stability of Andean, Mayan, and Central Mexican populations when compared to that of tropical forest populations suggests that, in the long-run, small-scale societies dependent on an extensive and dispersed resource
base are highly susceptible to disruption by external
agents (Wagley 1969).
This discussion should not be viewed as an attempt
to demean the practices of native Amazonians. The
strategies brought from outside by westerners have been
less productive, more destructive, less efficient and
less stable than native systems of production (Sanchez
1976; Chirif 1978; Scazzocchio 1980; Moran 1981, 1982).
On the other hand, native agricultural systems varied a
great deal in their use and knowledge of resources, in
efficiency and long-term stability, in gross production

potential, and in their isomorphism with microecological conditions.

We cannot assume, as has been done in the past, that Amazonian food production systems and social organization were simply determined by edaphic factors, primarily soil. Models have failed to give sufficient credit to native Amazonians for the complex choices they have had to make through time. Rather, the full range of resource management strategies needs investigation to elucidate the complex interactions between habitat characteristics, subsistence strategies, and the organizational and demographic characteristics of human populations. In this interactive process the population plays an important role. Choices are made daily between moving or not, exact relocation sites, and how best to provide for life and leisure.

ACKNOWLEDGMENTS

The research upon which this paper is based was made possible by grants from the Social Science Research Council, the National Institutes of Mental Health, National Science Foundation and Man and the Biosphere/UNESCO's project on Amazon Rain Forest Ecosystems. I am grateful to Daniel Gross, Nigel Smith, Anthony Stocks, William Denevan, William Vickers, and Anthony Seeger, for critical and constructive comments.

8
An Overview of Adaptation

Michael A. Little

Editors' Summary: Michael Little, in this chapter, discusses some basic principles of adaptation in the context of several other contributions to this volume. He focuses his discussion on environmental stress, the pitfalls of dealing with human sex ratios, and strategies of resource exploitation. Little emphasizes the complexity of adaptive processes and the problems of reconciling human adaptation at the individual level, which involves the aggregate behaviors of individuals each striving to maximize access to or control over limiting resources. Human adaptation at the population level, which involves a need to maintain ecosystem equilibrium, and the persistence in time of ecosystem resources are also discussed.

INTRODUCTION

That humans adapt to their biological and sociocultural environment is a major theoretical premise in ecological anthropology and human biology. However, there is considerable misunderstanding about adaptation as a concept, and the concept is subject to a spectrum of interpretations (Mazess 1975b, 1978). This is so because of the complexity of both the concept and the actual processes of adaptation leading to states of adaptation to the environment. In addition to uses of adaptation as a "process" and adaptation as a "state" (Medawar 1951), adaptation can also be equated with fitness, in the Darwinian sense, where adaptation involves a genetic state and is directly subject to the process of natural selection (Stern 1970). Adaptation as a state of being and as a process of achieving such a state can be viewed in at least two ways. The first is evolutionary, where natural selection, fitness, reproductive success, and differential survival of organisms and, particularly, genes are of prime interest. Evolutionary biology, ethology, and sociobiology are fields of investigation in which behavioral and biological adaptation are approached from evolutionary perspectives. The second may be thought of as secular or temporal, where survival and general well-

137

being of the organism and population are of interest
without a direct emphasis on genetic systems (Little
1982). This second legitimate approach to understanding
adaptation should be concerned with individual coping
mechanisms, behavioral and biological adjustments to
stress, relative merits of different individual and population strategies, physiological flexibility, and perhaps, genetic plasticity. Although evolutionary process
is always implied in this latter approach, it is not
necessary to demonstrate fitness of various systems or
reproductive advantage in order to document adaptation
within a human population.

In the sections that follow, a few selected topics
that deal with adaptation are discussed in the context
of some of the contributions to this volume.

TOPICS IN ADAPTATION

Environmental Stress and Adaptive Domains

The approach of Haas to study high altitude natives
according to multiple environmental stresses and response
evaluation according to adaptive domains is likely to be
a highly productive one. In order to understand this approach more effectively, I should like to discuss,
briefly, the concepts of stress and adaptation within the
context of the high altitude environment.

As noted at the beginning of this chapter, adaptation can be considered a process of adjustment or a state
of adjustment to environmental conditions. Implied in
the definition of adjustment is that there is no absolute
kind of adjustment to an environment, but that some organisms (or populations) are better adjusted than others.
This observation brings into the picture two important
points: (1) that we are considering relative benefit
when we deal with most adjustments, and (2) that an individual or population comparative approach is needed to
define the patterns of adaptation.

The force that stimulates the need to change or
modify a level of adaptation arises from the environment
and can be called a stress. A stress is then defined as
a perturbing force or a force that produces a deviation
from homeostasis or a dynamic state of balance. The deviation or imbalance itself is referred to as a strain,
and it is implied that a strained system impairs normal
function. A response may be adaptive or successful by
restoring normal function through (1) removal of the
stress directly, (2) returning the system to its previous
state of homeostasis by appropriate feedback controls,
or (3) accommodating to the strain by maintaining a new
homeostatic level. A response may be maladaptive by any
of the above responses being unsuccessful or by an over-
shoot effect or overcompensation of control mechanisms.

The flow pattern below illustrates the sequence of events:

(Stressor)   (Disturbance)   (Restoration or Failure)
 STRESS ————————➤ STRAIN ——————————————➤ RESPONSE
(Deforming   (Deviation from   (Adaptation or
 Force)   Homeostasis)   Maladaptation)

This is, of course, a simple model of a very complex process (see Baker 1974, 1975; Prosser 1964; Slonim 1974).

High-altitude hypoxia or hypobaric hypoxia (decreased atmospheric oxygen pressure) is a very potent environmental stress and can serve as an example of the stress/strain/response model at the single-stress level. First, since hypoxia strains the human physiological system most intensely during work or vigorous activity, it is possible to reduce the stress somewhat by becoming relatively inactive or by resting. Obviously, this is only a stop-gap kind of behavioral adaptation, since humans as members of social groups cannot terminate all activities and still hope to survive. Second, since effective oxygen delivery to body tissues and working muscles is limited at high altitude, then a variety of compensatory mechanisms can come into play to facilitate oxygen transport in the body. These mechanisms involve feedback controls in the heart, lungs, blood and the circulatory system. Third, the chest and lungs and the right side of the heart of individuals who have lived since infancy at high altitude are larger than in sea level residents. These permanent size differences might be considered as morphological or structural adaptations to hypoxia. The same stress/strain/response model can be used to inspect high-altitude cold adaptation, adaptation to nutritional deprivation, or adaptation to any other identifiable stress in the environment. A model of multiple stress interaction is presented in Figure 8.1. Here hypoxia and cold stimulate increased ventilation and blood flow to the skin surface, both processes enhancing heat loss. The elevated heat loss requires an increase in basal metabolic rate (BMR) which, in turn, increases the body's energy needs. Hence, it is likely that high-altitude natives require more food energy than sea level natives.

The importance of adaptive domains is, as Haas points out, to be able to evaluate the relative benefit conferred on individuals by showing variation or relative levels of adaptation. Mazess' (1975a, 1975b) adaptive domains of physical performance, nutrition, growth, reproduction, affective (emotional) function, and others, are categories of biobehavioral needs for health and normal functioning. We can then evaluate the effects of stress independently on different adaptive domains to define quite precisely the degree of adaptation.

140

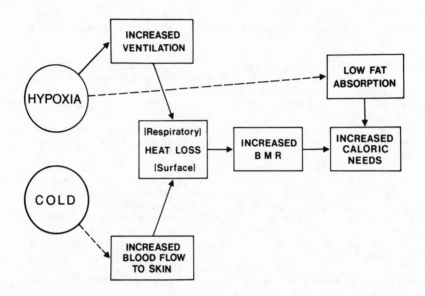

Figure 8.1. A flow diagram that illustrates how hypoxia and cold, as combined stresses at high altitude, produce an increased need for food energy (calories) in humans. Dashed lines are relationships in which documentation is good; solid lines indicate relationships in which documentation is very good. (From Little 1981; Picón-Reátegui 1978.) This is a deterministic model in that the flows move in one direction only. In fact, however, it is only a part of a complex interactive model, where increased caloric needs of Andean natives influence subsistence patterns, trade, and economy, and feedback to influence tolerance to cold and hypoxia.

The Human Sex Ratio

The contributions to this volume by May Jane Kellum and James Dow reflect the strong interest by anthropologists in sex ratio variations and causes of these variations in populations around the world. Kellum's chapter serves as an important update to a short, but comprehensive review by Teitelbaum (1972). Teitelbaum documented twenty-eight variables for which there is some evidence for an influence on the secondary or live-birth sex ratio in humans. Some of these include: birth order, family size, radiation exposure, physique of parents, frequency of coitus, socioeconomic status, and urban or rural residence. Hence, sorting out causes of secondary sex ratio variation is a difficult task, although a legitimate scientific one.

Rather than attempt to deal with the problem at this level, I should like to present an explanation for the universal human attribute of high secondary sex ratio (ratio at birth), and presumptive high primary sex ratio

(ratio at conception) from the viewpoint of reproductive
biology. My assumption is that once the basic biobehavioral factors leading to sex ratios at birth greater than
100 are known, then we shall be in a better position to
explain the conditions leading to their variation.

As Kellum noted (Chapter 4), several years ago the
generally observed secondary sex ratio of between 103 and
106 was believed to be caused by two factors. First the
primary sex ratio was thought to be very high, perhaps
200 or more, and second, this large number of males conceived was reduced in utero by a correspondingly high
male embryonic and fetal death rate. Recent observations
(Cavalli-Sforza and Bodmer 1971: 654ff.; Stern 1973:
530ff.) suggest that the primary sex ratio is not ex-
traordinarily high and that the sex ratio of spontan-
eously aborted fetuses appears to be close to 100 (equivalence by sex) or only slightly greater than 100 (more
male deaths). Nevertheless, a sex ratio at conception
of somewhat greater than 100 (predominance of males) is
still very likely in light of the evidence on near sex
equivalence of spontaneous abortions in association with
sex ratios at birth greater than 100 for nearly all human
populations.

Several lines of evidence are needed to construct a
model to explain a male conception rate greater than for
females. Figure 8.2 is a curve showing probability of
conception when coitus occurs at various times around the
period of ovulation in women. The curve was constructed
by Guerrero and colleagues (1979), where ovulation was
determined by variations in basal body temperature. If
coitus occurs before ovulation, the probability of conception is much higher than if coitus occurs after ovulation. Based upon this curve one could predict that
roughly 85 percent of conceptions would occur with coitus
taking place at or before ovulation, and 15 percent of
conceptions would occur with coitus at the time of or
following ovulation. This probability curve simply reflects the fact that human sperm cells may survive in the
female reproductive tract for three or more days (Hafez
1978, Guerrero et al. 1979), whereas ova or egg cells are
thought to survive only about one day unless fertilized
(Guerrero et al. 1979). Hence, there is a greater pre-
ovulatory than postovulatory period in which coitus can
lead to conception.

If all sperm cells had an equal probability of
reaching the egg cell in the oviduct following coitus,
then it would be unimportant whether coitus occurred before or after ovulation. However, there is good evidence
that motility of Y-bearing sperm cells (male-determining
chromosome carriers) is greater than X-bearing sperm
cells (female-determining chromosome carriers) (David et
al. 1977; Goodall and Roberts 1976). Therefore, if
coitus takes place in the period before ovulation, then
Y-bearing and X-bearing sperm cells have an equal chance

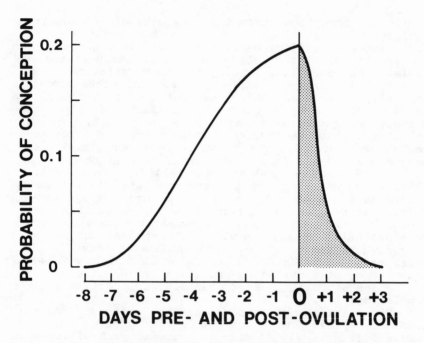

Figure 8.2. A curve giving the probability of human conception with respect to the time of coitus before or
after the time of ovulation. Time of ovulation was
determined by basal body temperature (BBT--early morning) and data were compiled by Vollman (1953). (From
Guerrero, Rojas and Cifuentes 1979.)

of fertilizing the ovum, since the more motile and rapid
Y-bearing and the slower X-bearing sperm cells are
likely both to be present in the oviduct when the ovum
is released from the ovary. Yet if coitus takes place
after ovulation, then the more rapid Y-bearing cells are
likely to arrive at the site of the ovum first and
consequently increase the chance of a male conception.
Referring back to the probability curve in Figure 8.2,
and assuming an equal frequency of coitus over the
eleven day period represented, then in approximately 15
percent of the conceptions (the shaded area of the
curve) male conceptions should occur with greater
frequency than female conceptions. The magnitude of
this greater frequency is not known.
    This phenomenon alone should increase the sex ratio
at conception, but there is additional evidence that Y-
bearing sperm cells are more successful in penetrating
the cervical mucus at the opening of the uterus than are
X-bearing cells (Broer and Kaiser 1978). Thus, greater

numbers of Y-bearing than X-bearing sperm cells may actually enter the female reproductive tract to increase
further the probability of male conceptions.

In order to understand more fully sex ratio from
conception to early childhood, a diagram is given in
Figure 8.3 that incorporates some of the best documented
variables influencing sex ratio. The magnitude of the
task to partition the variance and identify the most important variables is formidable. For example, the variables (1) socioeconomic status, (2) family size, (3)
birth order, and (4) ages of parents, interact in a number of ways. Low socioeconomic status persons are often
characterized as having larger families (thus, children
in higher ranks of birth order), and a greater age of
reproduction, all of which contribute to a mean sex ratio
that is relatively low. Although not documented, large
family size (many pregnancies) may sensitize the mother
to certain cell antigens and contribute to rejection reactions. Child sex ratios, which are the outcome of secondary sex ratio and subsequent mortality, are certainly
influenced by parental treatment and care.

The scientific problem of identifying causes of
human population variation in secondary sex ratio or
child sex ratio is as difficult as the problem of dealing
with human population differentials in fertility--the
numbers of variables involved are overwhelming. Adequate
sampling, particularly for child sex ratios, is essentially because of the wide, and often unbalanced age representation among populations of children. Hence, careful research design is needed, as well as acquisition of
solid demographic data to be used for hypothesis testing.

Resource Acquisition and Adaptation

A "resource" can be thought of as something useful
in which there is an available, but finite, supply that
can be procured when needed. Clearly, all resources are
"limited" in their availability, but some resources are
profoundly "limiting" in the ecological sense of the definition (McNaughton and Wolf 1973: 30), in which their
short supply constrains population growth, growth in body
size, mobility, technological advancement, or some other
definable characteristic. Resources, then, and particularly those that are limiting, are of special interest
to anthropologists, since human patterns of subsistence
and survival are really adaptive strategies for resource
exploitation and utilization (Little and Morren 1976:
20). The contributions of Boone and Moran to this volume
are concerned with resources, be they land or protein,
and their contributions reflect this special anthropological interest.

Boone makes a statement in Chapter 5 (p. 81) with
which I am in full agreement. It is ". . . that social
behavior is best explained in terms of the aggregate con-

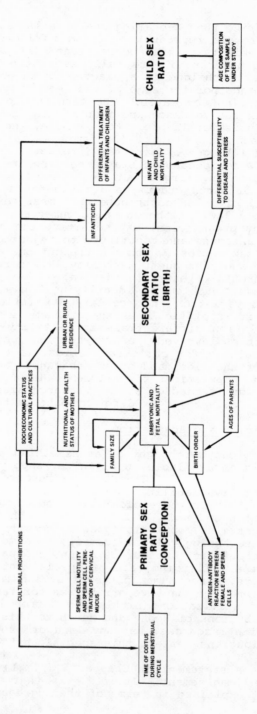

Figure 8.3. A model to document some of the variables affecting primary, secondary and child sex ratios.

sequences of individual behavioral strategies aimed at maximizing access to or control over limiting resources through competitive and cooperative interaction with other individuals." At the individual level, planning and intent are implied, but, as N. Dyson-Hudson (1980) suggested, "A population strategy may be inferred from the aggregate behavior of organisms without having to go into the question of their intentionality, rationality, or self-awareness . . ." In other words, we can define a human population or a culture as a reasonably well-adapted system of internal regulators (controls, if you will) if it has the characteristic of persistence through time. And also, we can refer to an overall population or adaptive strategy, despite the absence of a supreme planner or manager, as an outcome of interacting individual and small group behaviors. Perhaps the term "adaptive strategy" at the population level, which implies a plan, should be changed to "adaptive system," which seems more neutral, since anthropologists appear to have a problem conceptualizing population adaptation.

"Control" is also a term that can be conceptualized by many at the individual level because "control" implies "controller," but again there is a conceptual problem at the population level where the controller cannot be identified easily. For example, warfare may be viewed as not adaptive or not a population control because it does not benefit the group as a whole and is destructive. In fact, warfare, infanticide, epidemic disease or any other killer of people is a population control because it reduces the number of people in the population. The controllers are at the individual level but the effects can be viewed at the population level.

Extrapolation from individual to group behavior within an adaptation framework is a difficult conceptual task. Mazess (1975b) suggested several "population adaptive domains" to serve as evaluators of population adaptation. These are: reproductive success (being able to maintain or increase population numbers), demographic optimality (appropriate age and sex distribution and density), spacial-temporal spread (expansion of population in space and time), and energetic or ecological efficiency (efficiency of resource exploitation while maintaining the viability of the ecosystem and its resource productivity). In this latter domain, persistence in time of ecosystem resources has a direct affect on persistence in time of the human population. Also, it is certainly the case that the rate with which resources are exploited will influence ecosystem homeostasis. Therefore, the need to maintain ecosystem equilibrium or homeostasis is an important consideration when dealing with human strategies of resource exploitation in a given ecosystem. This is particularly true in the tropical wet forest where Moran (Chapter 7) suggests that mobility is only a short-term strategy to cope with the specific fea-

146

tures of this environment. There is the implication
that productivity should be increased, and that
increased productivity, the principal measure of
adaptation, is limited by mobility. My argument is that
level of productivity is only one measure of adaptation;
persistence of productivity can be another.

DISCUSSION

When all things are considered, the process of adaptation is incredibly complex. The reason for its complexity is that adapation is a fundamental property of
life itself. Organisms, including human organisms, adapt
to their environments in an infinite variety of ways and
with numerous mechanisms. The basic mechanisms are found
in the hereditary material or genes of the individual or
gene pool of the population. Some of these genes resist
environmental influences and provide a very rigid biological or behavioral set of instructions. Other genes are
markedly flexible in their reception to environmental
stimuli, while still other genes are in operation only
at specific times of the life cycle. Adaptation at this
genetic level is an evolutionary form of adaptation and
results from processes of natural selection.
    Genetic adaptations, as Dyson-Hudson outlined in the
first chapter, often limit biological and behavior flexibility, and it is those adaptive processes that occur in
the short-run or over an individual's life time that
truly enhance human adaptation. For example, human in-
telligence and behavior have a genetic basis for our
species, yet these constitutional abilities will not develop (or show adaptive properties) unless the proper
environment for acquiring knowledge, reasoning, and
developing behavioral skills occurs. This pattern of
latent genetic ability requiring environmental enhance-
ment characterizes human adaptation at the individual
level. Learning, developing athletic skills, acquiring
immunity to a disease, and acclimatizing to hot weather
or high altitude--all are examples of adaptive processes
in humans which illustrate this principle.
    It is, perhaps, the understanding of adaptation at
the population level where our greatest scientific chal-
lenges lie. At the population level is where social and
evolutionary scientists are in greatest conflict over
theoretical issues. These conflicts are reflected in the
chapters by Kellum, Boone and Dow. Modeling and modern
computer simulation is proving to be highly productive
in explaining adaptation at the population level. In
terms of society, however, there is the practical problem
of resolving what is adaptive for a population with per-
ceived individual needs and societal goals, some of which
may be incompatible with population adaptation.
    And last, we must not forget the environment or the
ecosystems of which humans are an integral, and often

perturbing, element. Smith, Haas, and Moran's chapters
on theory, human biology, and human subsistence, respectively, express these ecosystem considerations. It is,
of course, the interactions of humans within the ecosystem that stimulate adaptive responses in their sociocultural and biological systems. A greater understanding
of the limits and flexibility of human adaptation to the
environment may well be necessary to ensure human survival beyond the next few generations.

ACKNOWLEDGMENTS

Many of the ideas in this chapter were formulated
or stimulated by Paul T. Baker and Richard B. Mazess. I
acknowledge their intellectual contribution with thanks.
    Partial support was provided by National Science
Foundation Grant No. DEB-8004182 during the preparation
of this work. I wish to thank Sue McMahon for assistance
in manuscript preparation.

Bibliography

AASftP (Ann Arbor Science for the People). 1977. Bi-
ology as a Social Weapon. Minneapolis, Minn.:
Burgess Publishing Co.
Abelson, A. E., T. S. Baker, and P. T. Baker. 1974. Al-
titude, migration and fertility. Social Biology 21:
12-27.
Alexander, R. D. 1974. The evolution of social behavior.
Annual Review of Ecology and Systematics 5:324-383.
Alexander, R. D. 1979. Darwinism and Human Affairs.
Seattle: University of Washington Press.
Alexander, R. D. and D. W. Tinkle (eds.) 1981. Natural
Selection and Social Behavior. New York: Chiron
Press.
Alland, A. 1972. The Human Imperative. New York:
Columbia University Press.
Alland, A. 1975. Adaptation. Annual Review of Anthro-
pology 4: 59-73.
Alland, A. and B. McCay. 1974. The concept of adapta-
tion in biological and cultural evolution. In Hand-
book of Social and Cultural Anthropology, J. J.
Honigmann (ed.) Chicago: Rand McNally.
Andrews, P. and J. A. H. Van Couvering. 1975. Paleo-
environments in the East African Miocene. In Con-
tributions to Primatology: Approaches to Primate
Paleobiology, F. S. Szalay (ed.): 62-103. Basel:
Krager.
Ardrey, R. 1966. The Territorial Imperative. New York:
Dell Publishing Company.
Armstrong, R. A. and R. McGelee. 1980. Competitive ex-
clusion. American Naturalist 119: 151-170.
Baker, P. T. 1969. Human adaptation to high altitude.
Science 163: 1149-1156.
Baker, P. T. 1974. An evolutionary perspective in en-
vironmental physiology. In Environmental Physiol-
ogy, N. B. Slonim (ed.): 510-522. St. Louis:
Mosby.
Baker, P. T. 1975. Research strategies in population
biology and environmental stress. In The Measures
of Man: Methodologies in Human Biology, E. Giles

150

and J. Friedlaender (eds.): 230-259. Cambridge,
Mass.: Schenkman Publishing Co.
Baker, P. T. 1976. Work performance of highland natives.
In Man in the Andes: A Multidisciplinary Study of
High Altitude Quechua, P. T. Baker and M. A. Little
(eds.): 300-314. Stroudsburg, Pa.: Dowden, Hutchin-
son and Ross.
Baker, P. T. (ed.). 1978. The Biology of High Altitude
Peoples. New York: Cambridge University Press.
Baker, P. T. and J. S. Dutt. 1972. Demographic vari-
ables as measures of biological adaptation: a case
study of high altitude human populations. In The
Structure of Human Populations, G. A. Harrison and
A. T. Boyce (eds.): 352-378. Oxford: The Clarendon
Press.
Baker, P. T. and M. A. Little (eds.). 1976. Man in the
Andes: A Multidisciplinary Study of High Altitude
Quechua. Stroudsburg, Pa.: Dowden, Hutchinson and
Ross.
Balikci, A. 1970. The Netsilik Eskimo. Garden City,
N.Y.: The Natural History Press.
Barac-Nieto, M., G. B. Spurr, M. G. Maksud, and H. Lotero.
1978. Aerobic work capacity in chronically under-
nourished males. Journal of Applied Physiology 44:
209-215.
Barkow, J. H. 1977. Conformity to ethos and reproduc-
tive success in two Hausa communities: an empirical
evaluation. Ethos 5: 409-425.
Bates, D. G. and S. H. Lees. 1979. The myth of popula-
tion regulation. In Evolutionary Biology and Human
Social Behavior, N. A. Chagnon and W. Irons (eds.).
North Scituate, Mass.: Duxbury Press.
Bates, H. W. 1892. Naturalist on the River Amazons.
Berkeley: Univ. of California Press, 1962.
Bayham, F. E. 1979. Factors influencing the Archaic
pattern of animal exploitation. Kiva 44: 219-235.
Beall, C. M. 1981. Optimal birthweights in Peruvian
populations at high and low altitudes. American
Journal of Physical Anthropology 56: 209-216.
Beall, C. M., P. T. Baker, T. S. Baker, and J. D. Haas.
1977. The effects of high altitude on adolescent
growth in southern Peruvian Amerindians. Human
Biology 49: 109-124.
Beckermann, S. 1979. The abundance of protein in Ama-
zonia: a reply to Gross. American Anthropologist
81: 533-560.
Bennett, J. W. 1976. The Ecological Transition:
Cultural Anthropology and Human Adaptation. New
York: Pergamon Press.
Berlin, B. 1978. Bases empiricas de la cosmología
Aguaruna. In Etnicidad y Ecología, A. Chirif (ed.).
Lima: CIPA.
Berlin, B. and L. Berlin. 1979. Etnobiologia, subsis-
tencia y nutrición en una sociedad de la selva trop-

ical: Los Aguaruna. In Salud y Nutrición en Socie-
des Nativas, A. Chirif (ed.). Lima: CIPA.

Bernstein, M. E. 1948. Recent changes in the secondary
sex ratio of the upper social strata. Human Biology
20: 182-94.

Bertram, B. C. R. 1978. Living in groups: predators
and prey. In Behavioural Ecology, J. R. Krebs and
N. B. Davies (eds.), 64-96. Sunderland, Mass.:
Sinauer.

Blalock, H. M., Jr. 1972. Social Statistics, 2nd edition. New York: McGraw-Hill.

Blurton Jones, N. G. and R. M. Sibley. 1978. Testing
adaptiveness of culturally determined behaviour: do
Bushmen women maximize their reproductive success by
spacing births widely and foraging seldom? In Human
Behaviour and Adaptations, N. G. Blurton Jones and
V. Reynolds (eds.): 135-57. Symposium No. 18,
Society for the Study of Human Biology. London:
Taylor and Francis.

Boas, F. 1888. The Central Eskimo. Lincoln: University of Nebraska Press (reprint, 1964).

Bodmer, W. F. and A. W. F. Edwards. 1960. Natural
selection and the sex ratio. Annals of Human
Genetics 34: 239-44.

Boserup, E. 1965. The Conditions of Agricultural Growth.
Chicago: Aldine.

Boyd, R. and P. J. Richerson. 1980. Sociobiology, culture, and economic theory. Journal of Economic Behavior and Organization 1: 92-121.

Brazelton, T. B. 1969. Infants and Mothers: Differences in Development. New York: Delacorte Press.

Briggs, J. L. 1974. Eskimo women: makers of men. In
Many Sisters, Carolyn J. Matthiasson (ed.). New
York: The Free Press.

Broer, K. H. and R. Kaiser. 1978. The frequency of Y
chromatin positive spermatozoa in postcoital tests
and under various experimental conditions. In Human
Fertilization, H. Ludwig and P. F. Tauber (eds.):
137-142. Stuttgart: Georg Thieme Publishers.

Brown, J. L. 1964. The evolution of diversity in avian
territorial systems. Wilson Bulletin 76: 160-169.

Brown, J. L. and G. H. Orians. 1970. Spacing patterns
in mobile animals. Annual Review of Ecology and
Systematics 1: 239-262.

Brown, L. 1975. The Evolution of Behavior. New York:
W. W. Norton and Co.

Brožek, J. (ed.). 1979. Behavioral Effects of Energy
and Protein Deficits. Bethesda, Md.: Department of
Health, Education and Welfare (NIH), U.S. Govern-
ment.

Butzer, K. W. 1971. Environment and Archeology: An
Ecological Approach to Prehistory, 2nd ed. Chicago:
Aldine Atherton.

Carneiro, R. L. 1957. Subsistence and Social Structure: An Ecological Study of the Kuikuru. Ph.D. Dissertation: Univ. of Michigan, Dept. of Anthropology.

Carneiro, R. L. 1970a. A theory of the origin of the state. Science 196: 733-738.

Carneiro, R. L. 1970b. The transition from hunting to horticulture in the Amazon Basin. 8th Congress of Anthropological and Ethnological Sciences 3: 243-251.

Carneiro, R. L. 1974. Slash-and-burn cultivation among the Kuikuru and its implications for cultural development in the Amazon Basin. In Native South Americans, P. Lyon (ed.). Boston: Little Brown.

Carter, H. and P. C. Glick. 1976. Marriage and Divorce: A Social and Economic Study, Revised Edition. Cambridge, Mass.: Harvard University Press.

Cavalli-Sforza, L. L. and W. F. Bodmer. 1971. The Genetics of Human Populations. San Francisco: W. F. Freeman and Co.

Chagnon, N. A. 1968. Yanomamo social organization and warfare. In War: The Anthropology of Armed Conflict and Aggression, M. Fried (ed.). Garden City, N.Y.: Natural History Press.

Chagnon, N. A. 1973. The culture-ecology of shifting (pioneering) cultivation among the Yanomamo Indians. In Peoples and Cultures of Native South America, Daniel Gross (ed.). Garden City, N.Y.: Natural History Press.

Chagnon, N. A. 1974. Studying the Yanomamo. New York: Holt, Rinehart and Winston.

Chagnon, N. A. 1977. Yanomamo: The Fierce People, Second Edition. New York: Holt, Rinehart and Winston.

Chagnon, N. A. 1979. Is reproductive success equal in egalitarian societies? In Evolutionary Biology and Human Social Behavior, N. A. Chagnon and W. Irons (eds.): 374-401. North Scituate, Mass.: Duxbury Press.

Chagnon, N. and R. Hames. 1979. Protein deficiency and tribal warfare in Amazonia. Science 203: 910-913.

Chagnon, N. A. and W. G. Irons (eds.). 1979. Evolutionary Biology and Human Social Behavior, North Scituate, Mass.: Duxbury.

Chagnon, N. A. and W. Irons, organizers. 1981. Symposium: Human Sociobiology, New Research and Theory, Northwestern University.

Chagnon, N. A., M. V. Flinn, and T. F. Melancon. 1979. Sex ratio variation among the Yanomamo Indians. In Evolutionary Biology and Human Social Behavior, N. A. Chagnon and W. Irons (eds.): 290-320. North Scituate, Mass.: Duxbury Press.

Chapman, R. F. 1976. Biology of Locusts. London: Edward Arnold.

Charnov, E. L. 1976. Optimal foraging: the marginal value theorem. Theoretical Population Biology 9: 129-36.

Chasko, W. J., Jr. and E. Cashdan. 1978. Competitive interactions between human populations. Paper presented at the annual meeting of the American Anthropological Association, Los Angeles, November 1978.

Chirif, A., (ed.). 1978. Etnicidad y Ecología. Lima: Centro de Investigacion y Promocion Amazonica (CIPA).

Clarke, W. 1966. From extensive to intensive shifting cultivation: a succession from New Guinea. Ethnology 5: 347-359.

Clegg, E. J. 1978. Fertility and early growth. In The Biology of High Altitude Peoples, P. T. Baker (ed.): 65-116. New York: Cambridge University Press.

Clutton-Brock, T. H. and P. H. Harvey. 1978. Mammals, resources, and reproductive strategies. Nature 273: 191-95.

Christian, J. J. 1970. Social subordination, population density, and mammalian evolution. Science 168: 84-90.

Cody, M. L. 1974. Optimization in ecology. Science 183: 1156-64.

Cody, M. L. and J. M. Diamond (eds.). 1975. Ecology and the Evolution of Communities. Cambridge: Harvard University Press.

Cohen, Y. A. 1974. Culture in adaptation. In Man in Adaptation: The Cultural Present, Y. A. Cohen (ed.). Chicago: Aldine.

Colson, E. 1971. The Social Consequence of Resettlement. London: Manchester University Press.

Conklin, H. 1957. Hanunoo Agriculture. Rome: FAO.

Cooper, J. P. 1978. Patterns of inheritance and settlement by great landowners from the fifteenth to the eighteenth centuries. In Family and Inheritance: Rural Society in Western Europe 1200-1800, J. Goody, J. Thirsk, and E. O. Thompson (eds.). Cambridge: Cambridge University Press.

Cottrell, F. 1951. Energy and Society. New York: McGraw-Hill.

Crow, J. F. 1966. The quality of people: human evolutionary changes. BioScience (December): 863-867.

Daly, M. and M. I. Wilson. 1981. Abuse and neglect of children in evolutionary perspective. In Natural Selection and Social Behavior, R. D. Alexander and D. W. Tinkle (eds.): 405-416. New York: Chiron Press.

Damon, A. (ed.). 1975. Physiological Anthropology. New York: Oxford University Press.

Darwin, C. 1859. The Origin of Species, London: John Murray. (Facsimile edition, E. Mayr (ed.), Harvard University Press, 1964).

154

Darwin, C. 1874. The Descent of Man and Selection in
Relation to Sex, Second Edition. Philadelphia:
John Wanamaker.
David, G., C. Jeulin, A. Boyce, and D. Schwartz. 1977.
Motility and percentage of Y- and YY- bearing sperma-
tozoa in human semen samples after passage through
bovine serum albumin. Journal of Reproduction and
Fertility, 50: 377-379.
Davies, N. B. 1978. Ecological questions about terri-
torial behaviour. In Behavioural Ecology, J. R.
Krebs and N. B. Davies (eds.): 317-350. Sunderland,
Mass.: Sinauer.
Delgado, H. L., A. Lechtig, C. Yarbrough, R. Martorell,
R. E. Klein and M. Irwin. 1977. Maternal nutrition
--its effects on infant growth and development and
birth spacing. In Nutritional Impacts on Women,
K. S. Moghissi and T. N. Evans (eds.): 133-150.
Hagerstown, Md.: Harper and Row.
Denevan, W. 1966. A cultural ecological view of the
former aboriginal settlement in the Amazon Basin.
Professional Geographer 18: 346-351.
Denevan, W. 1973. Development and the imminent demise
of the Amazon rain forest. Professional Geographer
25: 130-135.
Denevan, W. 1976. Amazonia. In The Population of the
Americas before 1492, W. Denevan (ed.). Madison:
Univ. of Wisconsin Press.
Diamond, J. 1978. Niche shifts and the rediscovery of
interspecific competition. American Scientist 66:
322-331.
Dickemann, M. 1979. Female infanticide, reproductive
strategies, and social stratification: a preliminary
model. In Evolutionary Biology and Human Social Behavior, N. A. Chagnon and W. Irons (eds.): 312-367.
North Scituate, Mass.: Duxbury Press.
Divale, W. T. 1972. Systemic population control in the
middle and upper Paleolithic: inference based on
contemporary hunter-gatherers. World Archaeology 4:
222-243.
Divale, W. T. and M. Harris. 1976. Population warfare
and the male supremacist complex. American Anthropologist 78: 522-538.
Divale, W. T. and M. Harris. 1978a. Reply to Lancaster
and Lancaster. American Anthropologist 80: 117-118.
Divale, W. T. and M. Harris. 1978b. The male supremacist
complex: discovery of a cultural invention. American Anthropologist 80: 668-671.
Divale, W. T., M. Harris, and D. T. Williams. 1978c. On
the misuse of statistics: a reply to Hirschfeld et
al. American Anthropologist 80: 379-386.
Duby, G. 1977. The Chivalrous Society, Cynthia Postan,
trans. London: Edward Arnold.
Durham, W. H. 1976a. The adaptive significance of cultural behavior. Human Ecology 4: 89-121.

Durham, W. H. 1976b. Resource competition and human aggression, part 1: a review of primitive war. Quarterly Review of Biology 51: 385-415.

Durham, W. H. 1978. Toward a coevolutionary theory of human biology and culture. In The Sociobiology Debate, Arthur L. Caplan (ed.): 428-48. New York: Harper and Row.

Durham, W. H. 1979. Toward a coevolutionary theory of human biology and culture. In Evolutionary Biology and Human Social Behavior: An Anthropological Perspective, N. A. Chagnon and W. Irons (eds.): 39-58. North Scituate, Mass.: Duxbury Press.

Dutt, J. S. 1976. Altitude and Fertility: The Bolivian Case. Ph.D. Dissertation. University Park, Pa.: The Pennsylvania State University.

Dyson-Hudson, N. 1980. Strategies of resource exploitation among East African savanna pastoralists. In Human Ecology in Savanna Environments, D. R. Harris (ed.): 171-184. London: Academic Press.

Dyson-Hudson, R. 1979. Sociobiology as a political statement. The Cornell Review 7: 48-57.

Dyson-Hudson, R. 1980. Toward a general theory of pastoralism and social stratification. Nomadic Peoples 7: 1-7. Published by Commission on Nomadic Peoples, International Union of Anthropological and Ethnological Sciences.

Dyson-Hudson, R. and Smith, E. A. 1978. Human territoriality: an ecological reassessment. American Anthropologist 80: 21-41.

Easterlin, R. A. 1968. Population, Labor Force and Long Swings in Economic Growth. New York: National Bureau of Economic Research.

Eden, M. 1978. Ecology and land development: the case of Amazonian rain forest. Transactions of the Institute of British Geographers 3: 444-463.

Edwards, A. W. F. 1970. The search for genetic variability of the sex ratio. Journal of Biosocial Science, Supplement 2: 55-60.

Eibl-Eibesfeldt, I. 1971. Love and Hate: The Natural History of Behavior Patterns. New York: Holt, Rinehart and Winston.

Emlen, J. M. 1973. Ecology: An Evolutionary Approach. Reading, Mass.: Addison-Wesley.

Emlen, S. T. 1976. An alternative case for sociobiology. Science 192: 736-38.

Emlen, S. T. 1980. Ecological determinism and sociobiology. In Sociobiology: Beyond Nature/Nurture?, edited by George W. Barlow and James Silverberg, pp. 125-50. AAAS Selected Symposia, No. 35. Boulder, Colo.: Westview Press.

Emlen, S. T. and L. Oring. 1977. Ecology, sexual selection, and the evolution of mating systems. Science 197: 215-23.

156

Erickson, J. D. 1976. The secondary sex ratio in the
U.S. 1969-71: association with race, parental ages,
birth order, paternal education, and legitimacy.
Annals of Human Genetics 40: 205-12.
Etter, M. A. 1978. Sahlins and sociobiology. American
Ethnologist 5: 169-79.
Falesi, I. C., A. R. Camacho Baena, S. Dutra. 1980. Con-
sequencias da exploracão agropecuária sobre as con-
dicões físicas e químicas dos solos das microregiões
do Nordeste Paraense. Boletim de Pesquisa N° 14,
Belem: Embrapa/CPATU.
Fearnside, P. 1978. Estimation of Carrying Capacity
for Human Populations in a Part of the Trans-
amazon Highway Colonization Area of Brazil. Ph.D.
Dissertation: Univ. of Michigan.
Ferdon, E. H. 1959. Agricultural potential and the de-
velopment of cultures. Southwestern Journal of Anthropology 15: 1-19.
Ferroni, M. A. 1980. The Urban Bias of Peruvian Food
Policy: Consequences and Alternatives. Ph.D. Dis-
sertation. Cornell University, Ithaca, N.Y.
Fisher, R. A. 1930. The Genetical Theory of Natural
Selection. New York: Dover Press (Dover ed., 1958).
Fjellman, S. M. 1979. Hey, you can't do that: a
response to Divale and Harris's population warfare
and the male supremacist complex. Behavior Science
Research 14: 189-200.
Flannery, K. 1972. The cultural evolution of civili-
zations. Annual Review of Ecology and Systematics
3: 399-426.
Fried, M. 1967. The Evolution of Political Society: An
Essay in Political Anthropology. New York: Random
House.
Friedman, J. 1979. Hegelian ecology: between Rousseau
and the world spirit. In Social and Ecological
Systems, P. C. Burnham and R. F. Ellen (eds.):
253-270. London: Academic Press.
Frisancho, A. R. 1969. Human growth and pulmonary func-
tion of a high altitude Peruvian Quechua population.
Human Biology 4: 365-379.
Frisancho, A. R. 1975. Functional adaptation to high
altitude hypoxia. Science 187: 313-219.
Frisancho, A. R. 1978. Human growth and development
among high altitude populations. In The Biology of
High Altitude Peoples, P. T. Baker (ed.): 117-171.
New York: Cambridge University Press.
Frisancho, A. R. 1979. Human Adaptation: A Functional
Approach. St. Louis: Mosby.
Frisancho, A. R., C. Martinez, T. Velásquez, J. Sanchez
and H. Montoye. 1973a. Influence of developmental
adaptation on aerobic capacity at high altitude.
Journal of Applied Physiology 34: 176-180.
Frisancho, A. R., J. Sanchez, D. Pallardel, and L. Yañez.
1973b. Adaptive significance of small body size

157

under poor socioeconomic conditions in southern Peru. American Journal of Physical Anthropology 39: 255-262.

Frisancho, A. R., T. Velásquez, and J. Sanchez. 1975. Possible adaptive significance of small body size in the attainment of aerobic capacity among high altitude Quechua natives. In Biosocial Interrelations in Population Adaptation, E. S. Watts, F. E. Johnston, and G. W. Lasker (eds.): 55-64. The Hague: Mouton.

Frisch, R. 1978. Population, food intake, and fertility. Science 199: 22-30.

Frisch, R. and J. McArthur. 1974. Menstrual cycles: fatness as a determinant of minimum weight necessary for their maintenance or onset. Science 185: 949-951.

Furley, P. 1980. Development planning in Rondonia based on naturally renewable resource surveys. In Land, People and Planning in Contemporary Amazonia, F. Scazzocchio (ed.). Cambridge, UK: Cambridge Univ. Centre of Latin American Studies Publications.

Gage, T. B. 1979. The competitive interactions of man and deer in prehistoric California. Human Ecology 7: 253-268.

Gall, P. L. and A. A. Saxe. 1977. The ecological evolution of culture: the state as predator in prehistory. In Exchange Systems in Prehistory, T. Earle and J. E. Ericson (eds.): 255-268. New York: Academic Press.

Gama Barros, H. de. 1945-51. Historia da Administração Publica em Portugal nos Seculos XII a XV, 2nd ed., 11 vols. Lisbon.

Gardner, G. W., V. R. Edgerton, R. J. Barnard, and E. M. Bernauer. 1975. Cardiorespiratory, hematological and physical performance responses of anemic subjects to iron treatment. American Journal of Clinical Nutrition 8: 982-188.

Garfinkel, T. and S. Selvin. 1976. A multivariate analysis of the relationship between parental age and birth order and the human secondary sex ratio. Journal of Biosocial Science 8: 113-21.

Gaulin, S. J. C. and M. J. Konner. 1977. On the natural diets of primates, including humans. In Nutrition and the Brain, Volume I, R. Wurtman and J. Wurtman (eds.): 1-86. New York: Raven Press.

Giesel, J. T. 1976. Reproductive strategies as adaptations to life in temporally heterogeneous environments. Annual Review of Ecology and Systematics 7: 57-79.

Godinho, V. M. 1962. A Economia dos Descobrimentos Henriquinos. Lisboa: Sá da Costa.

Golovachev, G. D. 1970. Relation between human sex ratio and some clinical toxaemiae of pregnancy. Human Biology 42: 619-625.

158

Goodall, H. and A. M. Roberts. 1976. Differences in mo-
tility of human X- and Y-bearing spermatozoa.
Journal of Reproduction and Fertility 48: 433-436.
Gourou, P. 1953. The Tropical World. London: Long-
mans.
Gowaty, P. A. 1981. An extension of the Orians-Verner-
Willson model to account for mating systems besides
polygyny. American Naturalist 118: 851-859.
Greenwood, D. J. and W. A. Stini. 1977. Theories of cultural evolutionism. In Nature, Culture and Human
History: A Biocultural Introduction to Anthropology:
409-425. New York: Harper and Row.
Greenberg, R. A. and C. White. 1968. The sexes of con-
secutive sibs in human sibships. Human Biology 34:
374-404.
Gross, D. 1975. Protein capture and cultural development in the Amazon Basin. American Anthropologist
77: 526-549.
Gross, D., G. Eiten, N. Flowers, F. Leoi, M. Ritter,
and D. Werner. 1979. Ecology and acculturation
among native peoples of Central Brazil. Science
206: 1043-1050.
Guerrero, R., O. Rojas, and A. Cifuentes. 1979. Natural
family planning methods. In Human Ovulation: Mechanisms, Prediction, Detection and Introduction,
E. S. E. Hafez (ed.): 477-490. Amsterdam: North-
Holland Publishing Co.
Gulliver, P. H. 1955. The Family Herds. London: Rout-
ledge and Keagan Paul.
Haas, J. D. 1973. Altitudinal Variation and Infant
Growth and Development in Peru. Ph.D. Dissertation.
The Pennsylvania State Univ., University Park, Pa.
Haas, J. D. 1976. Prenatal and infant growth and devel-
opment. In Man in the Andes: A Multidisciplinary
Study of High Altitude Quechua, P. T. Baker and M. A.
Little (eds.): 161-179. Stroudsberg, Pa.: Dowden,
Hutchinson and Ross.
Haas, J. D. 1980a. High altitude adaptation. Review of
"The Biology of High Altitude Peoples," P. T. Baker
(ed.), Reviews in Anthropology 6: 437-451.
Haas, J. D. 1980b. Maternal adaptation and fetal growth
at high altitude in Bolivia. In Social and Biologi-
cal Predictors of Nutritional Status, Physical Growth
and Neurological Development, L. S. Greene and F. E.
Johnston (eds.): 257-290. New York: Academic Press.
Haas, J. D. 1981a. Maternal-fetal responses to pregnancy
as indicators of human adaptability at high altitude.
In Environmental and Human Population Problems at
High Altitude, C. Jest and P. T. Baker (eds.): 81-85.
Paris: C.N.R.S.
Haas, J. D. 1981b. Human adaptability approach to nutritional assessment: A Bolivian example. Federa-
tion Proceedings 40: 2577-2582.

159

Haas, J. D., E. A. Frongillo, C. D. Stepick, J. L. Beard, and L. Hurtado G. 1980. Altitude, ethnic and sex difference in birth weight and length in Bolivia. Human Biology 52: 459-477.
Haas, J. D. and G. G. Harrison. 1977. Nutritional anthropology and biological adaptation. Annual Review of Anthropology 6: 69-101.
Haas, J. D., G. Moreno-Black, J. Pabon, G. Pareja, J. Ybarnegaray, and L. Hurtado. 1982a. Altitude and infant growth in Bolivia. American Journal of Physical Anthropology (in press).
Haas, J. D., D. Small, J. Beard, and L. Hurtado. 1982b. Variacion en hemoglobina materna y peso al nacer en las grandes alturas. Revista del Instituto Boliviano de Biología de Altura (in press).
Hafez, E. S. E. 1978. Transport and survival of spermatozoa in the human female reproductive tract. In Human Fertilization, H. Ludwig and P. F. Tauber (eds.): 119-127. Stuttgart: Georg Thieme Publishers.
Halliday, T. R. 1978. Sexual selection and mate choice. In Behavioural Ecology, J. R. Krebs and B. Davies (eds.): 180-213. Oxford: Blackwell.
Hamburg, D. A. 1963. Emotions in the perspective of human evolution. In Expression of Emotions in Man, P. H. Knapp (ed.). New York: International Universities Press, Inc.
Hamburg, D. A. 1968. The evolution of emotional response. Science and Psychoanalysis 12: 39-53.
Hames, R. (ed.). 1980. Studies in hunting and fishing in the Neotropics. Bennington, Vt.: Bennington College. Working Papers on South American Indians No. 2.
Hamilton, W. D. 1963. The evolution of altruistic behavior. American Naturalist 97: 354-356.
Hamilton, W. D. 1967. Extraordinary sex ratios. Science 156: 477-488.
Hardesty, D. L. 1977. Ecological Anthropology. New York: John Wiley and Sons.
Hardesty, D. L. 1980. Ecological explanation in archaeology. In Advances in Archaeological Method and Theory, Vol. 3. M. B. Schiffer (ed.). New York: Academic Press.
Harner, M. 1972. The Jivaro. New York: Doubleday.
Harris, M. 1968. The Rise of Anthropological Theory. New York: Crowell.
Harris, M. 1974. Cows, Pigs, Wars and Witches: The Riddles of Culture. New York: Vantage Books, Random House.
Harris, M. 1975. Reply to Heinen. Current Anthropology 16: 454-455.
Harris, M. 1977. Cannibals and Kings: The Origins of Culture. New York: Random House.
Harris, M. 1979. Cultural Materialism: The Struggle for a Science of Culture. New York: Random House.

160

Harris, M. and M. Sahlins. 1979. Cannibals and kings:
an exchange. New York Review of Books, June 28:
51-53.
Heffley, S. 1981. Northern Athabaskan settlement patterns and resource distributions: an application
of Horn's model. In Hunter-Gatherer Foraging Strategies, B. Winterhalder and E. A. Smith (eds.). Chicago: University of Chicago Press.
Herlihy, D. 1973. Three patterns of social mobility in
medieval history. Journal of Interdisciplinary History, III: 622-47.
Herrera, R., C. Jordan, H. Klinge, and E. Medina. 1978.
Amazon ecosystems. Interciencia 3(4): 223-231.
Hesser, J. E., B. S. Blumberg, and J. S. Drew. 1976.
Hepatitis B surface antigen, fertility and sex ratio:
implications for health planning. In Anthropological
Studies of Human Fertility, B. Kaplan (ed.): 75-82.
Detroit: Wayne State University Press.
Hinde, R. A. and Y. Stevenson-Hinde. 1973. Constraints
on Learning: Limitations and Predispositions. New
York: Academic Press.
Hirschfeld, L. A. 1979. A reply to Divale et al. Amer-
ican Anthropologist 81: 349-350.
Hirschfeld, L. A., J. Howe, and B. Levin. 1978. Warfare,
infanticide, and statistical inference: a comment on
Divale and Harris. American Anthropologist 80: 110-
115.
Hirschman, C. and J. Matras. 1971. A new look at the
marriage market and nuptiality rates, 1915-1958.
Demography 8: 549-569.
Hoff, C. J. and A. E. Abelson. 1976. Fertility. In Man
in the Andes: a Multidisciplinary Study of High-
Altitude Quechua, P. T. Baker and M. A. Little
(eds.): 128-146. Stoudsburg, Pa.: Dowden, Hutchinson and Ross.
Holmberg, A. 1960. Nomads of the Long Bow. Chicago:
University of Chicago Press.
Horn, H. S. 1968. The adaptive significance of colonial nesting in the Brewer's Blackbird (Euphagus
cyanocephalus). Ecology 49: 682-694.
Horn, H. S. 1978. Optimal tactics of reproduction and
life history. In Behavioural Ecology, J. R. Krebs
and N. B. Davies (eds.): 411-30. Oxford: Blackwell.
Howe, J. 1978. Ninety-two mythical populations: a reply to Divale et al. American Anthropologist 80: 671-
673.
Howell, N. 1976. The population of the Dobe area. In
Kalahari Hunter-Gatherers, R. B. Lee and I DeVore
(eds.). Cambridge: Harvard University Press.
Howell, N. 1979. Demography of the Dobe !Kung. New
York: Academic Press.
Hurtado, A. 1964. Animals in high altitudes: resident
man. In Handbook of Physiology, IV. Adaptation to
the Environment, D. B. Dills, E. F. Adolph, C. G.

Wilber (eds.): 843-860. Washington, D.C.: American Physiological Society.

Irons, W. 1976. Emic and reproductive success. Paper presented in Symposium on Sociobiology and Human Social Organization at the Annual Meetings of the American Anthropological Association, 1976.

Irons, W. 1977. Evolutionary biology and human fertility. Paper presented in Symposium on Family Fertility and Economics, at the Annual Meetings of the American Anthropological Association, 1977.

Irons, William. 1979a. Introduction to II. Kinship. In Evolutionary Biology and Human Social Behavior. N. A. Chagnon and W. Irons (eds.). North Scituate, Mass.: Duxbury Press.

Irons, W. 1979b. Natural Selection, Adaptation, and Human Social Behavior. In Evolutionary Biology and Human Social Behavior, N. A. Chagnon and W. Irons (eds.). North Scituate, Mass.: Duxbury Press.

Irons, W. 1979c. Cultural and biological success. In Evolutionary Biology and Human Social Behavior: An Anthropological Perspective, N. A. Chagnon and W. Irons (eds.): 257-272. North Scituate, Mass.: Duxbury Press.

Irons, W. 1980. Is Yomut social behavior adaptive? In Sociobiology: Beyond Nature/Nurture? G. Barlow and J. Silverberg (es.). Boulder, Colorado: Westview Press.

Jelliffe, D. B. and E. F. P. Jelliffe. 1978. Human Milk in the Modern World. New York: Oxford University Press.

Jenness, D. 1922. The Life of the Copper Eskimo. Volume 12 of the Report to the Canadian Arctic Expedition, 1913-1918. Ottawa: F. A. Acland.

Jochim, M. A. 1976. Hunter-Gatherer Subsistence and Settlement. A Predictive Model. New York: Academic Press.

Jurion, F. and J. Henry. 1969. Can Primitive Farming be Modernized? London: Agra-Europe.

Kahn, A. M. and I. Strageldin. 1979. Education, income and fertility in Pakistan. Economic Development and Cultural Change 27: 519-548.

Kalmus, H. and C. A. Smith. 1960. The evolutionary origin of sexual differentiation and the sex ratio. Nature 186: 1004.

Kamil, A. C. and T. D. Sargent (eds.). 1981. Foraging Behavior: Ecological, Ethological, and Psychological Approaches. New York: Garland STPM Press.

Kang, G., S. Horan and J. Reis. 1979. Comments of Divale and Harris's population warfare and the male supremacist complex. Behavior Science Research 14: 201-209.

Keen, M. H. 1976. Chivalry, nobility, and the man-at-arms. In War, Literature, and Politics in the Late Middle Ages. New York: Barnes and Noble.

Keene, A. S. 1979a. Economic optimization models and the study of hunter-gatherer subsistence-settlement systems. In _Transformations: Mathematical Approaches to Culture Change_, C. Renfrew and K. Cooke (eds.): 369-404. New York: Academic Press.

Keene, A. S. 1979b. Prehistoric Hunter-Gatherers of the Deciduous Forest: A Linear Programming Approach to Late Archaic Subsistence in the Saginaw Valley (Michigan). Ph.D. dissertation, University of Michigan.

Kenne, A. S. 1981. Optimal foraging in a nonmarginal environment: a model of prehistoric subsistence strategies. In _Hunter-Gatherer Foraging Strategies: Ethnographic and Archeological Analyses_. Bruce Winterhalder and Eric A. Smith (eds.). Chicago: University of Chicago Press.

Kolman, Wilfred M. 1960. The mechanism of natural selection for the sex ratio. _American Naturalist_ 94: 373-377.

Konner, M. 1977. Infancy among the Kalahari Desert San. In _Culture and Infancy_, H. Leiderman, S. R. Tulkin, and A. Rosenfeld (ed.): 287-328. New York: Academic Press.

Konner, M. and C. Worthman. 1980. Nursing frequency, gonadal function, and birth spacing among !Kung hunter-gatherers. _Science_ 207: 788-791.

Krebs, J. R. 1978. Optimal foraging: decision rules for predators. In _Behavioural Ecology_, J. R. Krebs and N. B. Davies (eds.): 23-61. London: Blackwell.

Krebs, J. R. and N. B. Davies (eds.). 1978. _Behavioural Ecology: An Evolutionary Approach_. London: Blackwell (distributed in the U.S. by Sinauer, Sunderland, Massachusetts).

Krebs, J. R. and N. B. Davies. 1981. _An Introduction to Behavioural Ecology_. London: Blackwell.

Kurland, J. A. 1979. Paternity, mother's brother, and human sociality. In _Evolutionary Biology and Human Social Behavior_, Napoleon Chagnon and William Irons (eds.): 86-132. North Scituate, Mass.: Duxbury Press.

Lancaster, C. and J. B. Lancaster. 1978. On the male supremacist complex: a reply to Divale and Harris. _American Anthropologist_ 80: 115-117.

Lathrap, D. 1968. The hunting economies of the tropical forest zone of South America. In _Man the Hunter_, R. B. Lee and I. Devore (eds.). Chicago: Aldine.

Latham, M. C. 1974. Protein-calorie malnutrition in children and its relation to psychological development and behavior. _Physiological Reviews_: 54: 541-565.

Leach, E. 1965. _The Political Systems of Highland Burma_. Boston: Beacon Press.

Leatherman, T. L., L. P. Greksa, J. D. Haas, and R. B. Thomas, n.d. Anthropometric assessment of nutritional status in porters at high altitude, in prep.

163

Lebzelter, V. 1934. Eingeborenenkulturen in Südwest- und
Südafrika. Leipzig: Verlag Karl W. Hiersemann.
Lee, R. B. 1972. Population growth and the beginning of
sedentary life among the !Kung Bushmen. In Popula-
tion Growth: Anthropological Implications, B.
Spooner (ed.): 329-342. Cambridge, Mass.: MIT Press.
Lee, R. B. 1979. The !Kung San. Men, Women and Work in
a Foraging Society. New York: Cambridge University
Press.
Lee, R. B. and I DeVore, eds. 1976. Kalahari Hunter-
Gatherers. Cambridge: Harvard University Press.
Lees, S. H. and Bates, D. G. 1979. The myth of popula-
tion regulation. In Evolutionary Biology and Human
Social Behavior: An Anthropological Perspective,
N. A. Chagnon and W. Irons (eds.). North Scituate,
Mass.: Duxbury Press.
Leigh, E. G. 1970. Sex ratio and differential mortality
between the sexes. American Naturalist 104: 205-210.
Lenneberg, E. H. 1967. Biological Foundations of Lan-
guage. New York: Wiley.
Levins, R. 1977. Symposium on Sociobiology. Presented
at Summer Institute: Biological and Social Perspec-
tives on Human Nature. Colorado Springs: Colorado
College.
Lewontin, R. C. 1974. The analysis of variance and the
analysis of causes. American Journal of Human Gene-
tics 26: 400-411.
Lewontin, R. C. 1977. Caricature of Darwinism. (Review
of The Selfish Gene by Richard Dawkins.) Nature 266:
283-84.
Lewontin, R. C. 1978. Adaptation. Scientific American
239 (3): 213-230.
Little, M. A. 1981. Human populations in the Andes: the
human science basis for research planning. In
Unesco/UNEP State of Knowledge Report on Andean Eco-
systems, Vol. 1, A General Prospectus on the Andean
Region, M. A. Little (ed.). Mountain Research and
Development 1(2).
Little, M. A. 1982. Development of ideas on human
ecology and adaptation. In History of American
Physical Anthropology, 1930-1980, F. Spencer (ed.).
New York: Academic Press.
Little, M. A., R. B. Thomas, R. B. Mazess, and P. T.
Baker. 1971. Population differences and develop-
mental changes in extremity temperature responses to
cold among Andean Indians. Human Biology 43: 70-91.
Little, M. A. and P. T. Baker. 1976. Environmental adap-
tations and perspectives. In Man in the Andes: a
Multidisciplinary Study of High-Altitude Quechua,
P. T. Baker and M. A. Little (eds.): 405-428.
Stroudsburg, Pa.: Dowden, Hutchinson and Ross.
Little, M. A. and G. E. B. Morren, Jr. 1976. Ecology,
Energetics and Human Variability. Dubuque: Wm. C.
Brown.

Lizot, J. 1971. Aspects economiques et sociaux du
    changement culturel chez les Yanomami. L'Homme 11
    (1): 32-51.
Lizot, J. 1977. Population resources and warfare among
    the Yanomamo. Man 12: 497-517.
Lorenz, K. 1952. King Solomon's Ring. London: Methuen
    and Co. Ltd.
Lorenz, K. 1966. On Aggression. New York: Harcourt,
    Brace and World.
Lyon, P. (ed.). 1974. Native South Americans. Boston:
    Little, Brown and Co.
Lyster, W. R. 1970. Sex ratio in the Australian Capital
    Territory. Human Biology 42: 670-678.
Lyster, W. R. and M. W. H. Bishop. 1965. An association
    between rainfall and sex ratio in Man. Journal of
    Reproduction and Fertility 10: 35-47.
MacArthur, R. H. 1958. Population ecology of some warb-
    lers of northeastern coniferous forests. Ecology 39:
    599-619.
MacArthur, R. H. 1960. On the relation between reproduc-
    tive value and optimal predation. Proc. National
    Academy of Sciences 46: 143-145.
MacArthur, R. H. 1961. Population effects of natural
    selection. American Naturalist 95: 195-199.
MacArthur, R. H. and E. R. Pianka. 1966. On optimal use
    of a patchy environment. American Naturalist 100:
    603-609.
MacArthur, R. H. and E. O. Wilson. 1967. The Theory of
    Island Biogeography. Princeton: Princeton Univer-
    sity Press.
Marler, P. and M. Tamura. 1964. Culturally transmitted
    patterns of vocal behavior in a Sparrow. Science
    146: 1483-1486.
Mattoso, J. 1975. Clero. In Dicionario de Historia de
    Portugal, J. Serrão (ed.): 590-594. Vol. I: Lisbon.
Mattoso, J. 1981. A Nobreza Medieval Portuguese: A
    Familia e o Poder. Imprensa Universitaria, No. 19.
    Lisbon.
Malowist, M. 1964. Les aspects sociaux de la prémière
    phase de l'expansion coloniale. Africana Bulletin 1:
    11-40.
May, R. M. 1974. Stability and Complexity in Model
    Ecosystems, Second edition. Princeton: Princeton
    University Press (Monographs in Population Biology,
    No. 6).
May, R. M. (ed.). 1981. Theoretical Ecology: Principles
    and Applications. Oxford: Blackwell.
Maybury-Lewis, D. 1968. Akwe-Shavante Society. Ox-
    ford: Clarendon Press.
Maynard Smith, J. 1979. Game theory and the evolution of
    behavior. Behavioral Ecology and Sociobiology 7:
    247-251.

Maynard Smith, J. 1978. Optimization theory in evolution. Annual Review of Ecology and Systematics 9: 31-56.

Maynard Smith, J. 1976. Evolution and the theory of games. American Scientist 64: 41-45.

Maynard Smith, J. and G. A. Parker. 1976. The logic of asymmetric contests. Animal Behavior 24: 159-175.

Maynard Smith, J. and G. R. Price. 1973. The logic of animal conflict. Nature 246: 15-18.

Mayr, E. 1974. Behavioral programs and evolutionary strategies. American Naturalist 62: 650-659.

Mazess, R. B. 1969. Exercise performance at high altitude in Peru. Federation Proceedings 28: 1301-1306.

Mazess, R. B. 1975a. Biological adaptation: aptitudes and acclimatization. In Biosocial Interrelations in Population Adaptation, E. S. Watts, F. E. Johnston, and G. W. Lasker (eds.): 9-18. The Hague: Mouton.

Mazess, R. B. 1975b. Human adaptation to high altitude. In Physiological Anthropology, A. Damon (ed.): 167-209. London: Oxford University Press.

Mazess, R. B. 1978. Adaptation: a conceptual framework. In Evolutionary Models and Studies in Human Diversity, R. J. Meier, C. M. Otten, and F. Abdel-Hameed (eds.): 9-15. The Hague: Mouton.

McCay, B. J. 1981. Optimal foragers or political actors? Ecological analyses of a New Jersey fishery. American Ethnologist 8: 358-382.

McNaughton, S. J. and L. L. Wolf. 1973. General Ecology. New York: Holt, Rinehart and Winston.

McNeil, M. 1964. Lateritic soils. Scientific American 211(5): 86-102.

McClung, J. 1969. Effects of High Altitude on Human Birth. Cambridge, Mass.: Harvard University Press.

Medawar, P. B. 1951. Problems of adaptation. New Biology, 11: 10-26.

Meggers, B. 1954. Environmental limitations on the development of culture. American Anthropologist 56: 801-824.

Meggers, B. 1971. Amazonia: Man and Culture in a Counterfeit Paradise. Chicago: Aldine.

Meggers, B. and C. Evans. 1957. Archeological Investigations at the Mouth of the Amazon. Washington, D.C.: Smithsonian Institution.

Meggitt, M. F. 1968. Marriage classes and demography in Central Australia. In Man the Hunter, R. Lee and I. DeVore (eds.). Chicago: Aldine.

Miracle, M. 1973. The Congo Basin as a habitat for man. In Tropical Forest Ecosystems in Africa and South America B. Meggers et al. (eds.). Washington, D.C.: Smithsonian.

Montagu, A. (ed.). 1968. Man and Aggression. New York: Oxford University Press.

Moore, K. A. and S. B. Caldwell. 1976. Out of Wedlock Pregnancy and Childbearing, Working Paper 992-02. Washington, D.C.: The Urban Institute.

Moorman, F. R. 1972. Soil microvariability. In Soils of the Humid Tropics. Washington, D.C.: National Academy of Sciences.

Moran, E. F. 1973. Energy flow analysis and Manihot esculenta Crantz. Acta Amazonica 3(3): 28-39.

Moran, E. F. 1974. The adaptive system of the Amazonian Caboclo. In Man in the Amazon, C. Wagley (ed.). Gainesville: University of Florida Press.

Moran, E. F. 1975. Pioneer Farmers of the Transamazon Highway: Adaptation and Agricultural Production in the Lowland Tropics. Ph.D. dissertation: University of Florida.

Moran, E. F. 1976a. Manioc deserves more recognition in tropical farming. World Crops 28: 184-188.

Moran, E. F. 1976. Food, development and man in the tropics. Gastronomy: The Anthropology of Food and Food Habits, M. Arnott (ed.). The Hague: Mouton.

Moran, E. F. 1979. Criteria for choosing homesteaders in Brazil. Research in Economic Anthropology 2: 339-359.

Moran, E. F. 1981. Developing the Amazon. Bloomington, Ind.: Indiana University Press.

Moran, E. F. 1982. Human Adapability: An Introduction to Ecological Anthropology. Boulder, Colo.: Westview Press. (Originally published in 1979.)

Morris, D., P. Collett, P. Marsh, and M. O'Shaughnessy. 1979. Gestures, Their Origins and Distribution. New York: Stein and Day.

Mueller, W. H., F. Murillo, H. Palamino, M. Badziveh, R. Chakraborty, P. Fuerst, and W. J. Schull. 1980. The Aymara of Western Bolivia, V: growth and development in an hypoxic environment. Human Biology 52: 529-546.

Mueller, W. H., F. Yen, F. Rothammer, and W. J. Schull. 1978. A multinational Andean genetic and health program: VII: lung function and physical growth--multivariate analysis in high- and low-altitude populations. Aviation, Space, and Environmetnal Medicine: 49: 1188-1196.

Murra, J. 1972. El control vertical de un maximo de pisos ecológicos en La economia de las sociedades Andinas. Visita de la Provincia de Leon de Huánuco en 1562, J. Murra (ed.). Peru: Univ. Nacional.

Nam, C. B. and S. O. Gustavus. 1976. Population: The Dynamics of Demographic Change. Boston: The Houghton Mifflin Company.

NAS (National Academy of Sciences). 1972. The Soils of the Humid Tropics. Washington, D.C.: NAS.

NAS (National Academy of Sciences). 1977. World Food and Nutrition Study. Report to the U.S. Senate Select

Committee on Nutrition and Human Needs. Washington, D.C.: NAS.

Newitt, M. D. 1973. Portuguese Settlement on the Zambezi. New York: Africana Publishing Co.

Norton, H. 1978. The male supremacist complex: discovery or inventions? American Anthropologist 80: 665-667.

Novitski, E. and A. W. Kimball. 1958. Birth order, parental ages, and sex of offspring. American Journal of Human Genetics 10: 268-75.

Nye, P. H. and D. J. Greenland. 1960. The Soil under Shifting Cultivation. Harpenden, UK: Commonwealth Bureau of Soils. Technical Communication No. 51.

O'Connell, J. F. and K. Hawkes. 1981. Alyawara plant use and optimal foraging theory. In Hunter-Gatherer Foraging Strategies, Bruce Winterhalder and E. A. Smith (eds.). Chicago: University of Chicago Press.

Oliveria Marques, A. H. 1968. Introdução a Historia da Agricultura em Portugal: A questão cerealifera durante a Idade Media, 2nd ed. Lisbon: Cosmos.

Oliveira Marques, A. H. 1972. History of Portugal. New York: Columbia University Press.

Oliveira Marques, A. H. 1975. Nobreza. In Dicionario de Historia de Portugal: Vol. IV: 386-387. Joel Serrão (ed.). Lisbon.

Orans, M. 1975. Domesticating the functional dragon: an analysis of Piddocke's potlatch. American Anthropologist 77: 312-28.

Orians, G. H. 1969. On the evolution of mating systems in birds and mammals. American Naturalist 103: 589-603.

Orlove, B. S. 1980. Ecological anthropology. Annual Review of Anthropology 9: 235-273.

Osgood, C. 1936. Contributions to the Ethnography of the Kutchin. New Haven: Yale University Press.

Parker, G. A. 1974. Assessment strategy and the evolution of fighting behavior. Journal of Theoretical Biology 47: 223-243.

Peebles, C. and S. M. Kus. 1977. Some archeological correlates of ranked societies. American Antiquity 42: 421-438.

Pelto, P. J. and G. H. Pelto. 1975. Intra-cultural diversity: some theoretical issues. American Ethnologist 2: 1-18.

Perlman, S. M. 1976. Optimum Diet Models and Prehistoric Hunter-Gatherers: A Test on Martha's Vineyard. Ph.D. dissertation, University of Massachusetts at Amherst.

Peterson, W. 1975. Population. Third Edition. New York: MacMillan Publishing Co.

Pianka, E. R. 1970. On r and K selection. American Naturalist 104: 592-597.

Pianka, E. R. 1978. Evolutionary Ecology, 2nd edition. New York: Harper and Row.

168

Picón-Reátegui, E. 1976. Nutrition. In Man in the
Andes: A Multidisciplinary Study of High-Altitude
Quechua, P. T. Baker and M. A. Little (eds.): 208-
236. Stroudsburg, Pa.: Dowden, Hutchinson and Ross.
Picón-Reátegui, E. 1978. The food and nutrition of high-
altitude populations. In The Biology of High-Alti-
tude Peoples, P. T. Baker (ed.): 219-149. Cambridge:
Cambridge University Press.
Poewe, K. O. 1980. Universal male dominance: an ethnological illusion. Dialectical Anthropology 5 (2):
111-125.
Pollard, G. N. 1969. Factors influencing the sex ratio
at birth in Australia, 1902-1965. Journal of Biosocial Science 1: 125-44.
Popenoe, H. 1960. Effects of Shifting Cultivation on
Natural Soil Constituents in Central America. Ph.D.
dissertation, University of Florida.
Posey, D. 1982. Indigenous ecological knowledge and de-
velopment of the Amazon. In The Dilemma of Amazo-
nian Development, E. F. Moran (ed.). Boulder, Colo.:
Westview Press.
Prosser, C. L. 1964. Perspectives of adaptation: theoretical aspects. In Adaptation to the Environment,
Section 4, Handbook of Physiology, D. B. Dill, E. F.
Adolph, and C. G. Wilber (eds.): 11-25. Washington,
D.C.: American Physiological Society.
Pyke, G. H., H. R. Pulliam, and E. L. Charnov. 1977. Op-
timal foraging: a selective review of theory and
tests. Quarterly Review of Biology 52: 137-154.
Quinn, V. J. 1982. The relationship between hemoglobin
and iron status in primary school children living at
high altitude in La Paz, Bolivia. M.S. thesis, Cor-
nell University, Ithaca, N.Y.
RADAM (Radar de Amazonia). 1974. Levantamento de Recur-
sos Naturais, Vol. V. Rio de Janeiro: Ministerio de
Minas e Energia.
Radcliffe-Brown, A. R. 1948. The Andaman Islanders.
Glencoe, Ill.: The Free Press.
Ranzani, G. 1978. Alguns solos da Transamazonica da re-
giao de Maraba. Acta Amazonica 8(3): 333-355.
Rappaport, R. A. 1967. Ritual regulation of environment
among New Guinea people. Ethnology 6: 17-20.
Rappaport, R. A. 1971a. The sacred in human evolution.
Annual Review of Ecology and Systematics 2: 23-44.
Rappaport, R. A. 1971b. Ritual, sanctity, and cyberne-
tics. American Anthropologist 73: 73-76.
Rappaport, R. A. 1977. Ecology, adaptation, and the
ills of functionalism. Michigan Discussions in
Anthropology 2: 138-190.
Rapport, D. J. and J. E. Turner. 1977. Economic models
in ecology. Science 195: 367-373.
Raup, D. M. 1977. Stochastic models in evolutionary
paleontology. In Patterns of Evolution as Illus-

trated by the Fossil Record, A. Hallam (ed.): 59-78. New York: Elsevier.

Reichel-Dolmatoff, G. 1971. Amazonian Cosmos. Chicago: University of Chicago Press.

Reynolds, R. L. 1961. Europe Emerges: Transition Toward an Industrial World Wide Society 1600-1750. Madison: University of Wisconsin Press.

Richerson, P. J. 1977. Ecology and human ecology: a comparison of theories in the biological and social sciences. American Ethnologist 4: 1-26.

Richerson, P. J. and R. Boyd. 1980. Review of "Cultural Materialism" by Marvin Harris. Human Ecology 8: 171-75.

Riches, D. 1976. The Netsilik Eskimo: a special case of selective female infanticide. Ethnology 13: 351-361.

Riopelle, A. J. and R. Favrat. 1977. Protein deprivation in primates XIII: growth of infants born of deprived mothers. Human Biology 49: 321-33.

Roosevelt, A. 1980. Parmana: Prehistoric Maize and Manioc Subsistence along the Orinoco and Amazon Rivers. New York: Academic Press.

Ross, E. B. 1980. History of the ascendancy of beef in the United States diet. In Beyond the Myths of Culture, E. B. Ross (ed.). New York: Academic Press.

Rothenbuhler, W. C. 1964a. Behavior genetics of nest cleaning in honey-bees. I. Responses of four inbred lines to disease-killed brood. Animal Behavior 12: 578-593.

Rothebuhler, W. C. 1964b. Behavior genestics of nest cleaning in honey-bees IV. Response of F_1 and backcross generations to disease-killed brood. American Zoologist 4: 111-123.

Roughgarden, J. 1979. Theory of Population Genetics and Evolutionary Ecology: An Introduction. New York: Macmillan.

Sahlins, M. D. 1964. Culture and environment: the study of cultural ecology. In Horizons of Anthropology, S. Tax (ed.). Chicago: Aldine.

Sahlins, M. 1976. Culture and Practical Reason. Chicago: University of Chicago Press.

Sahlins, M. 1978. Culture as protein and profit. New York Review of Books, Nov. 23: 45-53.

Sanchez, R. 1972. Review of Soils Research in Latin America. Raleigh: North Carolina State University Press.

Sanchez, P. 1976. Properties and Management of Soils in the Tropics. New York: Wiley-Interscience.

Sanchez, P. and S. Buol. 1975. Soils of the tropics and the world food crisis. Science 188: 598-603.

Sarkar, S. 1960. Onge population and settlements. Anthropos 55: 561-563.

Scazzocchio, F. (ed.). 1980. Land, People and Planning in Contemporary Amnazonia. Cambridge, UK: Cambridge

University Centre of Latin American Studies Publications.

Schneider, H. K. 1974. *Economic Man*. New York: Free Press.

Schoener, T. W. 1971. Theory of feeding strategies. *Annual Review of Ecology and Systematics* 2: 369-404.

Schoolcraft, H. R. 1857. *History of the Indian Tribes of the United States*. Philadelphia: J. B. Lippincott.

Seligman, M. E. P., and J. L. Hager. 1972. *Biological Boundaries of Learning*. Englewood Cliffs, New Jersey: Prentice-Hall.

Sen, P. K. 1962. *Land and People of the Andamanus: A Geographical and Socioeconomical Study with a Short Account of the Nicobar Islands*. Calcutta: Post-Graduate Book Mart.

Shaklee, A. B. and R. B. Shaklee. 1975. Ecological models in relation to early hominid adaptations. *American Anthropologist* 77: 611-615.

Sharp, R. L. 1940. An Australian Aboriginal population. *Human Biology* 12: 481-507.

Shettleworth, S. J. 1972. Constraints on learning. *Advances in the Study of Behavior* 4: 1-68.

Sioli, H. 1951. *Alguns Resultatdos e Problemas da Limnologia Amazonica*. Boletim Tecnico do Instituto Agronomico do Norte No. 24. BELEM: IAN.

Siskind, J. 1973. *To Hunt in the Morning*. New York: Oxford University Press.

Slatkin, M. and J. Maynard Smith. 1979. Models of co-evolution. *Quarterly Review of Biology* 54: 233-63.

Slobodkin, L. and Rapoport, A. 1974. An optimal strategy of evolution. *The Quarterly Review of Biology* 49: 181-200.

Slonim, N. B. 1974. Introduction. In *Environmental Physiology*, N. B. Slonim (ed.): 1-9. St. Louis: Mosby.

Smith, E. A. 1979. Data and theory in sociobiolgoical explanation: a critique of van den Berghe and Barash. *American Anthropologist* 81: 360-363.

Smith, E. A. 1980. Evolutionary Ecology and the Analysis of Human Foraging Behavior: An Inuit Example from the East Coast of Hudson Bay. Ph.D. dissertation, Cornell University.

Smith, E. A. 1981. The application of optimal foraging theory to the analysis of hunter-gatherer group size. In *Hunter-Gatherer Foraging Strategies*, B. Winterhalder and E. A. Smith (eds.). Chicago: University of Chicago Press.

Smith, E. A. and B. Winterhalder. 1981. New perspectives on hunter-gatherer socioecology. In *Hunter-Gatherer Foraging Strategies*, B. Winterhalder and E. A. Smith (eds.). Chicago: University of Chicago Press.

Smith, N. 1976. Transamazon Highway: A Cultural Ecological Analysis of Settlement in the Lowland Tropics.

Ph.D. Dissertation: University of California at
Berkeley.
Smith, N. 1978. Agricultural productivity along Brazil's
transamazon highway. Agro-Ecosystems 4: 415-432.
Smole, W. J. 1976. The Yanomama Indians: A Cultural
Geography. Austin: University of Texas Press.
Sombroek, W. G. 1966. Amazon Soils. Wageningen: Centre
for Agric. Publ. and Doc.
Southwood, T. R. E. 1981. Bionomic strategies and popu-
lation parameters. In Theoretical Ecology, R. M. May
(ed.): 30-52. Oxford: Blackwell.
Southwood, T. R. E., R. M. May, M. P. Hassell, and G. R.
Conway. 1974. Ecological strategies and population
parameters. American Naturalist 108: 791-804.
Spencer, P. 1973. Nomads in Alliance. London: Oxford
University Press.
Spurr, G. B., M. Barac-Nieto, and M. G. Maksud. 1977.
Productivity and maximal oxygen consumption in sugar
cane cutters. American Journal of Clinical Nutri-
tion 30: 316-321.
Stearns, S. C. 1976. Life-history tactics: a review of
the ideas. Quarterly Review of Biology 51: 3-47.
Stearns, S. C. 1977. The evolution of life history
traits: a critique of the theory and a review of the
data. Annual Review of Ecology and Systematics 8:
145-71.
Stern, C. 1973. Principles of Human Genetics, Third
Edition. San Francisco: W. H. Freeman and Company.
Stern, J. T., Jr. 1970. The meaning of "adaptation" and
its relation to the phenomenon of natural selection.
In Evolutionary Biology, Vol. 4. Th. Dobzhansky,
M. K. Hecht, and W. C. Steere (eds.): 39-66. New
York: Appleton-Century-Crofts.
Sternberg, H. 1973. Development and conservation.
Erkunde 27: 253-265.
Stevenson, A. C. and M. Bobrow. 1967. Determinants of
sex proportions in man, with consideration of the
evidence concerning a contribution from X-linked
mutations to intrauterine death. Journal of Medical
Genetics 4: 190.
Steward, J. H. 1939-46. Handbook of South American In-
dians, 7 volumes. Washington, D.C.: Smithsonian
Institution/Bureau of American Ethnology.
Steward, J. H. 1955. The Theory of Culture Change. Ur-
bana: University of Illinois Press.
Stinson, S. 1981. The growth of middle and upper class
children in La Paz, Bolivia. American Journal of
Physical Anthropology 54: 281.
Stott, D. H. 1962. Cultural and natural checks on popu-
lation growth. In Culture and the Evolution of Man,
M. F. Montague (ed.). New York: Oxford University
Press.

Taylor, K. 1974. *Sanuma Fauna Prohibitions and Classifications*. Caracas: Fundación La Salle de Ciencias Naturales.

Teitelbaum, M. S. 1972. Factors associated with sex ratio in human populations. In *The Structure of Human Populations*, G. A. Harrison and A. J. Boyce (eds.): 90-109. Oxford: Clarendon Press.

Teitelbaum, M. S. and N. Mantel. 1971. Socio-economic factors and sex ratio at birth. *Journal of Biosocial Science* 3: 23.Terrell, J. 1977. Biology, biogeography, and man. *World Archaeology* 8: 237-47.

Thomas, R. B. 1976. Energy flow at high altitude. In *Man in the Andes: a Multidisciplinary Study of High Altitude Quechua*, P. T. Baker and M. A. Little (eds.): 379-404. Stroudsburg, Pa.: Dowden, Hutchinson and Ross.

Thomas, R. B., B. Winterhalder, and S. D. McRae. 1979. An anthropological approach to human ecology and adaptive dynamics. *Yearbook of Physical Anthropology* 22: 1-46.

Tiger, L. 1970. Dominance in human societies. *Annual Review of Ecology and Systematics* 1: 287-306.

Tinbergen, N. 1951. *The Study of Instinct*. Oxford: Clarendon Press.

Trivers, R. L. 1971. The evolution of reciprocal altruism. *Quarterly Review of Biology* 46: 35-57.

Trivers, R. L. 1972. Parental investment and sexual selection. In *Sexual Selection and the Descent of Man 1871-1971*, B. Campbell (ed.): 136-179. Chicago: Aldine Publishing Company.

Trivers, R. L. 1974. Parent-offspring conflict. *American Zoologist* 14: 249-264.

Trivers, R. L. and D. E. Willard. 1973. Natural selection of parental ability to vary the sex ratio of offspring. *Science* 179: 90-92.

Tufts, D. A. 1982. *Iron, Hemoglobin and Work Capacity at High Altitude*. M.S. thesis, Cornell Universssity, Ithaca, N.Y.

Tufts, D. A., J. L. Beard, J. D. Haas, and H. Spielvogel. 1981. Contribution of polycythemia and anemia to the hemoglobin distribution in a high altitude male population. *American Journal of Physical Anthropology* 54: 285.

UNESCO. 1978. *Tropical Forest Ecosystems*. Paris: UNESCO.

US AID. 1975. *Bolivia: Health Sector Assessment*. La Paz, Bolivia: U.S. Agency for International Development.

Uvarov, B. P. 1966. *Grasshoppers and Locusts*. Cambridge: Cambridge University Press.

van den Berghe, P. L. 1978. Bridging the paradigms. In *Sociobiology and Human Nature: An Interdisciplinary Critique and Defense*, M. S. Gregory, A. Silvers, and D. Sutch (eds.): 33-52. San Francisco; Jossey-Bass.

Van Liere, E. J. and J. C. Stickney. 1963. Hypoxia. Chicago: University of Chicago Press.

Vayda, A. P. 1961. Expansion and warfare among swidden agriculturalists. American Anthropologist 63: 346-358.

Vayda, A. P. and R. A. Rappaport. 1968. Ecology, cultural and noncultural. In Introduction to Cultural Anthropology, J. Clifton (ed.): 477-97. Boston: Houghton-Mifflin.

Verner, J. and M. F. Willson. 1966. The influence of habitats on mating systems of North American passerine birds. Ecology 47: 143-47.

Vickers, W. 1975. Meat is meat: the Siona-Secoya and the hunting prowess-sexual reward hypothesis. Latin Americanist 11(1): 1-5.

Vickers, W. 1976. Cultural Adaptation to Amazonian Habitats. Ph.D. Dissertation: University of Florida.

Visaria, P. M. 1967. Sex ratio at birth in territories with a relatively complete registration. Eugenics Quarterly 14: 132.

Vollman, R. F. 1953. Über Fertilität der Frau inherhald des Menstruationscyclus. Archiv fur Gynockologie 182: 602.

Wagley, C. 1969. Cultural influences on population: a comparison of two Tupi tribes. In Environment and Cultural Behavior, A. P. Vayda (ed.). New York: Natural History Press.

Wagley, C. (ed.). 1974. Man in the Amazon. Gainesville: University of Florida Press.

Wagley, C. 1977. Welcome of Tears: The Tapirape Indians of Central Brazil. New York: Oxford.

Wallace, H. R. 1895. Travels on the Amazon and Rio Negro. Fifth edition. London.

Wallerstein, I. 1974. The Modern World System. New York: Academic Press.

Wambecke, A. van. 1978. Properties and potentials of soils in the Amazon Basin. Interciencia 3: 233-241.

Watters, R. F. 1971. Shifting Cultivation in Latin America. Rome: FAO Forestry Development. Paper no. 17.

Welty, J. C. 1975. The Life of Birds, 2nd ed. Philadelphia: W. B. Saunders Company.

Werner, D. 1979. Trekking in the Amazon forest. Natural History 87: 42-55.

West Eberhard, M. J. 1975. The evolution of social behavior by kin selection. Quarterly Review of Biology 50: 1-33.

Weyer, E. M. 1962. The Eskimos: Their Environment and Folkways. Hamden, Conn.: Archon Books.

WHO 1973. Energy and Protein Requirements. Report of Joint FAO/WHO ad hoc Expert Committee WHO Technical Report Series No. 522. Geneva, Switzerland: WHO.

White, L. A. 1943. Energy and the evolution of culture. American Anthropologist 45: 335-356.

174

White, L. A. 1959. <u>The Evolution of Culture</u>. New York: McGraw-Hill.

White, L. 1975. <u>The Concept of Cultural Systems</u>. New York: Columbia University Press.

Wiens, J. A. 1976. Population responses to patchy environments. <u>Annual Review of Ecology and Systematics</u> 7: 81-120.

Wiens, J. A. 1977. On competition and variable environments. <u>American Scientist</u> 65: 590-597.

Williams, G. C. 1966. <u>Adaptation and Natural Selection</u>. Princeton: Princeton University Press.

Wilmesen, E. N. 1973. Interaction, spacing behavior, and the organization of hunting bands. <u>Journal of Anthropological Research</u> 29: 1-31.

Wilson, E. O. 1971. Competitive and aggressive behavior. In <u>Man and Beast: Comparative Social Behavior</u>, J. F. Eisenberg and W. S. Dillon (eds.): 183-217. Washington, D.C.: Smithsonian Institution Press.

Wilson, E. O. 1975. <u>Sociobiology: The New Synthesis</u>. Cambridge, Mass.: Belknap Press of Harvard University Press.

Wilson, E. O. 1978. <u>On Human Nature</u>. Cambridge, Mass.: Harvard University Press.

Winston, S. 1931. The Influence of social factors upon the sex ratio at birth. <u>American Journal of Sociology</u> 37: 1-21.

Winterhalder, B. 1977. Foraging Strategy Adaptations of the Boreal Forest Cree: An Evaluation of Theory and Models from Evolutionary Ecology. Ph.D. dissertation, Cornell University.

Winterhalder, B. 1980. Hominid paleoecology: the competitive exclusion principle and determinants of niche relationships. <u>Yearbook of Physical Anthropology</u> 23: 43-63.

Winterhalder, B. 1981a. Optimal foraging strategies and hunter-gatherer research in anthropology: theory and models. In <u>Hunter-Gatherer Foraging Strategies</u>, B. Winterhalder and E. A. Smith (eds.). Chicago: University of Chicago Press.

Winterhalder, B. 1981b. Foraging strategies in the boreal environment: an analysis of Cree hunting and gathering. In <u>Hunter-Gatherer Foraging Strategies</u>, B. Winterhalder and E. A. Smith (eds.). Chicago: University of Chicago Press.

Winterhalder, B. 1981c. Hominid paleoecology: Limiting similarity, foraging and niche differentiation, and the effects of cultural behavior. <u>Yearbook of Physical Anthropology</u> 24: 101-121.

Winterhalder, B. and E. A. Smith (eds.). 1981. <u>Hunter-Gatherer Foraging Strategies: Ethnographic and Archeological Analyses</u>. Chicago: University of Chicago Press.

Wittenberger, J. F. 1979. The evolution of mating systems in birds and mammals. In <u>Handbook of Be-</u>

havioral Biology, P. Marler and J. Vandenbergh
(eds.), Vol. 3, 271-349. New York: Plenum Press.
Wittenberger, James F. 1981. Time: a hidden dimension
in the polygyny threshold model. American Naturalist 118: 803-822.
Wolpoff, M. H. 1971. Competitive exclusion among Lower
Pleistocene hominids. Man (n.s.) 6: 601-614.
Woods, F. A. 1939. Inheritance of strong parental instinct. Journal of Heredity 30: 237-244.
Wrangham, R. W. 1979. On the evolution of ape social
systems. Social Science Information 18: 335-368.
Wright, H. T. 1977. Recent research on the origin of
the state. Annual Review of Anthropology 6: 379-397.
Wynne-Edwards, V. C. 1962. Animal Dispersion in Relation to Social Behaviour, Edinburgh: Oliver and Boyd.
Yellen, J. E. 1977. Long-term hunter-gatherer adaptation to desert environments: a biogeographical perspective. World Archaeology 8: 262-274.
Yesner, D. R. 1981. Archaeological applications of optimal foraging theory: harvest strategies of Aleut
hunter-gatherers. In Hunter-Gatherer Foraging Strategies, B. Winterhalder and E. A. Smith (eds.). Chicago: University of Chicago Press.

Contributors

James L. Boone
Department of Anthropology
State University of New York
Binghamton, New York 13901

James Dow
Department of Sociology and Anthropology
Oakland University
Rochester, Michigan 48063

Rada Dyson-Hudson
Department of Anthropology
Cornell University
Ithaca, New York 14853

Jere D. Haas
Division of Nutritional Sciences
Cornell University
Ithaca, New York 14853

Mary Jane Kellum
Department of Anthropology
University of North Carolina
Chapel Hill, North Carolina 27514

Michael A. Little
Department of Anthropology
State University of New York
Binghamton, New York 13901

Emilio F. Moran
Department of Anthropology
Indiana University
Bloomington, Indiana 47401

Eric Alden Smith
Department of Anthropology
University of Washington
Seattle, Washington 98195

Index